4-H STORIES
from the HEART

Edited by Dan Tabler

iUniverse, Inc.
Bloomington

4-H Stories from the Heart

iUniverse books may be ordered through booksellers or by contacting:

iUniverse
1663 Liberty Drive
Bloomington, IN 47403
www.iuniverse.com
1-800-Authors (1-800-288-4677)

ISBN: 978-1-4502-7154-7 (pbk)
ISBN: 978-1-4502-7155-4 (hbk)
ISBN: 978-1-4502-7156-1 (ebk)

Library of Congress Control Number: 2010916416

Printed in the United States of America

iUniverse rev. date: 2/23/11

Dedication

4-H Stories from the Heart is dedicated to those who, for over 100 years, have helped "To Make The Best Better" by inspiring, teaching, and guiding millions of 4-H youth as they developed into successful, happy, caring, capable, and contributing adults.

Contents

Preface

Within the pages of *4-H Stories from the Heart* you will find wonderful stories from the whole 4-H family. Over the years a number of books have been written about 4-H, but to our knowledge this is the first book of stories written by current and former members, volunteers, staff and others. These stories were from the heart, not by professional writers. An intentional effort was made to preserve the tone and integrity of each story with a minimum of editing. While you will not find a common voice throughout this book, you will find a common theme. That theme is the positive impact 4-H and 4-H people have had on the lives of millions of young people for more than 100 years. It is an amazing story and we have done our best to capture a small portion of it.

4-H Stories from the Heart has truly been a labor of love. The inspiration was the heartfelt stories shared by the laureates as they were being inducted into the National 4-H Hall of Fame. Their stories were inspiring, sometimes "tear-jerkers," and sometimes funny, but always from the heart. We knew it was important to preserve those stories and others like them from the people who know 4-H best.

The dedication and tireless efforts of the editorial team made *4-H Stories from the Heart* possible. This group of friends from across the nation have more than 500 years of combined 4-H experience. They have consistently promoted the project, recruited authors, evaluated and edited stories, and provided thoughtful advice on every part of the book. You will find "The Team" listed in the acknowledgments.

Another group that made this book possible is the Publisher's Club. The editorial team provided, in addition to countless hours or work, funding to get the project started. Other 4-H friends who believed in this project also contributed. Thanks to the generosity of these folks we were able to publish the book debt free which will enable us to use the proceeds to create the National 4-H Hall of Fame Endowment. Members of the Publisher's Club are also listed in the acknowledgments.

We hope *4-H Stories from the Heart* will be the first in a series, as it is impossible to tell the whole 4-H story in a single volume. At the end of this book you will find instructions for submitting your story. We would also like to hear your ideas for improving future books. Please see the "Tell Us What You Think" page at the end of the book.

On behalf of the editorial team, I would like to thank everyone who shared a story, encouraged us, and supported the dream. If you enjoy the stories half as much as we did, please tell all of your 4-H friends.

Dan Tabler, Editor

Acknowledgments

A hardworking and dedicated editorial team made *4-H Stories from the Heart* possible. Two team members were recruited from each of the four U.S. regions to help collect stories from all over the nation. These Associate Editors include: Lynn Garland, New Hampshire, and Mark Manno, Delaware, from the Northeast; Kia Harries, Minnesota, and Niki Nestor McNeely, Ohio, from North Central; Janet Fox, Louisiana, and Betty Gottler, Alabama, from the South; and Jeff Goodwin, Colorado, and Diane Russo, Washington, from the West. Ron Drum and Nancy Valentine represented National 4-H Council and 4-H National Headquarters, respectively.

A very special thanks to our technical editors Nikki Manno, a former Delaware 4-H'er, and Ellen Butler, Colorado State 4-H Office Program Assistant. Nikki did the initial editing and Ellen did the final editing reading each story at least three times. Thanks to NAE4-HA Marketing Vice President Bob Peterson, NAE4-HA Public Relations and Information Committee Chair Cheryl Varnadoe, and NAE4-HA Executive Director Jody Rosen for their encouragement, wise counsel, and strong support.

We also thank our assistant editors who were most helpful in recruiting authors from their states, providing information to enhance stories or assisting with communications. Assistant Editors included Justin Crowe, Tennessee; Jim Kahler and Bianca Johnson, 4-H Headquarters; Jim Nichnadowicz, New Jersey; and Sheri Seibold, Illinois.

Members of the Publishers Club made it possible to "jump start" the project and publish our book debt free. Every member of the editorial team contributed, along with many other friends who believed in the book. Contribution levels were $300 for Gold, $200 for Silver and $100 for Bronze. Gold contributors were Ron Drum, Lynn Garland, Jeff Goodwin, Betty Gottler, Mark Manno, Bob Peterson, Nancy Rucker, Dan Tabler, Pam Van Horn, and

Betty Wingerter. Mary Jean Craig was a Silver donor and the following were Bronze donors: Travis Burke, Bryan Chadd, Janet Fox, Dorothy Freeman, Kia Harries, Lena Mallory, Niki Nestor McNeely, Diane Russo, Nancy Valentine, and Cheryl Varnadoe. Thanks to each person for their faith in the project and generous contribution.

Thanks to Maria Barga, a graphic artist and former Maryland 4-H'er, for providing all of the original sketches. Thanks also to those who submitted photos, especially professional photographer Edwin Remsberg of the College of Agriculture and Natural Resources, University of Maryland. Other photos were provided by Cheryl Varnadoe, Diane Russo, and others as noted in the photo captions.

Lastly, thanks to everyone who shared their 4-H story as we could not have published a book without stories. We received nearly twice as many stories as could be used. Stories not selected will be saved for future use. Those who submitted stories, whether selected or not, are welcome and encouraged to submit additional 4-H stories, as we know you have more than one to share.

Special 4-H Friends

A Golden Story
Lexa Loch, Montana

I did not cry when I fell off my bike and split my lip when I was four. I did not cry when I bumped my head going down the slide at six. I did not even cry the numerous times I was hit with the ball by my not-so-perfect-pitcher twin brother as I played catcher for him in little league. At 12 years old, I, Lexa Loch, cried like a baby when my 4-H market pig was sold. Whoever said crying will not help did not have my parents. As a result of my *devastating* loss, I was able to talk them into letting me have a puppy of my own. This was my start to an incredible 4-H adventure.

Everyone at some time will have something special come into their life that changes them forever. It may be an event, person, gift, or day. Life from that moment on will be different for you. For me, that time came on my 13th birthday. It was a day I will never forget because I received the dog of my dreams; an eight-week-old, nine-pound ball of fur—a Golden Retriever puppy. She soon became the love of my life and the best 4-H project I could have ever taken.

I named her Avalentine's Golda Gabrielle, Gabby for short. Her name fit her perfectly; she was born on Valentine's Day, a natural sweetheart and she loved to talk to everyone. From the start she changed my world. She was my responsibility. She was so beautiful and such a charmer that I loved showing her off.

In order to do it properly, we took obedience training and conformation classes. I even learned how to groom Gabby by volunteering at a dog grooming shop. My vet knew me on a first name basis and gave me lessons on proper feed, exercise, and care. He took the time to show me X-rays, which explained hip dysplasia and other hereditary and environmental health issues with my dog's breed.

With all the great advice, training, and care, Gabby was growing into a very well-behaved, beautiful, healthy dog. Without even realizing it, I was also growing. The once shy girl was gradually disappearing. As a result of showing Gabby in AKC shows and 4-H, and having her OFA (Orthopedic Foundation for Animals) testing completed, I got to travel throughout Montana, spending many cherished hours with my mom and grandmother and creating many unforgettable memories.

After learning to show and perform obedience with her, I finally felt I had obtained enough knowledge to assist younger 4-H members in the dog project. With Gabby at my side my confidence grew. She helped me to earn the privilege of attending Montana 4-H Congress, winning state awards in the Dog and Leadership projects—which also enabled me to attend National 4-H Congress. Through Gabby, I discovered I could make a difference in the lives of others.

Gabby even gave me my vocation in life. Without her I would never have known how rewarding teaching others could be. I am now studying to be an elementary school teacher. Her puppies have even helped to provide me with college funds, allowing me to work less and devote more time to my studies. The acquaintances and friends I have met through selling her pups will be with me for life. Gabby and I were a perfect team and the doors to success just kept opening. With Gabby as my partner we were invincible. Our accomplishments after seven years together were just the start.

Life throws us curves sometimes and mine was losing Gabby on December 30, 2007, from complications from ACL surgery. Heartbroken, I did not think my world would ever be the same. She was not just a 4-H project, a dog, or another pet to me. She was my mentor who taught and gave me more than I could ever imagine. She was a shoulder to cry on and a friend to depend on, always giving her unconditional love. The hurt of her loss is still with me; yet it fades a little more each day. I will never forget her, nor could I ever replace her. No matter how many other dogs I will have in my life, the special bond we shared was once in a lifetime. I am sure a lot of the magic had to do with my age and meeting the challenges of growing up, but in my heart I know if it were not for my Gabby and my 4-H project, many things in my life would have turned out very differently!

I did not cry when I hit the tree, smashing my new car when I was fifteen. I did not cry when I broke up with my first boyfriend. I did not even cry when I graduated, knowing my life would be changing and I would probably never see some of my high school friends again. But, at 20, I cried like a baby when I lost my Gabby. Whoever said 4-H is not that special of a program was apparently never really involved. As a result of my years in 4-H, I learned some very important life skills. I learned determination, self-esteem, and career skills. I made great friends and had the best experiences of my life. To top it off, I got to share them with a very special pal who will always be a part of me—Avalentine's Golda Gabrielle, Gabby for short.

Special Friends – Photo/Edwin Remsberg

Kindness Never to be Forgotten
Amy Dykes, Maryland

The following heart-warming story was shared by 4-H'er Amy Dykes at the Harford County (Maryland) Volunteer Banquet in November 2008. Amy is a Harford County 4-H teen and member of the Maryland 4-H Teen Council.

"Good Evening…

As many of you will recall, this time last year I had just undergone surgery to remove a large tumor in my brainstem and cerebellum. The surgery at Johns Hopkins Hospital was successful and, thankfully, the tumor was benign. The plan was that I would be discharged to go home five days after the surgery.

But then the unexpected happened: two days after surgery, my neurologic status rapidly deteriorated. My doctors were not sure exactly why this was happening. I did not recognize my parents or family, I began hallucinating, and my body had complete loss of function. No one knew at that point if I would ever be able to blink my eyes, swallow, eat, walk, remember, or think rationally again. Thankfully my heart and lungs continued to function normally.

After several weeks at Johns Hopkins, I was transferred to the Traumatic Brain Injury unit at Kennedy Krieger Institute (Baltimore, Maryland) for rehabilitation. During the seven weeks that followed, the medical team there collaborated and worked together to implement a course of action that restored my life.

The part of my hospitalization that I would like to bring to your attention, though, is the influence that 4-H had upon my recovery. Early on when it became apparent that my memory had significantly declined, the medical team suggested that my family surround me with reminders of some of the most important elements of my life. My parents brought in my 4-H ribbons, along with 4-H pictures from throughout the years, and hung them on my bulletin board. Next, the get-well cards started pouring in from Harford County 4-H, Maryland 4-H, 4-H volunteers, ambassadors, the Leaders' Association, and Teen Council members. Then the banners filled with well wishes from 4-H circles began to pour in and soon my walls were covered with everything 4-H.

Within a matter of days there were signs that my memory was improving. My neuropsychologist came in one morning and asked my mom if she thought I would be able to recite a poem such as "Jack and Jill" or "Hey Diddle Diddle." I quickly answered for myself that I could do better than that; I could recite the 4-H Pledge. So I did! The doctor looked to my mom to verify what I recited was correct. It was right, and at that point we realized I was recovering my memory significantly.

The days passed, and little by little there continued to be improvements in my health. On December 5, a most amazing event took place. The hospital called my home at 6:30 a.m. and reported that I had woken up that morning asking for the bed rails to be put down so I could get up and use the bathroom and get myself dressed. I had not done any of those things in two months! I had not even thought of doing things independently. My mom and brothers came right away to witness what was indeed a Christmas miracle. The hospital team began planning my discharge and in just a few days I was home.

Along with the get-well cards, banners, prayers, calls, emails, and text messages, several clubs made generous donations of gift cards, checks, and gasoline cards to help with our expenses. We were also blessed when the Leaders' Association supported us with a very generous check that was directly applied to the medical expenses our health insurance did not cover. Faithful as ever was my club leader and friend, Ms. Kim Sexton, who came to visit every Monday and Tuesday from beginning to end.

In closing, we would like to thank each of you for your support. It is because of our faith in God, as well as the love and support of friends such as you, that we have a success story to tell! Just when we thought that Harford County 4-H was already *the best*, you made the best better!

Many thanks from our family. We will never forget the kindness you have extended to us!"

Finding My Best Friend
Victoria Kronenberg, Illinois

When I started my 4-H career in 2001 as a shy, little eight-year-old girl, I never dreamed I would be as involved as I am today. I wanted to learn more about horses. My mother thought my interest in horses could be investigated further if I joined 4-H. I have always had a great affection for animals. I have been enrolled in animal projects my entire eight-year 4-H career. I started with the Small Pets project and my hamster Calico. I experimented with rabbits, chickens, and goats when we moved to our farm in Milledgeville, Illinois. After reading nearly every Marguerite Henry novel, I realized my great love was for horses. They are magnificent creatures!

My horse, SGF Jonquil (Jo), is a great Arabian mare. She had been broken to ride when she was younger, but had lived on pasture most of her life. Jo and I were paired four years ago by the wonderful owners of the stable where she was kept. My whole first year working with my horse was filled with patience. I wanted to just hop on her back and ride, but since she had not been worked in a while I had to spend several months ground training her to build up her muscles for riding. Once I started riding, we decided that she would make a fine Country English Pleasure horse. In my previous year I rode Western Pleasure, so this was a bit of a change in riding style. But with the help of my instructors, I was able to get Jo in shape for show season.

When we competed in our first horse show, she was very brave and we placed in all our classes. Through the show season we began clicking together more and more. We ended with a bang at our last show of the season, the Illinois State Fair. We placed second! I was so proud of my girl!

Our next year, however, was a bit more challenging. I spent a great deal of time throughout the winter experimenting on different tack, equipment, and riding techniques. Since my horse had gained strength and experience over the year, she had changed, so I needed to change too. We did not have the greatest showing that year. We would "butt heads" quite often. Then one day I was reminded, "It is always best to end on a good note." I stopped giving up and realized I should not be angry or disappointed with my horse. It would not help the situation.

She felt the difference in my attitude and gradually changed hers as well. I saw how wonderfully my horse could move when we worked as a team. I had been told that horses can "feel your mind." I suppose I did not understand how sensitive a horse could be to my actions. We needed to work together and have mutual respect for one another. That lesson applies to my relationships with people too. Cooperation and teamwork are essential life skills that I have learned in the 4-H program.

Now that I understood my horse, I wanted to try again. So I worked with my girl through the winter, spending a lot of time with her in the barn. I was really looking forward to the upcoming horse show season. The owners of the stable, who were also my instructors/4-H leaders, had many 4-H'ers that leased or boarded horses with them. Through the years I have done lots of exciting 4-H horse activities with friends I will never forget. We had the best times showing together. The barn became my "home away from home" and they were my "horse family."

Then one day I found myself out in Jo's pasture, feeding her treats, and giving her pats and hugs. But this time it was different. I was upset. I never imagined it would be so hard to say goodbye to a horse. There was a sudden change in plans. The next spring our family was to move six hours north due to my dad's work as an engineer. I did not want to leave, I just could not. It was not easy saying goodbye. However, I was comforted with the thought of visiting soon. I was able to finish my 4-H year in Carroll County. I came back a few times, once each month for our club meeting and, of course, to see my girl! She looked so happy to see me and worked beautifully each time. Then July came along and I was able to stay for five weeks to participate in three shows: the Illinois State 4-H Jr. Horse show, Carroll County 4-H Show, and the Illinois State Fair. Boy was I excited! I have always loved just being at the barn with my horse and the people I loved so much. Besides, I really missed our group trail rides out in the hayfield.

2009 was by far the best year Jo and I have had together! We got along so well. She was just a peach. We did excellent at our three shows, receiving first place for the first time together…and then another! Being away for three months was tough, but there was no change between me and Jo or my fellow 4-H'ers. The farewell was hard to swallow again, but this time I felt assured that I would not be forgotten and was always welcome back home. It always amazes me how much a person, or an animal, can make such a difference in your life.

When I came back for my first visit since August, I kept thinking to myself,

"I cannot wait to see her!" It had been a long two months. I burst into the barn and hollered out, "Jo!" She nickered at me and there she was, waiting by her stall door, covered in dry mud, just waiting for me to open the door (and probably brush her off). Oh, I was so happy I could have whinnied.

We had the best time together. I groomed her to perfection, as usual, and we had a wonderful ride. The November weather was too chilly and windy to have a nice trail ride, but the indoor arena was just fine as long as we were together.

I told Jo that I would bring her up north with me soon, but that was the last time I saw my girl. She passed away later that winter. It was hard news for me to hear, but I will never forget my best friend and everything she taught me. I love my Jo!

Here is a poem I wrote for her:

My horse Jo is the cutest thing,
She is in my heart and is sure to cling.
To hear her whinny is a wonderful sound,
And it takes my breath away to see her gallop across the ground.
She sure does know when she's being good or bad,
And can push all the right buttons to make me mad.
Even when our friendship goes through a rough patch,
I somehow smooth things over with a treat or a scratch.
When I see that sparkle in her eye,
It calls me to climb up onto her back, so high.
I feel I'm flying when we ride as one,
Together in rhythm it can be so fun.
I don't really like to be apart,
Because she brings joy and happiness to my heart.
But the most important thing of all:
Is to always get back on when I take a fall.

4-H has given me the opportunity to develop my interests and has given me great life skills. I have made friendships that will last a lifetime through the horse project. I hope to be like my horse instructors who give their time unselfishly to teach others.

I have very joyful memories of 4-H in Illinois. I hope 4-H in my new state will be just as much of a blessing to my life.

Julie & Christine–4-H Friends Forever
Christine M. Boerner, Minnesota

In the tiny, chilly Minnewaska Township Hall near rural Starbuck, Minnesota, we sat on folding chairs, dangling our legs that could not quite reach the floor. The gavel was about to strike to convene the business meeting of the Pleasant Hill Troopers 4-H Club. In January of 1972, Julie and I were eight. We had reached the day we had been anticipating with excitement for the past several years. We could finally join 4-H!

Julie and I lived in the country, as we used to say, three miles outside of Glenwood. We lived just down the road from each other. Julie was the youngest of four and her older sister Teri was a club officer. Enjoying her second year of 4-H, my older sister Shelly was a good friend of Julie's cousin Jill, who was also in the club. Julie and I had tagged along with these older role models for trash pickup, the county fair, meetings, picnics, and tours for several years until we were old enough to join, observing all the fun and all the headaches.

My family had an even stronger connection to 4-H since Dad was Pope County's agricultural Extension agent. It was almost a sure thing his kids would be involved in 4-H. After all these years, I cannot overemphasize how grateful I am that I joined. My 4-H memories, especially those from the 1970s, when Julie and I were so actively involved together, are some of the fondest of my life.

Tall, slim, and a brown-eyed blond, Julie hung out with me, a petite, brown-eyed brunette. We had much more in common than our brown eyes. Since kindergarten we had established ourselves as quite a pair. Mrs. Bredeson, our second grade teacher, created "Julie and Christine's Reading Group," allowing the two of us to read quickly at our own pace. Later in school, Julie and I were inseparable in extracurricular activities that included band, speech and track. No doubt about it, she was my best friend. Despite our close ties in school, I would cite my 4-H memories with Julie as even more memorable to look back on and among the strongest bonds of my life.

I recall it like it was yesterday: her cotton skirt and that coordinating top with tiny pink and black flowers. Julie sewed it all by herself for the dress revue.

Unlike Julie, I began sewing with extra supervision and help from Mom and a passion for it all my own. I used to create countless garments for myself and my four siblings, every year for many years. The clothing project was my favorite. Not as much for Julie. Up close, her work revealed crooked stitching, uneven hemlines, and unfinished seams; yet Julie often looked outstanding as she modeled her creations. Fortunately, there are numerous options to explore in 4-H. About that time, she tried team demonstrations with me.

Julie and I were unstoppable as team demonstrators. We competed for six consecutive years and, by the end, had our act down to a science. Before the infamous *Demonstration Day* in July we would prepare and practice for hours. Our posters were elaborate and creative. Once we spent nine straight hours on posters alone. We laugh as we look back on our unique obsession. After practicing until midnight, I would tell Julie to go home and get a little sleep but return to my house the next morning for some extra "brush-up" rehearsal. My requirement was that she had to walk over a half mile up the road in the dark and arrive back at my house no later than 3:00 a.m. so we could get another practice in!

Our first demonstration was how to make puppets from gourds. At one point, I could not get the glue bottle open and the two of us lost it in giggles. Julie had to take over when I doubled over in laughter and could not continue. Despite the performance, our home economics agent asked us to repeat the demonstration on television. Another demo was entitled, "The Costumes that Grow on You." I still have pictures of the two of us on that state fair stage, Julie dressed as a Sunkist orange and me, a giant cob of yellow corn. Our final demonstration, "Rapping about Wrapping," earned a purple ribbon at the Minnesota State Fair in 1981. I will never know who might actually take the time to wrap a birthday gift to look like an ornate house, but we had the time of our lives.

Sometimes I still have dreams about Julie and me dressed as cheerleaders in short skirts with long, swingy pigtails, dancing to a brass band on a 4-H Share-the-Fun stage; strolling down the state fair cement sidewalk past the Space Needle leading to the Mexican Village, grape snow cones in hand; picking up pop cans together from the ditch of a dusty township road; standing next to Julie in the food stand with her white paper hat on, taking someone's order for a hamburger, a tiny bead of sweat on her forehead on a hot July Saturday afternoon; barefoot on the green grass of a June 4-H Field Day, crossing the finish line first in the three-legged race (again for another year!), a blue bandana tying my left leg to Julie's right leg.

I live in Watertown, Minnesota, now with my husband and our two kids. Casey our oldest, is ready to graduate and will soon start college. It was gratifying to see her receive the Carver County 4-H Federation scholarship. (For eleven years I had fun serving as leader for our club, the Waconia Whiz Kids. I did not want our kids to miss out on the 4-H experience for all the world!) Julie has three children including a daughter Gina, the same age as Casey. Julie is now a citizen of the Netherlands. We, of course, are still friends. I do not see her enough, but when we do, we laugh heartily or shed tears of joy and nostalgia over the 4-H times we shared.

I am a true believer that if more youth would simply join 4-H, the world would be a better place with fewer problems. Leadership, teamwork, an orientation toward service and volunteerism, a quest for knowledge, and of course, acquisition of wonderful communication skills are just some of the gifts we gain from 4-H.

But let us not forget my favorite 4-H gift: *Forever Friendship.*

When Life Gets Ruff
Jennifer M. Johnston, Colorado

Many people have said that they have experienced a miracle. I must say that I believe them. I have seen what I believe was a miracle. It all happened a long time ago.

Okay, not *that* long ago, maybe five years. It all began with the birth of a very special dog. Okay, so maybe she was not *that* special. Being born in a thunderstorm, now *that* is special. Being born with six toes, *that* is special. When my old dog Bullet died, my family decided to get a new puppy. Wonder of wonders, we ended up with two brown bundles of chocolate Lab, named Chip and Hershey. My parents decided that I would have to train my new puppy. That is how I ended up in 4-H.

Dog training is *hard.* For five years my dog Hershey and I got very well acquainted with each other. I could interpret anything she said, and she could understand me. You *can* have a lovely conversation with your dog. After five years in your dog project, you know when something is wrong, really wrong.

It was a normal day, a few days after a dog show. I was incredibly impressed with Hershey's performance at that show. We had actually won a Reserve Champion in showmanship, a nearly impossible feat for me and a *really* impossible feat for Hershey. As I fed her that evening, she just looked at me. She did not dive into her food like she normally did. Something was really wrong. She was fine at the show and that was just a few hours ago.

For several days she became more and more lethargic. Finally we went to the vet. At this point, she was eating nothing and growing weaker every hour. The vet had the absolute worst news for me and my family. Hershey was dying. I refused to believe this, but I could see all the truth I needed in the face of my beautiful dog.

I prayed and prayed and prayed, even as the ravishing effects of her sickness carried my dog further and further away from me. And finally, neither she nor I could stand the suffering any longer. It was time.

With the heaviest heart you can imagine, we went to the vet to end the most wonderful friendship I have ever had. I knelt on the floor in the vet's office and held her as she slipped painlessly away. I do not remember all the final words I said to her. The ones I do remember were "I love you" and "I *will* see you again." My love for Hershey was the most prominent love I have ever known. I shed very few tears after that. Most of those went to Chip, Hershey's littermate. Slowly, the pain began to fade.

I became president of my 4-H club that year. And I also went to the state fair. As it turned out, that final show Hershey went to, and practically conquered, was enough for me to go to state, something Hershey and I had achieved only once before. But I did not have a dog! How could I compete without a dog? It was then that I realized I had Chip.

Although Chip was rather chunky, he could still trot slowly around a ring. With the state fair looming, my club trainers and I raced to put five years of knowledge into a dog that had never even seen a ring before. We did it! Hershey must have had much more confidence in my previous training than I did. We went to state.

But where is the miracle? Well, I am getting to that part. It was at the state fair. The dog show was being held indoors due to a killer heat wave. The miracle I observed was when I was actually in the ring. I had just finished trotting around the ring, and the other competitors and I had lined up for the judge to inspect us. That was when the miracle happened.

As we stood there, a small sparrow landed on the ring gate, about two feet away from Chip and me. All it did was land there, look back once, and was gone. Now I must remind you, this was in an indoor stadium. I never saw that little bird again. I am sure she had many other things to do. She knew Chip and I were going to be all right. I am convinced it was Hershey's spirit, in a form of pure innocence. To me it was a miracle.

I now have two more puppies, Tucker and Drake. Chip is still my showmanship dog and I have Drake for obedience. No dog though, no matter how many I have or will have in the future, will ever take the place of Hershey. Hershey gave me more than I can ever give back. She taught me to live, love, and to love life. She gave me so much, a debt I can never repay. She and I were puppies together.

This story is written in honor of the greatest, most spoiled, most *un*-obedient, and most loving dog I have ever known. Hershey gave me the greatest gift of love, passion, and friendship. That beautiful, wonderful dog left paw prints on my heart.

And Yet, There They Are
Reana Jean Bye, Nevada

They were, simply put, the popular kids. Their hair was always done perfectly, their clothes always in style, their makeup always immaculate. Just looking at them, one would never guess that hidden in the back corners of their yards were market lambs. Just looking at these girls, one would expect to see them at high school dances and football games, not livestock shows. Yet, there they were.

They walked onto the fairgrounds in designer jeans, looking like they were headed to another day at school, or perhaps a day hanging out with friends, laughing together and talking. New 4-H'ers and families must have thought they had made a wrong turn and had accidently stumbled upon a livestock show. As everyone watched their progress from the parking lot, there was no mistaking the animals following behind them. Leading the lambs, they moved with confidence and ease. Their strides were purposeful, and they did not miss a step as they were surrounded by a storm of youth. In fact, their smiles grew bigger, their laughter more audible.

The younger 4-H'ers in the club adored and idolized them. Here was a group of girls who were popular, fun, and hanging out with them! They often spent weeknights at 4-H meetings, and the occasional weekend at workshops working with lambs. They were not afraid of hard work and constantly helped with the younger kids.

At meetings, this group of girls sat at the front, middle table. It was always the same table and it was always full of people. Those who got to the meetings early or on time silently fought over the remaining seats, everyone wanted to sit with them. Of course, during the meetings, the girls wandered from table to table helping everyone, and with a club as big as theirs, that help was greatly appreciated. But even while they moved throughout the room, their table was still theirs, and it became a novelty. Everyone wanted to sit there.

And yet, despite all of their hard work and dedication, there was always that underlying feeling that defined them as "cool;" the feeling that they were doing this now, but when they were done, they would move on. They would be too old to raise market animals for 4-H and there was nothing to keep them there or even from coming back. The club had seen this happen with many kids, even those who grew up doing nothing but market animals. There was a university in town and upon graduating high school, many of the former 4-H'ers attended school there. Life got busier, and with so many other things going on, there just was no time to go to the meetings and help.

The club leaders and the parents would be especially sad to see this group of girls leave. There was a wide age gap between them and the next older group of kids. Not only would the youth be losing their role models, they would be losing many who had been in a leadership position the past few years. More importantly, this group of girls helped show the youth not to believe or put emphasis on stereotypes.

Stereotypically, these girls were the last group one would think would raise 4-H market animals. But there they were. They showed the younger members they could do anything they wanted without worrying about the opinion of others and proved you could accomplish anything you worked hard for. As the new 4-H year started, everyone arrived at the first meeting early. They had not seen each other or been together since the beginning of summer and there was much to catch up on. Stories of the summer were told, laugher was heard from all corners of the room, and the front middle table filled up quickly.

When the four girls walked into the room, nothing changed. Greetings were called out and the stories and laughter continued. They had been such a strong part of the club, no one questioned or even thought about why they were there. It was not until they sat down that an understanding went through the room. All of the 4-H'ers looked a little confused at first, but soon went back to their stories, content simply with the fact that the girls were there. What did it matter if they sat at a different table? As they made their way to a table, not the front middle one, but rather one on the side by the leaders, a smile spread across the faces of all of the parents. Here were four girls, the world at their fingertips. They were popular, stunning, outgoing, and well into their second month of college and the demands that go with it, and they were here. It was not because their parents had made them come, or because they were going to make money by raising a market animal. No longer living at home and too old to raise an animal, they were here because they wanted to be. They were here to help.

This year, when they walked onto the fairgrounds, anybody who does not know them, and quite possibly some that do, will think they took a wrong turn; that they were on their way to the university and had to pull over, laughing as they walked towards the show. As everyone watches them make their way from the parking lot with their designer jeans and cute hair, there will be no mistaking the group of youth surrounding them.

They were, simply put, the popular kids. But they are so much more than that. Just looking at them, one would never guess they would be up that early in the morning. Just looking at them, one would never guess they would be happily joking with the youth around them. Just looking at them, one would never guess they would be at a livestock show, simply helping. And yet, there they are.

4-H is for "Cool Kids" Too! - Photo/Reana Jean Bye

Because of 4-H I Can Do Anything
Rebecca Gordon, Illinois

Animals affect people's lives daily: dogs allow the blind to see, a little kitten is a friend to a child who has none, watching a tiny fish swimming helps a baby drift to sleep. Who would have known my story would come in the form of a horse? Not just any horse, a horse named Kibbles. The effect this 36-inch horse had on me was much larger than her size.

My journey started when I was six years old. In May of 2002, I was diagnosed with a chronic illness called Crohn's disease, an incurable disease of the digestive system. After taking medicine and having tests, I was fine for a little while. A year later, my older sister got a gentle horse named Cricket. This was the start of my love for horses. The size of Cricket scared me even though she was close to the size of a pony. I was then introduced to miniature horses used for in-hand events and sometimes carting.

My family started looking for a horse my size. At the 4-H horse show my sister had entered, I was invited to see a jet-black miniature. She was beautiful and I had a feeling something great was about to happen. Her name was Kibbles.

I told my parents how much I wanted her. Kibbles had been used in carting and in-hand, and it was the perfect fit. After seeing her twice we all knew she would be my little horse. I worked hard with her and learned carting and how to show for in-hand events. It was fun to get to know her skills while I learned how to handle her. The next year I showed her in all of the classes I could enter. It was my first 4-H show. We learned a lot and had a lot of fun even though we did not receive blue ribbons.

The following year I was once again sick with my illness and admitted to the hospital in hopes of getting the right medicines needed to avoid surgery. After being in the hospital a few days on an IV, I was sent home and feeling fine. A few days later, though, I was sicker than ever. I returned to the hospital, packed for a long stay. After being back in the hospital for over a week, my mom convinced me to go to the play room. They had a lot of art stuff, so I asked if I could draw.

I drew Kibbles at home in her little pasture. Every day I went down to the play room and most of the time drew Kibbles. When I was finally feeling well enough after my surgery, I went back to the play room and again I drew Kibbles. The hospital was having an art show and I was asked to participate. I painted Kibbles telling me to get better and come home. Then I made a picture that I wanted to keep forever. It was a drawing of my family; and of course Kibbles, Cricket, and our other horse, Angel. I could not wait to see the horses—even more than my "people" family. My sisters and parents were able to visit me, but my horse family had not seen me for a long time.

I was released from the hospital after almost two months. I was so happy to see the horses, especially Kibbles. Years later, I am well and showing Kibbles in 4-H. The best part of my summer is going with Kibbles and my new horse, Snickers, to the county 4-H show. Though we are getting better year by year, we still have lots to learn.

Little did anyone know this horse was one of the things that kept me going, constantly reminding me of the fun we would have when I got better. Because of that 4-H show, because of that horse, because of being inspired everyday, I know I can do anything.

Anything is possible in 4-H! - Photo submitted by Rebecca Gordon

It Started With a Camp Scholarship
Nancy Rucker, Tennessee

Through 4-H it is possible for all children to have similar opportunities through which they can grow and excel. A challenge that many 4-H professionals face; however, is that some children lack the funds needed for them to enjoy these opportunities.

Several years ago in a casual conversation I had with Tony Young, a 4-H volunteer leader, I mentioned that I was seeking funds for camp scholarships so that 4-H members who could not afford it would be able to spend a week at 4-H camp. Tony said that was a lofty goal but suggested a few people and groups I might contact. A couple of days later Tony called again. He had been thinking about my problem and had thought of someone who might want to help—a local businessman named John E. Mayfield. Tony asked if I knew Mr. Mayfield and I said I did not. There was a long pause, and then Tony said, "Good luck."

I went to see Mr. Mayfield about a scholarship. I did not know him and our paths had never crossed, even though we lived in a small community and he owned the used bookstore and trading card shop in town. I must admit I was nervous going to ask someone I had never met for money. I had no idea if he even knew anything about 4-H or our camping program.

I turned the doorknob, slowly swung the door open, and saw boxes and boxes of used books. Like all good used book stores, books of every kind were protruding from boxes stacked more than four feet high. I made my way though the stacks of boxes and up a couple of steps into the next part of the store. There he sat on his stool behind a counter filled with sports cards. He said hello and I introduced myself. I told him what I did and then I asked him if he would be interested in supporting our 4-H camping program. He proceeded to ask questions about the 4-H program and camp.

I answered all his questions and explained I was making this request because I felt passionate about making it possible for as many kids as possible to spend a week at a great camp. The camp registration fee that year was $125 and he gave me a check for that exact amount right then and there. Then he asked if I had all the scholarships we needed. I told him no, but that I still had a few more people to ask who had provided scholarships in the past. He told me if I did not get all the money I needed, to come back and see him.

A few days later, John called and asked me to come by and see him again. I went to the bookstore and we talked about Extension and the 4-H program. We shared information and got to know each other better. He told me it was his life-long dream to own a bookstore. He said he had not been a 4-H member as a youth but that he had been asking questions of the youth who came into his store and had learned a lot about 4-H. He said he had visited our county 4-H website and the state 4-H website. He said he liked what he was learning about the program.

Then he asked me a question that really shocked me! He asked me about establishing an endowment for the county 4-H camping program through the Tennessee 4-H Foundation. Was he kidding? A few days earlier I was happy to leave his store with a check for one camp scholarship and now he wanted to discuss an endowment for the whole program! Was this for real?

It was! He continued to ask questions about the endowment opportunities and I began taking notes so I could get him some answers. When I left the bookstore I went directly back to the office to call Extension Specialist Mark Gateley, who worked with the Tennessee 4-H Foundation. It was not long before Mark was driving out to Cheatham County to meet with John.

In 2002, John E. Mayfield donated $25,000 to the Tennessee 4-H Foundation to establish the Cheatham County Endowment Fund and the John E. Mayfield 4-H Scholarship Fund. The county endowment supports 4-H youth and volunteer leader awards, programming efforts, and leadership opportunities. The Mayfield Scholarship is awarded to one or more graduating 4-H members who will continue his or her education. So far, ten 4-H members have received this honor. In 2004, John E. Mayfield established the Cheatham County 4-H Camp Endowment. Many of the campers who received a scholarship have written thank you notes to John filled with appreciation, fun stories, and evidence of new skills gained throughout the week.

John, joined by other donors, has continued to support the county 4-H program. The endowments now total more than $110,000. These funds have made "the best better" in Cheatham County. John is a true believer in endowments. These funds will continue to support 4-H long after we are gone. John made a difference with one camp scholarship but did not stop there. He has made a difference in the lives of many young people and his continued generosity will positively impact the lives of many young people for many years to come.

A Young Girl's Far-Fetched Dream
Jessica Poole, Nevada

Nearly every little girl wants a horse sometime while growing up, but there was one little girl who never stopped talking about them. Through elementary, middle, and high school she would draw pictures of horses, have folders with horses on them, read horse books like *The Black Stallion*, and do school projects on horses. There was a point in her life when close relatives would ask her to talk about something else as they were tired of hearing about horses. But she never stopped dreaming; in fact, her biggest dream was to own a horse. Unfortunately, this little girl's family was unable to afford a horse but she continued to dream her far-fetched dream.

When she was about 13 years old, the girl's mother brought home a skinny, one-year-old, mixed breed, female dog from a co-worker. One day after school the girl found the dog in the garage, hiding in a corner, shaking with anxiety, and unwilling to approach her. She was thrilled to have another living creature in her household that was not human, but she was a little worried about the dog's behavior. The dog, known as Kesha, began acclimating to her new family but still exhibited unacceptable behavioral characteristics. For example, Kesha would have "accidents" on the carpet, leave shredded clothing on the floor, and was very rambunctious. The girl's mother decided Kesha needed some training or she would have to go. While searching for affordable dog training, the girl's mother found a 4-H dog club in Carson City, Nevada, that provided obedience training for youth willing to work with their dogs. The girl's mother asked her about joining the 4-H club, and after a little thought she agreed. This was her first 4-H club, but it would not be the last!

As Kesha and her owner's skills grew, the girl became more involved in 4-H. She started showing in 4-H dog shows and later had the opportunity to attend and participate in some big leadership events including National 4-H Conference, National Canadian 4-H Conference, and the Nevada State 4-H Ambassador program. She even landed a job at the Carson City/Storey County Cooperative Extension Office at the age of 16. Her involvement with 4-H was intensive, time-consuming, and costly, but was very beneficial. The girl's dog training skills would be put to good use when her mom got another dog.

Unlike Kesha, this dog was a puppy, playful and full of energy. But this mixed breed female also needed some behavioral adjustments. The new dog's name was Mesha and while initially a cute name, it made it difficult to train the dogs together since Kesha and Mesha sound so much alike. Once the name problem was resolved, the two dogs became phenomenal in obedience and agility classes, and they and the girl won many grand champion and reserve champion ribbons. While she loved her dogs immensely, her dream of owning a horse began to emerge again.

The spark that reawakened the girl's dream is attributed to the Parelli Conference she attended with her 4-H group in the summer of 2003. The Natural Horsemanship methods and skills they demonstrated "blew her away." She had never seen anything like it before and it motivated her to find a horse to begin practicing these methods. While working at the Cooperative Extension office in Carson City, she learned of a BLM Wild Horse project in progress. Sadly, the group had already started and was filled to capacity when she asked about joining. While a "bummer," it did not stop her from moving forward with other options. Sandy Wallin, the girl's 4-H boss and Extension agent, told her about a group known as Least Resistance Training Concepts (LRTC). This group worked closely with feral horses and used Natural Horsemanship methods. Since the girl was determined to work with horses no matter what, she decided to join and learn the skills needed to work with feral horses. The whole time, the girl (who by now was about 17) never forgot her dream of owning a horse. She was fully supported by her mother, as it had once been her mother's own long-lost dream. Not only was the girl able to work with horses, meet new friends, and attend horse events, but she also developed a close bond with her mother as they participated in these activities together. From a rekindled dream to a work in progress, the girl finally believed her far-fetched dream could come true.

Participating with LRTC enabled the girl to do a 4-H independent horse project that gave her the opportunity to practice her natural horsemanship skills. At the 2004 Western States Wild Horse and Burro Expo in Reno, Nevada, LRTC encouraged her to give a demonstration with Mackey, a horse she had been working with. It turned out Mackey's owner, Lacy J. Dalton (the professional singer), watched the girl work with her horse and was extremely impressed with her horsemanship skills. She quietly told the girl's mother and Willis Lamm, then President of LRTC, she would like to give the girl one of her horses. The girl's mother considered the offer and when Ms. Dalton and Mr. Lamm said they would provide the necessary support, she agreed to allow the girl's dream of owning a horse to become a reality. After the Expo, mother and daughter were eating at a local restaurant when her mother told the girl that Lacy J. Dalton was giving her a horse. She sat there in shock, finding such generosity hard to believe, but when her mother assured her it was true she began crying tears of happiness!

My name is Jessica Poole and as you have probably guessed, that young girl was me. My far-fetched dream of owning a horse became a reality because of 4-H. My horse Bebe and I are still together. Even the most far-fetched dreams can come true!

Cloverbuds and Horses
Shawna Gordon, Illinois

God's blessings come in many ways, some of which we would never expect, but nonetheless appreciate and love. My blessings came when my older sister, Gabrielle, decided it was time for me to start riding her old horse Cricket. This was not just a horse to her, but her best friend who had always taken care of her on all of her riding experiences. That is, up until now. Gabrielle knew that Cricket was getting too old and frail for her to keep riding, and also knew that Cricket could be her little sister's best friend. After much anguish, care, and thought, Gabrielle relinquished her old Crick-A-Moe to me. I am now old enough to be a 4-H Cloverbud, with a story to tell of friendship and love. Beth Gordon, my mom, helped me share my story.

My two teenage sisters have horses and have been teaching me about them since almost the day I was born. Their first horse was a mini, named Angel, with a wild personality and inquisitive attitude. To our surprise, she grew to be a pony who challenged all of her handlers, except for Gabrielle. Since I did not have my own horse they let me adopt her and consider her my own, though Gabrielle and Becca showed her at the 4-H county show. I loved Angel with all of my heart, and now she is gone. I know that somebody else is enjoying her friendship.

I have since moved on to be Cricket's best friend. My dreams came true; I was finally learning to ride with my older sisters. Gabrielle was a great teacher and Becca was always helpful and encouraging. My sisters have always been there to teach me how to sit in the saddle, how to mount and dismount, how to be gentle with the reins, and, most of all, how to be a loving, and caring rider.

Last year I was hoping to ride Cricket at our county 4-H show. I learned that because of state rules I had to wait until I turned eight to show my horse. The adults in my county knew all of the Cloverbuds were heartbroken, so we had a show of our own. We could not ride the animals we loved and cherished, but we did have a lot of fun making stick horses to fill-in for our friends. My stick horse was black with a black mane and tail. To me she was identical to my friend Cricket.

It was one of the happiest days of my life. I was going to ride in the 4-H county show. Everyone was going to watch me ride Cricket. The arena was emptied so that all of the Cloverbuds could enter for our competition. I entered the arena a bit nervously, but soon became more at home, showing off my beaming smile, and of course my riding abilities. We walked, trotted, and cantered our horses. We competed in barrels, poles, and flags. We showed our horses proudly, with all of the other 4-H kids and parents watching us. It was a great day. Who knew that we could have so much fun riding stick horses at the 4-H horse show? Though they looked like stick horses to others, to us they represented our best friends.

That was the day I won my first trophy for riding. I was given all sorts of prizes for riding in that competition, but the trophy was the best one of all. I have treasured that small trophy, knowing that in the future I will ride in the county 4-H show atop my best friend, Cricket.

This is my story, but I needed some help from my mother Beth Gordon to write it because I am just six years old.

Cloverbuds Are Horse Lovers - Drawing/Maria Barga

Bleeding Green

4-H Has It All!
Gus Kronberg, North Dakota

When you are five years old, *everything* seems big! This includes the "talks" my mom gave us. My mom always wants us to do the best we can at everything we do. She is more like a coach. I think it is because she actually was a coach. She says she is my biggest fan and cheerleader, just without the pom-poms.

I was five years old and being nosey and listening to one of my mom's "talks" that was supposed to be just for my big sisters. It was getting close to fair time and they had projects they needed to finish. I think they were watching TV instead of working on their projects. My mom told them that whatever they do in life, they need to follow through with it. "If you are going to get anywhere in life, you can't be a quitter. You cannot rely on anyone other than yourself to make things happen for you. There are some people who are really good athletes. Some people are really good in school. They might get athletic scholarships or academic scholarships, but it's because they have worked hard at what they do. We are good at a lot of things, but what we are *really* good at is 4-H. It gives you more opportunities than you will find anywhere else. If you are going to get anywhere in your life and if you are going to get out of this town after you graduate, you need to count on no one other than yourself. You need to give 100 percent in 4-H. You need to find out what you like, what you are good at, and do the best you can at it." Well, that "talk" must have done the job. My sisters were up and working on their projects before Mom could even finish her last sentence.

I have never forgotten that talk my mom gave my sisters. I am 12 years old now and I can remember everything she said that day. Now, I do not think it would be fair of me to go on with this story without mentioning I have received my fair share of Mom's famous "talks." My mom is great at getting us fired up and inspired about a lot of things but when it comes to anything related to 4-H, she is something else! There have been a lot of times that I did not want to finish something or follow it through, but my mom always found a way to help me turn that around. I know it is because she believes in me, but I also know it is because she believes in 4-H.

I have learned a lot by just trying new project areas and have found there are some things I like and am good at. There are also some things I do not like or am not great at and, for safety reasons, should only try once. But even if I am not good at something, I am glad I tried it. Thanks to 4-H, I am a pretty good cook, I can sew, and I can grow a pretty amazing flower garden. Most guys my age would not find these things very exciting, but I sure do. Why would any guy my age get excited about things like that? Well, I think it is the feeling of accomplishing something and giving it my best effort. I have made cookies and fudge that did not look anything like cookies or fudge the first time I tried to make them. But after the second or third try, they were great. I remember not being happy about the way things turned out the first time I tried to make them. I also remember being determined not to give up until I got it right and hearing my mom say, "I knew you could do it!"

"Some people dream of success while others wake up and work hard at it." I am not sure who said that first, but we sure like that phrase at our house. Well, *like* might be a "stretch" especially on those mornings I would like to sleep in. When I say *we*, it is really my mom who enjoys using that phrase the most. Who really wants to get up at five in the morning, drive for three hours on icy roads and through snow just to get to a livestock judging contest? Usually, I do not. Once I am there, though, and I see all of my 4-H friends and get into my "judging mode," I am really glad I am there. Who wants to get up early on any morning and do chores? Usually, I do not. I am always glad I have my animals and once I am up and going, it is not bad at all. I am busy, I am a kid, and I am involved in a lot of things. So, really, the hardest part of 4-H for me right now is waking up. Other than that, it is a piece of cake! Anyone who thinks 4-H is hard work and does not have anything you are interested in, well; I dare you to try it! This year I became a Junior 4-H Ambassador. I have created and participated in community service projects. I have been to camps. I have been involved in speaking contests. I have been involved in over 40 different project areas and I have learned a lot and have also *liked* every single one of them. I have been to county fairs and state fairs. I have seen a lot and I am only 12 years old. Where else can you get anything like this? Nowhere.

4-H has it all! Whatever you want to do, 4-H can help you. Whatever it is that you want to be when you grow up, 4-H gives you everything you need to become whatever you want to be. I do not know what I want to be when I grow up yet. I still have time to work on that, but the one thing I do know is that 4-H is going to help me be great at it!

I Want to be a Leader
Alvin G. Davis, Texas

When I became a 4-H member
It was with a very great joy
Just like a small child
With a brand new toy.

I cared for my project
From day to day
Just like the child
In his daily play.

And I gradually grew
In my childish way
Till I made some money
Which was more than pay.

But much more important
Than the money I made
Was the knowledge I gained
In my 4-H Club trade.

My projects were entered
In our many 4-H shows
But they weren't very good
As far as that goes.

So I learned to take defeat
With a rock hard chin
And I sure didn't quit
Because I didn't win.

I just kept on trying
Like the old sayings go
If you don't succeed
It just goes to show.

I Want to be a Leader

You've not done your best
And there's further to go
If you never have won
And the top you're below.

I kept up my work
That grew better each day
Till at last I succeeded
The long, hard way.

A few honors I won
Which weren't very high
But to me were like stars
In an almost empty sky.

And these few successes
Though small they may be
Served a very good purpose
By putting spirit in me.

So now I'm striving harder
Even harder than before
With the strength and wisdom
That I may have in store.

Though my goals are higher
Than most 4-H'ers are
I think I may reach them
And add to my sky a star.

But the thing I want most
In this 4-H Pilgrim Land
Is to guide a young member
And to lend a helping hand.

So that when his work is over
And his 4-H life is done
That I may say in earnest
I helped him when he won.

And if I'm enabled to do this
By our Creator with grace
I think it would be a star
That would fill all the space.

In my sky of 4-H honors
To glow o'er me each night
And be a shining memory
Of my 4-H days, so bright.

Alvin Davis wrote this poem in 1943 following the first of three trips to National 4-H Congress. He was named the nation's outstanding 4-H boy in 1948. Alvin's many accomplishments and years of service to 4-H have been recognized with his induction into the National 4-H Hall of Fame Class of 2010.

4-H Is...
Emily Tebbe O'Neill, Illinois

What do you think of when you hear someone mention 4-H? Many people think of 4-H as "cows, plows, and sows." When I joined 4-H 20 years ago, 4-H was taking projects to the fair and receiving ribbons. Believe me, I soon realized 4-H was much more than that!

4-H is perseverance. My first cooking project, an apple crisp, became a family favorite. Unfortunately, my biscuits or 'hockey pucks' as my brothers called them, did not. Dad joked about surviving the cooking projects of his three sisters and figured he would make it through mine, too. The ladies in Mom's office were always willing to try one of my new recipes and tell me how they rated.

4-H is creative expression. I always took visual arts projects since they gave me a chance to be creative and design something original, and it also helped Mom decorate our home and save money at the same time. One Christmas I made plant hangers for several relatives. It meant so much to them because I made them.

4-H is appreciating one's history. The citizenship projects required a lot of time, doing research at libraries, historical societies, churches and cemeteries, and were usually a lot of fun, (except when the air conditioner went out in the car and we had to walk for help in 100 degree plus heat). I discovered several interesting facts about my ancestors, my community, my county, and my state. These projects brought to light the suffering some people had to endure to obtain a better way of life. I have a better understanding of Mother Jones, fighting for better working conditions in the mines. I located a house in our county that served as part of the Underground Railroad. My search for interesting facts and trivia paid off as I watched people read my display and walk away saying "I didn't know that!"

4-H is local and global. One thing that had been stressed over the years was community service. For several years our club collected socks at Christmas. Some of the socks would go to the veterans to put in their baskets. The rest were taken to the school nurse in case a child would need a pair of socks. Canned goods and paper products were collected for the local Care

Center, the veterans to help fill their baskets at Christmas, and also for the victims of the flood of 1993. We all knew someone who was helped by these contributions. Maybe it was a neighbor, or maybe it was Mom's best friend from college who lost everything in that flood. No matter who it was, we helped contribute to the effort.

Tony, a friend of my mom's, became involved with an orphanage in Haiti. Several years ago a group from the orphanage came to visit and perform. We collected clothing for the boys to wear while they were here and also to take back with them. They were in need of personal items such as soap, shampoo, and toothpaste, as well as school supplies and linens. In all, our club collected seven boxes of clothing and supplies to be taken back to Haiti. Most of the boys spoke very little English, but the words they all knew were "Thank You!" They meant it.

<u>4-H is community in action.</u> Environmental awareness is a focus of many 4-H clubs. We participated in the Adopt-A-Highway program where we picked up trash from a two-mile stretch of road. Sometimes it was hot; sometimes it was cold and wet. Sometimes we came away with poison ivy. It was hard work but we still had fun.

One of the first things our 4-H Voices in Action group organized was a county-wide paper drive that was held in conjunction with 4-H week. Our goal was to "Save a Tree." As a member of Voices in Action, I presented the idea to our local club. I contacted the mayor to inquire about "wrapping" a tree and displaying a sign in the city park. I also received permission from local business owners to use their business as a drop off point for papers. The response from the community was unbelievable! In only a week's time, our club collected three pickup loads of paper! The response was similar all over the county. In all, we saved more than 50 trees!

Our mayor saw a need. If the community responded that well to a paper drive held by a 4-H group, how would the city respond to a city-sponsored recycling project? It took time, but within six months the city opened its own recycling center. Because of our success with the paper drives, the mayor approached our club and asked if we would be willing to volunteer a few Saturday mornings to assist with the recycling. Of course we were willing! The mayor scheduled the community organizations and then I prepared a schedule for our club. Again, the response was unbelievable. Mom said because of the success of the program, the recycling center hours were increased to give citizens more opportunities to drop off their recycling.

<u>4-H is making a difference.</u> One year our club held a Halloween story hour at our local library in conjunction with "Make a Difference Day." I read a "scary" story to the children. Then we helped them make a lollipop ghost and treated them to goody-filled treat bags! With the assistance from a local store, we were also able to present our local library with several new children's books.

Being employed at a local nursing home, I knew first-hand how the residents appreciated visits from children. At my suggestion, our club wrote over 100 Christmas cards. The residents' faces lit up as our club members presented them with a card, leaving them with a little bit of Christmas cheer.

<u>4-H is a personal commitment.</u> Our club has helped with many community service activities and I have done a few on my own. I assisted and taught at Vacation Bible School for several summers and made lap robes for children in wheelchairs in a Haitian orphanage. Within a week, my grandmother, Mom and I had six brightly colored lap robes sewn and ready to go to Haiti.

My favorite service was volunteering as a candy striper at the local hospital. For four summers and over 500 hours, I transported patients, filed X-ray films and paperwork, and filled water pitchers. I wanted to be a nurse and what better way to find out what it was like on the floor of a hospital than to volunteer!

In a world where violence and drugs seem to be the norm rather than the exception, some of us try to make this world a better place. In 2000 I attended National 4-H Congress in Atlanta. I attended seminars and worked on community service projects while I was there. But the most awesome moment during that entire event was to hear 1200 people say, "I pledge my head to clearer thinking, my heart to greater loyalty, my hands to larger service, and my health to better living for my club, my community, my country and my world." 4-H gives young people a chance to give something back to their community.

Today I am a nurse, just like I always wanted to be, and a new mom. In seven years I hope my daughter will have the opportunity to join 4-H and find out for herself what 4-H really is!

The National 4-H Hall of Fame
Dan Tabler, Maryland

The idea for the National 4-H Hall of Fame came to me in the early 70s while driving home from a regional staff meeting in Morgantown, West Virginia. A news item on the radio about a sports hall of fame triggered an epiphany; a hall of fame to *"celebrate those who have made a significant impact on 4-H."* I had the opportunity to share my idea with the leader of one of our national 4-H organizations later that summer at Jackson's Mill (West Virginia's legendary state 4-H camp). I happened to be seated across from him at dinner one evening and as we chatted I mentioned my idea. He said a 4-H Hall of Fame had merit but would never happen, as it would be impossible to reach a consensus on whom to include. Ironically, that gentleman was inducted into the Centennial Class. He was right about the consensus issue, as that discussion continues.

I had been a 4-H member for ten years and a 4-H agent for several more but did not fully understand how 4-H "worked" at the national level. Once the roles of the three national partners (National 4-H Council, what is now known as 4-H National Headquarters and the National Association of Extension 4-H Agents) were more clear, I began to understand why finding consensus can be challenging. Starting with NAE4-HA appeared to be the best option. I joined NAE4-HA in 1972 and in 1975 chaired a task force that became the Public Relations and Information Committee the following year. As PR&I chair in 1977, followed by two years as Northeast Regional Director, I had the opportunity to "sell" my hall of fame idea. Unfortunately, the typical response was, "That's a nice idea." As a 4-H'er, I had learned the value of persistence and over the next 25 years kept the dream alive.

In 1999, with the the 4-H centennial on the horizon, I again proposed the National 4-H Hall of Fame. Apparently my idea had been ahead of its time, but with the centennial approaching the timing was finally right. When the PR&I Committee broke into task forces, I was no longer a "committee of one." I was joined by a small cadre of kindred spirits who proved to be a very dedicated group that continues to be the heart of the 4-H Hall of Fame committee more than ten years later.

While there was now a committee to work with, we needed someone with good computer skills. The first person I thought of and recruited was my friend Jim Kahler, a Maryland co-worker. Jim soon left Maryland to work at 4-H National Headquarters but continued providing his technical expertise. The initial committee decided we needed to expand our membership to include two representatives from each region and one each from National 4-H Council and 4-H National Headquarters. During the early planning years, committee membership remained relatively stable with a few new members joining and some leaving for other projects. The founding Hall of Fame Committee included Karen Gagne (Maine) and me from the Northeast; Travis Burke (North Carolina) and Cheryl Varnadoee (Georgia) from the South; Jo Turner (Missouri) and Betty Wingerter (Ohio) from North Central; and Bryan Chadd (Arizona) and Mary Jean Craig (Idaho) from the West. Several program assistants represented National 4-H Council initially until Carolyn Fernandez joined us. Jim Kahler represented 4-H National Headquarters. Pam Van Horn (Kansas) joined us and Dorothy Freeman (Minnesota) was recruited to replace Jo Turner. Dorothy also represented state leaders, as had Jo, and additionally represented past national presidents. Betty Wingerter and Karen Gagne are now also past national presidents, making this a very distinguished group.

As the Hall of Fame plans evolved I shared them with then National 4-H Council President and CEO Dick Sauer and COO Don Floyd. It was Don who suggested a virtual hall of fame rather than a room full of dusty pictures. Don's recommendation was enthusiastically endorsed and, thanks largely to Jim Kahler's efforts, the virtual National 4-H Hall of Fame became a reality. You can view it at http://www.nae4ha.com/hof/

The goal for the 2002 Centennial Class was to induct 100 laureates, one for each year of 4-H's existence. Every state was invited to nominate three "favorite sons and daughters" with a promise of having at least one nominee inducted that the state could identify. The three national partners each nominated ten people. The intent from the beginning was to create a National 4-H Hall of Fame that included members of the whole 4-H family from volunteers, to faculty and staff at all levels, to major donors, and others who had made a significant impact on 4-H from the club to the national level.

The Hall of Fame committee selected the Centennial Class. Beginning with the Class of 2003, a separate 16 person selection committee was appointed to serve a two-year term. In an effort to provide continuity and avoid "gate keeping," half of the committee is replaced each year with new members. The selection committee includes two representatives from each of the four regions, a representative from 4-H National Headquarters and one from

National 4-H Council, three laureates, a past national NAE4-HA president, and a 4-H member. HOF Classes typically celebrate about 20 laureates. There is no set number of laureates selected each year.

After keeping the dream alive for so many years, the Centennial Class induction was especially meaningful. As expected, a significant number of those inducted in the first several years of the Hall of Fame were deceased, some for many years. A family member often attended the ceremony to represent the laureate, including J. C. Penney's daughter in 2002. It was truly inspiring to see how deeply the Centennial laureates valued their recognition as it took a considerable effort for many to attend, especially those in wheelchairs or relying on walkers and canes. National 4-H Council has served as the ceremony's host from the beginning and consistently does a wonderful job of making the laureates feel special and appreciated.

I was invited to serve as the master of ceremonies for the Class of 2003 ceremony. I had carefully rehearsed the script detailing each laureate's achievements and service to 4-H. At the last minute, I decided to ignore the script and have the laureates tell their own stories. With no time for preparation, each laureate shared a brief, heartfelt story that often brought tears, was sometimes funny, and was always inspiring. Those stories became the inspiration for this book and were such a valued part of the ceremony that Travis Burke and Pam Van Horn, who followed me as HOF chairs, have continued the practice.

For more than 50 years, 4-H has provided me with many wonderful opportunities and experiences. The National 4-H Hall of Fame, serving as editor of *4-H Stories from the Heart* and helping create the Diamond Clover Award are among my most cherished accomplishments. Dreams do come true, but persistence is often required.

Dan Tabler's years of service to 4-H and NAE4-HA have been recognized with his induction into the National 4-H Hall of Fame Class of 2010.

The National 4-H Hall of Fame Class of 2010 - Photo/Edwin Remsberg

Operation Military Kids

Sharon K. B. Wright, National 4-H Headquarters

On a cold November evening I accompanied my husband to the Maryland 4-H Volunteer Forum in Ocean City, Maryland. He promised that Maryland teens were going to feature Operation: Military Kids (OMK), a program that had been initiated with Army Child and Youth Services while I served as a National Program Leader at National 4-H Headquarters, USDA.

OMK is a collaborative effort of the US Army and 4-H to support the children and youth of military service members who are impacted by deployment, and to build understanding among citizens of the challenges faced by military families.

4-H has designated a State 4-H Military Liaison in each state to coordinate programs with children of service members in all military branches. The State 4-H Military Liaison directs OMK in each state by building a state team of representatives from 4-H Extension, National Guard, Military Reserve components, schools, and various community and state organizations. These state teams build infrastructure and sustainable support services to youth in military families before, during, and after family members are deployed. OMK programs focus on integrating active-duty and guard/reserve youth into local youth programs. OMK programs create community support networks for military youth by delivering recreational, social, and educational programs and integrating military youth into ongoing 4-H and other youth development programs.

Major OMK program components include Speak Out for Military Kids, Hero Packs, and Ready, Set, Go! training. Speak Out for Military Kids is a community service opportunity where military and non-military teens are trained to establish speakers bureaus to advocate for military-connected youth affected by deployment. The teens raise community awareness of issues faced by geographically dispersed military children and youth, and foster community understanding of the sacrifices that military families make. In the process, the teens acquire knowledge and skills in developing creative and informative presentations using various media as well as leadership, research, organizational, and public speaking skills. Hero Packs are OMK knapsacks filled with teddy bears, stationery, books, bracelets, key chains, and a variety of items, and are given to military youth as a "Thank You" for the sacrifices that they make while their parents are deployed. Ready, Set, Go! is a comprehensive training designed to educate youth workers, educators, counselors, and other community service agencies on military culture, the deployment cycle, fostering resilience in kids, influence of the media, and building community capacity. The intent of Ready, Set, Go! training is to increase ordinary citizens' understanding of the unique issues facing military youth and to assist them in creating state and local OMK support networks. School personnel, youth-serving agency staff, and civic groups find Ready, Set, Go! training especially beneficial.

Officially launched in April 2005, OMK has touched 88,000 military youth and provided information to 21,000 community members across the United States.

Shortly after I entered the exhibit area in the Ocean City hotel, I met Brittany, who eagerly explained OMK to me. She talked fast and directed me to the table where she and a couple of other teens were busy sewing. "We're making fleece scarves for military kids whose parents are going to Iraq. There are two different fabrics. This is how they are made. It's easy. Do you want to make some?" Before I could respond, Brittany had me involved as she went on to explain their plans for distribution at an upcoming National Guard event. "The kids miss their parents and we want to show them that we care and invite them to join our 4-H Club." She clearly understood the mission behind OMK and was an enthusiastic promoter. That evening I met teens whose parents were in the Army and also National Guard members who were serving as 4-H volunteers for this conference. I was delighted to see how this program that I knew from a 4-H Headquarters perspective worked at the community level. When I left, Brittany sent me home with two bolts of fleece, sewing instructions, and a deadline for completing the project in time for the event.

Sharon Wright has retired and lives in Delaware with her husband, former Maryland State 4-H Program Leader, Dick Byrne.

My Favorite Holiday
Holli Jo Kronberg, North Dakota

I was recently asked what my favorite holiday is, and after thinking about it for a while, I had almost determined that I do not have a favorite. I am equally passionate about all of the holidays. Each one has a special feeling that is evoked at the very moment it arrives, a special smell that is in the air outside or emanating from the kitchen. Each holiday also has its own meaning that makes it special. There is no possible way that I could pick one to be my favorite! So, I began to wonder why this person would ask me such a question. Could it be that I go a little *overboard* with the enthusiasm and décor I display when a holiday rolls around? Was it that obvious and should I be embarrassed? Before I could even begin to explain or answer the question, my daughter was kind enough to answer the question for me. Without an ounce of hesitation my daughter said, "My mom's favorite holiday is National 4-H Week. We celebrate it at our house like most people celebrate Christmas!" Well, that holiday was not included when I was initially asked about my favorite, but my daughter, sensing my *distress*, was quick to come to my rescue. On the way home, I asked her why she answered as she did, and the conversation that followed was one I will never forget.

"Who else do you know shops for anything and everything that comes in green, white, and gold?" she said. Well, I guess she is right. I do hit the clearance aisles after Christmas to pick up everything I can in those glorious colors. I think I am also in love with St. Patrick's Day because it sports the same colors as 4-H. Honestly, I am Irish, and we are *obligated* to celebrate, but how lucky am I that I can use those decorations twice in one year! "Who else do you know gets as excited as you, and does a happy dance in the middle of Walmart, because you found bags of green and white M&M's?" she said next. Well, she is right again. I do get excited about those things. Do you know how many incredibly cool 4-H things you can make with green and white M&M's? We like to make little favors that have 4-H stickers on them and hand them out to everyone during National 4-H Week. We have used green and white gum, green and white hard candies, and now we have M&M's to work with. She was right. I did do a happy dance. National 4-H Week is such a wonderful opportunity to share with others all of the wonderful things that 4-H has to offer young people. I have been a member, a leader, and a volunteer for many years and now I have children who are in the 4-H program. It is my goal to let others know what a wonderful program 4-H is and if it means passing out a million green and white M&Ms, then that is just what I will do! National 4-H Week is also the perfect time to thank those who administer the 4-H program, because without them, we would not have the amazing opportunities that 4-H provides.

My daughter had quite a few examples of how I get "worked up" over this holiday more so than the other holidays we celebrate. I was unhappy with myself that I had not put this holiday on the mental list I had made earlier as I was trying to make a selection from those "traditional" holidays such as Christmas, Thanksgiving, Easter and so on. How could I possibly forget to include this holiday, which is equally as important to me as all of the other holidays—well, with just a bit more importance than the others? While my mind was racing with all of these thoughts and questions, I stopped and faced my daughter. Was she embarrassed by all of this? Were any of my children embarrassed by my over abundant and zealous display of "holiday-ism?" I had never questioned this before. Did my daughter's quick response to the question asked of me mean more than I had initially thought? I wanted to ask her, but did not want to put her on the spot. It seemed like forever since she had made her last comment regarding my happy dance at Walmart. In fact, it was just a breath or two and then, "Mom, why *do* you get so into the holidays?" What a relief. Now I could explain myself.

My childhood was not that perfect childhood you hear about in storybooks. There was never much holiday spirit or decorations. I do recall some happy holiday memories, but they were sparse. I knew it would be important to celebrate holidays with my children when I became a parent. I wanted my children to be able to tell wonderful stories about the holidays they experienced and I wanted to start traditions they could pass on to their children. So, for the past 23 years I have tried to make the most of each holiday. I decorate, but not to extremes. The main joy and experience I like to take from each holiday is letting those around me know I am thinking of them. I cannot imagine not taking the time to celebrate all that is important in my life. I have so much to celebrate and to be thankful for.

After explaining why I like to do a little extra to celebrate the holidays, she just smiled. She did not say another word. She understood and I knew she had not been embarrassed by my "holiday-ism" and, in fact, I think she might be proud of the fact that I do those extra things to make the holidays, including National 4-H Week, special. We are a family that is very proud of our 4-H heritage and my children love celebrating that holiday just as much as I do, maybe even just a little bit more. How do I know? They are the first ones to head for the green boxes that hold all of the decorations for that week-long holiday, and in those boxes are the largest pair of sparkling green four leaf clover sunglasses (picture Elton John in the 70s), green, white, and gold beads, crazy tie-dyed green t-shirts that have the 4-H emblem front and center, and the craziest green hat selection. They find different 4-H-themed outfits for every day of the week and wear them proudly. They make phone calls to see if they can paint windows full of clovers and 4-H-isms for the upcoming celebration. They actually put a lot of thought into the activities and plans for National 4-H Week. I think with all the effort they put into this holiday they are proud. They must be. Why would children go to such great lengths to show their support for something if it did not involve pride? I know that my children are not embarrassed by my desire to share my "holiday-ism" with others. Honestly, they would be the first ones to tell me if they were embarrassed. I think they have learned its "OK" to be passionate about something and its "OK" to show others you care. Just one more of the wonderful "life lessons" taught and learned through 4-H that in itself is worth celebrating! I would recommend you take the opportunity to enjoy all the traditions and celebrations you can. I know this is one tradition I am glad I started and I know my children and I will continue to share it with others for quite some time.

Wally Jerome, Entrepreneur
Gloria Hafemeister, Wisconsin

"4-H has always meant a great deal to me," Wally Jerome recently said. Mr. Jerome is the perfect example of a 4-H success story.

Back in 1922, young Wally became fascinated with turkeys and bought his first turkey eggs. That started his life-long career in turkey production, culminating in the sale of his Turkey Store Company to Hormel for over $334 million in 2001.

While in grade school, Jerome persuaded his parents, twin brother, and sister to raise turkeys and become involved in the Maple Grove 4-H Poultry Club in Barron County. In those days it was typical to have 4-H clubs that focused on a specific animal, project or activity. He won honors in 4-H club work in the poultry field and became the leader of the club. His club also had a demonstration team at the Wisconsin State Fair.

In 1941 Wally Jerome formed Jerome Turkey Farm. In 1952 he raised 15,000 turkeys. In 1953 he began a hatching operation and in 1959 hatched over 2.5 million poults. In 2001 the renamed Turkey Store Company became the sixth largest turkey operation in the United States.

As one of Wisconsin's oldest 4-H alumni (Jerome was 96 in 2005), he sees 4-H as one of the sparks that laid the foundation of his hugely successful business.

"It (4-H) has a tremendous influence on youth," said Mr. Jerome. "If they diligently pursue 4-H and all the things 4-H teaches, they're not only going to be more successful in life, but happier and more creative in every respect." Jerome knows that it does not take much in the way of encouragement and information to help a child get started in a life-long interest.

Wally Jerome's family members have all been active in 4-H and remain so to this day.

In addition to his business success, Mr. Jerome displays the 4-H emphasis on community service as a strong supporter of the Coalition for a Tobacco-Free Wisconsin and the Barron community. He has been an annual contributor to the Wisconsin 4-H program since the 1960s, helping to support 4-H youth across the state.

4-H's emphasis on leadership, communication and citizenship were a factor in the development of Wally Jerome—businessman, philanthropist, and community leader.

This story previously appeared in the Wisconsin 4-H Foundation's booklet "4-H... Impacts & Shapes Lives."

Vermont 4-H Teen Congress Launches a Career
Mary Carlson, Vermont

During my years on the University of Vermont State 4-H Staff, one of my favorite things was watching teens grow and develop through their teen leadership experiences. One example especially stands out in my memory. It was February 1996. The Vermont 4-H Teen Board was holding a teen congress planning meeting when Derrick Cram, a quiet new board member, approached me that morning saying he would like to be the DJ (disc jockey) during the dance at our annual Vermont 4-H Teen Congress the following summer. He was a 14-year-old eighth grader, had been to Teen Congress once, and was new on the board. To top it off he was really shy, but he was also determined to DJ the big Teen Congress dance on our annual Lake Champlain cruise. His dad did some DJ work as a hobby and Derrick had already been working with him for a couple of years. He said he was sure he could do a super job. I was nervous because we always hired a professional DJ for the cruise. It was our biggest teen event of the year. I looked at Derrick and said something like, "Do you know what you're asking? These kids will eat you alive!" We had always put the dance in the hands of a much older, professional DJ. Just the thought of putting the dance in the hands of a 14-year-old shy kid made me very nervous. He looked at me and said in a quiet voice, "I *know* I can do it; I *know* I can." I looked back at him and said, "Why don't you talk to the teen board right after lunch and see what they say."

The quiet teen shared his idea with his fellow board members that afternoon. They seemed pretty surprised to have this young, quiet new board member make such a request. They held back a bit, and then Derrick made them an offer they could not refuse. He said, "I'll do it *for free* and we can use my equipment for other activities during Teen Congress." That sealed the deal. Budgets were always tight, so *free* was the magic word.

The evening of the summer cruise arrived, and buses loaded with excited 4-H Teen Congress delegates pulled up at the dock on Lake Champlain. The big boat was waiting, and coming from that boat was dynamite music. Derrick was already onboard and working. The air was electric. For the next three and a half hours the teens danced non-stop. Derrick knew his audience and knew the kind of music they liked. With a majority of the delegates being girls, he knew he had to avoid the slow dances and intersperse lots of group numbers like the "Chicken Dance," "Cotton Eyed Joe," "The Electric Slide," and of course, the "Limbo." If he played some fast songs and got the girls dancing, the boys would follow...and they did. Best of all, he knew a lot of the boys because most of them were fellow 4-H dairy members. If Derrick could be involved with this dance thing, well, they could too.

It was the most successful Teen Congress cruise we had ever had. Under that introverted exterior was an outstanding DJ just waiting for a chance to prove himself. Derrick says high school and 4-H were completely different. In high school he was shy, embarrassed, and afraid to take a step. The 4-H teen board accepted him and let him be who he wanted to be. By getting that support he was able to transition into the business. After 4-H Teen Congress he had many referrals to DJ high school dances throughout the state. He also went on to be the DJ for New England 4-H Teen Congress held at the various land-grant universities in the other New England states.

Derrick graduated from college with a degree in music technology. Today he owns his own DJ business and has eleven staff working for him, including two younger brothers and several 4-H'ers. The business, Jam Man Entertainment, has three divisions—one focusing on parties, school dances and nightclubs; another that focuses on weddings and formal events; and a third that is karaoke-based. His business takes him all over New England. In addition, he is one of a group of top nationally recognized DJs who provide mixes for entry level DJs throughout the country.

Vermont 4-H Teen Congress is still very much in his family. He continues to take his music there every year and teaches a popular DJ workshop for congress delegates. His younger brother is about to serve his final year as DJ for 4-H Teen Congress, but a cousin is coming along with the skills to carry on the family tradition.

Derrick's dream is to continue to expand and grow his business. Every year he attends the International DJ Expo in Atlantic City, New Jersey, and takes one of the younger DJs with him. He says going to this professional conference is a carryover from his 4-H days. The educational opportunities provided through 4-H gave him an appreciation for the benefits of continuing to learn and grow. Derrick is a shining example of "Making the Best Better."

Mary Carlson was inducted into the Centennial Class of the National 4-H Hall of Fame in 2002.

First Place
Albert Aguilar, Arkansas

It was a hot, June morning the day we went to Southwest Arkansas Regional O'Rama. We were up at the crack of dawn, 0630 to be precise, because we had a long day ahead. My younger brother, Cheairs, and I had been chosen to represent Garland County 4-H at the contest. Cheairs was competing in the sewing division and I was in sportfishing. I had been reading everything I could on the subject, and felt sure the trophy was mine. Cheairs had made a spectacular three-piece hiking outfit, and felt the same as I did.

When we were preparing to leave, I noticed I had forgotten to have my denim shorts washed. I commented about my forgetfulness to Momma, who said, "Well, I'm sorry, but it will look like you just went fishing." So, Cheairs and I got in the car and, bidding farewell to our little brother Oliver and our sister Lisa Jane, we departed to undying fame, glory, and triumph or our Waterloo.

By the time we reached Malvern High School where the contests were to be held, it was already close to eighty degrees. We instantly headed for the auditorium where the contestants were to assemble. After some speeches and waiting, they announced we would be voting on who was to be the new vice president of the Southwest Region. There were two candidates, one of whom was a good friend of mine. After the votes were counted, it was announced my friend had won. That was the first victory for Garland County.

Finally, the time came for us to compete. All the events except bait casting and biking were held inside separate classrooms. Daddy went with me and Momma with Cheairs, each of us wishing the other the best of luck. There is one thing that we do in our family when it comes to competitions—if you win, it is a win for the whole family; if you do not win, then you did your best. We walked over to the sport fishing room where Daddy waited outside in the hall while I went in and sat down. After everyone was in the room, the game and fish commissioner who was in charge told us what we were to do and gave us the test papers. I felt a little nervous at first, but after I looked over the test, I was put at ease. I started on the test, my confidence growing with every question I answered. There were; however, two thoughts that kept recurring in my mind: *Am I going to win* and *how is Cheairs faring?* I felt especially cocky when it came time to tie the knots. I do not know whether it was my accuracy or my speed, but the other kids looked the same way a catfish does after you land it—dazed.

The test was over. We sat in our seats waiting to hear the words that would either mean Utopia or Waterloo. I can still hear the commissioner's voice: "First place, Albert Aguilar." I wanted to yell or jump for joy, but I did not. Instead, I walked up, received my ribbon and tackle, and sat back down. I was so preoccupied thinking about when I would be able to use my tackle and how happy Momma would be, that I did not even hear who else won.

After we were dismissed, Daddy and I walked to the other side of the building where Momma and Cheairs were waiting. Before we got there Daddy and I decided to play a joke on Momma. He hid the ribbon in his pocket, and I put on my most down-hearted face. Momma and Cheairs were waiting for the judging to be finished when we arrived.

Momma was on the phone with Grandma, but when she saw me, she said, "Oh, Albert's here, and it looks like he won something." She could see I was carrying some tackle (an Uglystik combo, to be precise), which gave her a hint.

Then, turning to look at me, she said, "Second?"

"No ma'am," I replied in a quavering voice. "First!" When Momma heard that, she nearly shouted right there in the hallway, "You got first?"

The rest of the day was history. Cheairs also won first, and he was the only boy that competed in the sewing division. Not surprisingly, he became a celebrity of sorts. Several ladies were leading him around introducing him to different leaders in 4-H, including one from the Arkansas State 4-H Office. All in all, our county won five first places, the spirit award, and the vice-presidency. And so ended my best day in 4-H.

4-H Builds Tomorrow's Leaders Today! - Photo/Jenny Jordan

Ewe Never Know Where It Will Lead
Natasha Lehrer, Illinois

Just two little sheep started it all. Okay, it was two little sheep and a spinning wheel. In the spring of 2000, as the world was embracing the newness of a millennium, we were getting acquainted with a Cheviot ewe and her lamb. And, like all kids, of course we had to give them names—"Lily" and "Tulip." They were quite fitting names for the snow-white, wooly beings that brought us our first real glimpse of responsibility.

The chores were fun all summer. The grass grew green, the sun shone brightly and our "girls" grew in stature and, I do believe, in their fondness for us. Sheep have very distinctive personalities. To really gain their trust, you must earn it. Our mentor, a lovely neighbor named Flo who had been raising sheep for better than 60 years, told us this early on. Pulling us aside, she placed a hand on my shoulder and said very solemnly, "You must talk to them, honey, just like they are people. Get to know 'em, go ahead." With that seasoned bit of advice, Lily and Tulip entertained many long conversations with me, and were greeted daily with a cheery "Good morning, girls!" To this day, I still have to chuckle when I see people who walk up to a sheep and start to "baa" at them, instead of just having a chat.

Summer waned into fall, glorious, beautiful fall. The leaves crunched beneath our feet when we walked, and the lingering scent of bonfires mingled in the air. A golden aura washed the earth, and enveloped our own spirits with a sense of glowing warmth. The girls' rich, wooly fleeces grew downy in preparation for the cold winter ahead. It was time for breeding, and we rented a friendly ram from the neighbors to take care of that aspect of the season. Just a few weeks back we took on another ewe we called "Rosie." As they spent their evenings together, we waited for the five month gestation that would bring those precious little lambs to our barn.

Winter's sharp winds can never be anticipated, and we were surprised by the frozen buckets we encountered one morning. Needless to say, it was a trip to the local farm store; a cart heaped with heaters, buckets, and extension cords. We spent much time working in the barn with numbed fingers until the sheep had their water warm. Then the snow came and found all the cracks in the barn, much to our surprise. Blankets and straw made perfect caulking for drafty areas! There was ice, snow, cold, snow, and cold fingers. Did I mention snow? Chores were done quickly, and in a rather fashionable array of hats, scarves, mittens, and barn coveralls. Even then, it did not stop the chill from permeating our bones. The sheep, at least, had all that wonderful wool to keep them warm.

As spring came, the ground thawed (and so did we!) and the lambs arrived. It was not that easy for us first-timers though, and we ended up with two challenging births, one of which led to bottle-feeding a bummer lamb. But it was such fun for us kids! We had our own little ram lamb named "Paulie" who would follow us everywhere; he was practically attached to our legs. His pitiful bleats reached to my core, and I think it was that spring that I absolutely fell in love with sheep. Even today, when I meet people who used to raise sheep, there is such a glimmer of joy in their eyes when they recollect their experiences; I know it touched them like it did me. I spent a lot of time in the barn and the path wore down quite well.

During all this, my brother discovered 4-H and insisted we join. In the midst of becoming acquainted with all the records, rules, and responsibilities that are associated with the program, I discovered the fair! In the depth of the cold winter, our leader spoke of projects we could choose from, and of the fair where we could show our efforts. I had been to a few county fairs in the past and had fond memories of funnel cakes and talented handiwork, shiny ribbons and pork sandwiches. This sounded like a fantastic idea, and I was sold. I signed up for about 20,000 projects and began to see visions of blue ribbons dancing in my dreams.

Perhaps 20,000 projects is a bit exaggerated, but I had so many interests! The cooking and canning pulled me one way and the garden and horticulture in another direction. Then there was sewing, photography, natural resources, and so many other enticing, interesting areas that I wanted to explore. There was even a whole area devoted to sheep, both to show them at the fair, as well as a veterinarian project and a general project! The opportunities are quite endless and a crucial part of helping develop the well-rounded individual I am today.

I have to give credit for the way that 4-H encourages you to try new things. If we look a few more years down the road, you will find me hunched over the sewing machine. The bobbin threads were mucking, and time and patience were certainly not abundant at that moment in time. I was trying to reconstruct a wool coat and things were just not working out. Though I worked out the kinks in time to show it at the fair, and even model it in the fashion revue, reflection causes me to laugh and be thankful. The couple of years I took sewing projects in 4-H showed me that was something I really did not want to pursue! If you sew, please do not take offense, but sewing frankly made me scared to death of sewing machines. To this day, I still have strong feelings against that contraption. When I tell my customers that, they laugh because they know by looking at the work I create I found my niche. For the time being, I am a much more creative and happy person without a sewing machine in my life.

But back to the past! Our sheep got sheared and with all that wool and a spinning wheel, it was just too intriguing. I taught myself to spin, then knit (after all, what are you going to do with all that yarn?), then weave, dye, and felt. One thing just snowballed into another. Each year, as I looked to draw our sheep into my 4-H project for the fair, it became evident that the fiber was definitely my discipline. Wool, in all its capacities, represents a terrific fiber for a vast array of applications. My goal was to dabble in it all as much as possible. I did a lot in the community by demonstrating and sharing my interest in fiber, and even formed a fiber arts guild on our farm. Other sheep raisers in the area became aware of my efforts and I had the opportunity to try different types of fibers and learn about their various characteristics. My thirst for knowledge was like a sponge and, needless to say, I did not run out of subject matter for my projects!

Even though what I did was quite different than the average sheep project (because most kids I knew showed their sheep), I was accepted for National 4-H Congress in 2005 in the area of Animal Sciences. That was the culmination of my 4-H career, which was vast and varied with serving my club, county, and state. It was such an honor (and not to mention a great time!) and I am so thankful for the opportunity I had to be a part of it. The year 2005 was monumental not only because of National 4-H Congress, but because I graduated from high school that year and my whole future was right there in front of me.

Thank goodness to 4-H for all the years of drilling into me the importance of reading directions. As I focused my career on entrepreneurism with the goal of teaching fiber arts, a door opened. In my mailbox a grant application unexpectedly arrived from the USDA for producers interested in adding value to their agricultural products. To make a long story short, many hours of visionary planning and ninety pages of directions later culminated in a grant proposal. The premise was to add value to fiber by turning it into a useable product, developing labeling and marketing for Illinois fiber producers, and fostering an educational environment in fiber arts. This was a major undertaking, but 4-H gave me the backbone I needed to tackle projects with a short deadline, and to perform my best under pressure.

We celebrated our four-year anniversary of Esther's Place in March of 2010. What had been a fuzzy vision has grown into a thriving community of creativity, inspiration, and camaraderie. Each day when I wake up and go to work, I remind myself of how blessed I am to be doing what I love every single day. It is an enormous amount of work and responsibility, but the pleasure far outweighs the pain. I teach, travel, and, most importantly, create and keep encouraging my customers to do the same. Our sheep flock has grown beyond my dreams, and I now have several spinning wheels. I am now a 4-H alumnus and give the program credit for the many aspects of my character. Whenever I happen to be in town for the county fair, I get a funnel cake and enjoy checking out the work of enthusiastic and eager 4-H members. I feel a smile creeping into the corners of my mouth and have to chuckle. "Ewe" just never know where life is going to lead.

Making a Difference

Changing Their World
Gloria Seward, Mississippi

I want to tell you our story. It is an amazing story about a group of little kids and an old teacher who come from a poor, rural area in East Central Mississippi. Because of an organization called 4-H and a corporation known as JCPenney, these kids had the opportunity to change their world.

I am a teacher of talented and gifted (TAG) students in the poorest state in the union. Our school districts have been hit extremely hard by the recession and have had our education budgets slashed to the bone—I mean, *marrow*—by our state legislature. There is no money for anything extra. When teachers and staff were getting furloughed, or even worse, "pink-slipped" daily, I dared not ask for any funds for my students to have an opportunity such as being involved in *FIRST* (For Inspiration and Recognition of Science and Technology) Lego League (FLL) Robotics.

But I wanted to find a way. I went online and started looking for ways to fund my dream for my kids to get this kind of opportunity. When I found the national "4-H JCPenney Afterschool Fund *FIRST* Robotics Team Mini-Grants," I went wild. I read the requirements and I knew this was for us.

As a child growing up in rural Mississippi, 4-H was a very important part of my life. I still remember my little green and white seersucker dress with the green 4-H emblem on the pocket. I learned so much practical knowledge from 4-H, things I still use today. I knew my fifth grade gifted students needed this organization as much as I did when I was their age. So, I first checked out the state policy to see if it was against the law to have a 4-H club in school. Well, it was not!

Then I looked to see if it fit in with the state and federal guidelines for the teaching objectives for gifted education. Bingo! The skills of "Independent Study" based on student preference jumped right out for me to grab, because the materials offered by 4-H are definitely individualized learning according to preference. So I decided to start a 4-H club right in my classroom and hold monthly meetings with the kids. County 4-H Agent Mike Reed was ready to help me and has been a great friend to us.

Now it was time to make my dream of getting funding for the FLL team a reality, but the deadline was in 48 hours. Our state 4-H leader at Mississippi State University told me there was no way I could get all the information I needed from JCPenney, my school district, National 4-H Council, or from them (Mississippi 4-H), much less get a proposal written and submitted in time to be considered for a grant. She just did not know how big my dream was for these kids!

When we were awarded the grant she told me I must have misunderstood because our name was not on the list. I asked her to look again. Sometimes in life, things are just meant to be. This was one of those special times.

I never knew $1000 could make such a difference in the lives of 45 kids and their families in one of the poorest economic areas of the poorest state in the union. Because of the JCPenney Afterschool Fund and National 4-H Council, these children got to have hands-on experience building NXT robots and programming them to do tasks, just like the kids from the "rich" prep schools. I have children who never knew the talents and abilities they had in engineering or computer technology until we received this grant!

One of my girls, until this program, had never done more than simple keyboarding to answer multiple-choice tests. Through this project she discovered she has a gift in computer technology. She learned to fix her teacher's computer instead of calling the school's tech guy and is now the class web master. She wants to be a computer engineer and help her little sister go to college.

I have another student who is gifted, but autistic. Until now, he had never been able to focus and socialize with others to work as a group. Now he loves to build, program, and run the robots *with* his classmates. His parents are thrilled with how the doors of communication and socialization have been opened for him through this project.

Parents of all 45 kids became involved, an unusual thing for any school. Kids begged to stay with me longer on their TAG day, and we made school last from 7:30 a.m. to 6:30 p.m. (Yes, five days a week, every week, from the time we got the grant until January when we competed in the state tournament. I had nine kids for 11 hours a day work on this project.)

At 57, I am no spring chicken having taught for 37 years. In all that time, I have never seen anything do as much good as this $1000 grant did for this bunch of kids, their parents, and their community.

It helped their community because in *FIRST* FLL, students are asked to develop a community improvement plan and to present their research and recommendations for improving their communities at the FLL tournaments. This year's topic was very broad, "transportation problems." My kids are from a place where the only transportation they know anything about is what they see daily—school buses.

We are a consolidated county district with around 2,650 students being transported daily by school buses. Just prior to this project all school budgets were cut five percent, then eight percent, followed by ten percent and finally 12 percent. My students decided they wanted to learn how much it cost to run the buses and to see if there was a way to reduce costs. (In other words, they were afraid I might be one of the teachers who lost his or her job because of budget cuts. God bless the little fellows!)

First they interviewed their bus drivers, then the school's transportation director, who, because of public record accessibility had to answer all their questions truthfully and/or give them the weekly records for all buses (student number, mileage, fuel usage, driver salaries, insurance costs, maintenance costs, bus costs, trade-in value, etc.). From these weekly records, my students calculated the data for the entire year. They found that some children in our district have a daily round trip bus ride of 106.9 miles while others ride just 4 miles. My kids tried every way possible to make cost reductions, but nothing seemed to be enough of a savings. Then, a group of five children discovered a "secret." I mean a big secret, passed down from one elected superintendent to the next for about 40 years. The kids kept running the numbers but could not find a bus 49. They looked on the line daily for it. They made me take them to the bus barn to find it. It was not there. Then one child asked the "right" question of our transportation coordinator: "If bus 49 is not here and we are paying for it, where is it?"

He had to tell the truth and did. For 40 years our school district, against normal policy, had been granting transfers to a group of families who live on the other side of the county, within 12 miles of a school in the next county, yet only 20 miles from us (40 miles round trip). Our district pays for the bus (a new bus was just purchased last year at a cost of $74,000), the driver, the fuel, and maintenance and insurance costs, yet we never see the bus because it is parked at the other school in the neighboring county. The bus even has our district's name on it. To make matters worse, that bus is used to transport that county's students to all tournaments and other places to save their county money. Some of my kids had their parents drive them to the school to see if the bus was there, and it was!

When the kids finished their cost reduction research, they found that bus 49 costs our district, on average, $46,556 per year. The students reported their cost reduction findings to our "top brass," in a cute political commentary skit about superintendents, school board members, and big secrets like bus 49. When the students showed how eliminating the cost of bus 49 could save the jobs of several teachers there was dead silence. Finally, the students were told bus 49 is a "complicated matter." That news infuriated the parents of my students. There are a lot of new people who have qualified as candidates for this year's school board elections.

My kids took their presentation to our Mississippi State FLL Tournament along with our 4-H decorations, signs, streamers, suckers, temporary tattoos, and 4-H emblems on our pockets. As a rookie team we won the Project Presentation, one of the three top prizes. That was a first for a Mississippi rookie team, especially when most of the teams that usually win in our state have mentors that include former astronauts or rocket engineers who work at the Stennis Space Center in Bay St. Louis. At the awards ceremony the presenter kept going on and on about a team that took a real life problem and changed a community with its findings.

That $1000 purchased a robotics set and task mat and paid the FLL team registration fee and transportation costs (by school bus) for all 45 students to the Mississippi Gulf Coast for the Mississippi FLL Tournament. By the way, this was the first time 29 of the students had seen the Gulf of Mexico! We sold Pizza Hut cards to pay for meals and hotel rooms. This was the first time 23 of the children had stayed in a hotel.

Even though we could only afford to have one team of ten to represent us, we squeezed still more from the grant for a special side trip to the Stennis Space Center. The students learned about our country's space program and got hands-on experience with real robots. We stopped at every free museum on the Gulf Coast (where I am originally from) and we debriefed our fieldwork on the beach. We even brought back wet Gulf Coast sand in plastic bags for each child because the majority could not afford souvenirs. We made an experiment with the "beach sand in the plastic bag" for the entire class. The kids are still running tests at home checking the hypothesis that salt will separate from the sand if you continually add water and then let it evaporate. (Yes, as a 4-H project!)

It was a great honor to have received this grant. How could JCPenney Afterschool Fund, National 4-H Council, or any other entity know that a $1000 grant could make such a profound difference in the lives of 45 ten-year-olds, their families and the community of Philadelphia, Mississippi? Lives have been touched and changed forever. As an educator, I can never fully express my gratitude for having had the opportunity to make a real and lasting difference in the lives of my students.

Someday when we are dead and gone, these former students will tell their children and grandchildren about learning lots of practical skills in 4-H they still use, even in old age. They will fondly remember their green 4-H emblem as they relate how a group of young 4-H member students discovered a secret that changed their world.

Science Engineering and Technology - Photo/Edwin Remsberg

Like Coming Back to My Roots
Lynn Bailey, Florida

At 16, there I was, then known as Lynn Bonnette, on South Carolina's WIS TV's live morning show, using flip charts, food samples, and a doll to demonstrate my knowledge of nutrition. My nutrition knowledge had earned me a trip to the 1965 National 4-H Congress and my hometown of Wagener, South Carolina (population 1000), was busting its buttons with pride as they watched me, the local girl who had bested thousands of kids from bigger towns to win at the state level. A few weeks later they celebrated my success, cheering me on as I boarded a plane in Columbia, South Carolina. I remember vividly the heels and feathered hat I wore to represent them at the national event in Chicago. I was so proud to represent my hometown and state at National 4-H Congress. When I returned to Wagener I was even more enthusiastic about pursuing nutritional science as a career.

Even after all that success, my first casual mention that I might like to become a university professor someday did not get much serious consideration. All of my friends thought the idea was hilarious. Wagener kids did not grow up to think big thoughts in ivory towers. They worked as store clerks or laborers in the Wagener Shirt Factory; or maybe at the nuclear power plant, like my dad, who put in many hard hours as a steamfitter.

My mother went to college for a year to be a librarian, but was called back home to pick cotton. She eventually started the town's library that still bears her name. Fortunately, my 4-H agent, Alpha Jenkins, did not think it was silly for a young girl to hope for a career in academia. She told me, "Yes Lynn, I think you can do this." I was so inspired that someone believed in me that her positive influence really stayed with me. It would not be the last time an influential mentor would make a difference in my life.

I earned my undergraduate degree at Winthrop in 1970, a master's at Clemson two years later, followed by a Ph.D. in 1975 at Purdue. I had begun working at Purdue, studying protein as a means to find ways to create more nutritious corn for developing countries. My long-term goal was to help end world hunger, but without an on-campus medical school, the logistics of my human metabolic studies were challenging. The University of Florida had a hospital on campus.

At the age of 28 I was a successful applicant for a faculty position in the University of Florida's Food Science and Human Nutrition Department, a part of the Institute of Food and Agricultural Sciences. Arriving in Gainesville, Florida, I actively sought another mentor who would listen to my research ideas, someone who would have my best interest at heart. I found that mentor in Dr. Jim Dinning, a world-renowned folate expert who had retired from a dean's post in Thailand. He had seen the data on the number of children in developing countries with birth defects and felt "in his gut" that folate would be the key to reducing those numbers. Instead of malnutrition, Dinning argued I needed to change the whole focus of my research to folate and birth defects. I did. He was right.

My research group generated data instrumental in establishing folate-intake recommendations, including those for pregnant women, and the focus of my scientific investigation was folate and its role in optimizing health. By the early 1990s I was named to a Food and Drug Administration committee whose recommendations were adopted as law in 1996, mandating that all enriched foods in the United States be fortified with folic acid. It was not until the late 1980s-early 1990s that we received the evidence showing Dr. Dinning had been right.

I was humbled to receive the honor of being named the 2008 University of Florida's Teacher/Scholar of the Year. This award was given in recognition of the success of my folate research program and government advisory work which had led to major changes in recommended folate intake. This shared effort resulted in significant drops in neural tube birth defects, like spina bifida, around the globe.

Now just two years away from retirement, I hope to stay actively involved in my ongoing research, as well as folate-related work at the national and international levels as a professor emeritus. I am enjoying the payoff of years spent mentoring young academic minds like Marie Caudill, now on the faculty at Cornell, and Karla Shelnutt, who earned her Ph.D. under my tutelage. Karla, who now teaches a nutrition and metabolism class with me at University of Florida, honored me in a recent interview by stating, "Everything I know I've learned from that woman. She's amazing!"

Looking back on my career, I realize landing at University of Florida's Institute of Food and Agricultural Sciences was an ideal fit. I love working in a place where Cooperative Extension knows how to get research out to the public, especially to inquisitive kids from one-stoplight towns. Growing up, I thought that a college education would enable me to answer just about any question.

Being at IFAS has been rewarding, as I know we are providing opportunities for kids in rural communities to be inspired by a county 4-H agent as I was. It is like coming back to my roots. I am looking forward to sharing this story with my childhood county agent. She is now blind and will enjoy me reading it to her. I know she will be delighted to hear she inspired one of her young 4-H members, nearly a half century ago, to work hard and achieve the goals that many thought were just silly dreams of a small-town teenager.

Once in a Lifetime
Darlene Scott, Utah

As the cold chill of the morning air hits her exposed face, she wakes startled and disoriented. Trying to make sense of her new surroundings only takes a few minutes, but allows the time for her mind to race through events of the past few years. It is strange how emotions and feelings are so easily resurrected in the early morning hours when awakening from a near sleepless night.

Wanting to get involved, having lots of fun, and making good friends were all part of the decision to become involved in extracurricular school and community activities. Several small events over the past few years seemed just part of normal growing up; but combined, added up to a once-in-a-life-time opportunity for her. And that was the reason Kelcie Thomas of little Oak City, Utah, was waking to the chill of a Canadian winter morning.

Kelcie's introduction to 4-H was accompanied by few opportunities. At least that is how it seemed at the time. At first it was deciding to attend a teen council meeting, which evolved into becoming an officer for four years. Serving as secretary, vice-president, and president provided opportunities to plan, conduct, instruct, and carry through with projects that benefited the community and citizens of Millard County.

Watching youth at the community 4-H dance clubs and becoming aware of the joy that dance movement brings, awakened a desire in Kelcie to reach out and share her talents and skills with others. The realization that one person can make a difference became deeply embedded in Kelcie as she realized some of these young people had very few opportunities for dance instruction.

For Kelcie, this was the beginning of reaching out to others. Having a choice to do whatever you wanted was not a gift everyone possessed. Others in the world have limitations placed upon their bodies that take away their choice to walk or run. Kelcie realized this as activities were planned for those with special needs in the community. Four times each year teen council played, mingled, danced, dined, and celebrated Easter and Christmas with some very special people. The Easter Bunny always made an appearance after the annual Easter Egg hunt. Hugs and laughter were shared by all as teenagers spent time with those who could not do it without them. Tears filled many eyes as wheel chairs were pushed to square dancing music, and smiles appeared on the faces of everyone in the room. That dancing and fitness is for everyone, no matter what your lot is in life, danced through Kelcie's thoughts, along with a burning desire to do something to spread this knowledge.

Then it happened. An opportunity not considered an opportunity at first, but rather more of a curse and nuisance. It was her junior year in high school and a health class research paper was assigned. This was the dreaded research paper that interfered with all of life's activities. It would not go away, so the only thing to do was dig in and get it done. Obesity was of great concern in Kelcie's life as she struggled with situations in her own family that were a direct result of obesity. That would be her research theme. After completing the paper Kelcie decided to use the knowledge she gained to begin educating young children all over Utah about the importance of eating right and exercising.

Kelcie began to think of all the programs she had attended and the leadership and values she had learned. Being a regional ambassador for two years had given her the opportunity to organize and carry out retreats for others. Attending mock legislature, teen leadership training, state contests, fashion revues, and being a junior 4-H leader had given her skills she could now use to implement a program to reach all of the elementary children in Utah. This would be her service project for Dance Sterling Scholar! *Wow,* that is a big undertaking but she had prepared well and was confident it could be done.

Organization was the key to Kelcie's success. By delegating responsibilities and assignments to many volunteers, donations were received, fundraisers were conducted, and brochures were printed and distributed to spread the word throughout Utah.

Physical education classes in 111 schools (80,000 children) received information and jump ropes. Kelcie created a brochure containing information related to childhood obesity, fun ways to exercise, and ideas for nutritious snacks. Another 163,350 children received the brochure for a total of 245,858 Utah children reached. In addition, public and private schools in the states of Washington, Kentucky, Pennsylvania, and Mississippi were using Kelcie's brochure as part of the Gold Medal Schools program for health and fitness.

Kelcie has used dance to teach over 300 children about exercise and nutrition. More than 1200 exercise toys (balls, hula-hoops, and jump ropes) have been donated to three local elementary schools, along with boxes of exercise toys for the physical education departments. These donations were possible because of Kelcie's contacts with local businesses. She also planned and conducted numerous fundraisers to obtain the funding needed for her project to succeed.

The crisp Canadian air brings Kelcie back from her memories. Now wide-awake, Kelcie is fully aware of the once-in-a-lifetime opportunity that awaits her as a torchbearer for the 2010 Winter Olympics. She was one of two 4-H'ers chosen by the Coca-Cola Company for this great honor. Kelcie will run with the torch for 300 meters through Calgary, Canada. Excitement fills her soul as she realizes all of the little events that led to the opportunity of a lifetime.

**Olympic Torchbearer Kelcie Thomas - Photo
submitted by Darlene Scott**

Practicing the Four Hs
Diane McLean Russo, Washington

Close your eyes and imagine. Imagine living your life with your eyes closed, and getting around with the help of a Seeing Eye dog. Imagine grocery shopping without your sight, folding clothes, crossing the street, or exercising at the gym. How would it make you feel if someone saw your daily struggle and offered to help? Now open your eyes and picture the gift that members and leaders of Othello 4-H clubs gave Johnny Villarreal.

Johnny was born a twin. He was three months premature, weighing two pounds, nine ounces. Johnny lived in an incubator for his first 45 days until he grew stronger, but the sight in his right eye was permanently damaged and his left eye was replaced with a prosthesis. When he grew up, Johnny developed cataracts. "I didn't notice a difference until 1999, when I started to notice it was getting dimmer," Johnny said. "When I really started to notice was in 2005. I could no longer ride a bike; my vision just wouldn't cooperate as things came up on me too fast."

By 2007 Johnny could no longer watch television. He describes his vision at that time as dark and blurry, like looking through a glass of muddy water. He enrolled in the Seeing Eye Program in Morristown, New Jersey. This is where he met Ivan, a Seeing Eye Dog 4-H project. Ivan became Johnny's eyes. "A good working dog—they do it with all they have!" Johnny said. Ivan and Johnny made a great team for three great years.

Janelle Andersen, an Othello Top Cut Ranchers 4-H Club leader, knew Johnny through her business, Anytime Fitness. She had watched him put Ivan on a sit-stay command, and then feel his way along the wall to the exercise equipment. She marveled at his positive attitude and surviving spirit. She began to visit with him about the possibility of cataract surgery. His greatest barrier was finances. Janelle went to the Area Six Leader's Council to explain the situation. They wanted to help. Several Grant and Adams area 4-H clubs rallied to raise money for Johnny's eye surgery. They made it happen. Johnny says, "I'm very thankful. A lot of this would not have been possible without people like Janelle Andersen. It is amazing and really touching to have them there for someone like me. I have been lucky. I've always had good people around me."

The surgery was successful. Johnny's eyesight returned and he no longer needed Ivan's help. He felt that Ivan was such a good guide dog that it would be unfair not to share that special talent. "I decided giving him back was the best thing, so somebody can use him to his full potential. If Ivan can begin working with someone else, that would make me happy." Johnny has since accepted a full-time job and moved out of the state of Washington. The generosity of the Othello 4-H clubs using their heart, head, and hands really helped "To Make the Best Better."

4-H Leader Pearl Gerwig
John L. Gerwig, New Jersey

Pearl Gerwig was a tireless community worker. She was active in her church and community for all of her adult years. She founded the Chapel Hi-Flyers 4-H Club in the latter part of the 1920s and was its adult leader for some 65 years. It was through her efforts that multiple generations of youth were involved in the 4-H experience. The club met from its beginning on the second floor of the country store operated by her husband. In recognition of her leadership and service, she received the honor of being named a West Virginia 4-H All Star.

She raised six kids, losing a son as a teenager to appendicitis and another son who was killed in action in World War II. Her faith in God carried her through troubled times and she never lost hope or became discouraged. She learned canning and food preservation at an early age. Traveling by horseback and taking her pressure cooker, she rode 12 miles to attend a Cooperative Extension class on food preservation. Going into winter she always had 600 gallons of canned food to feed her family.

Mrs. Gerwig had limited formal education but was a strong believer in it and was determined to see all of her children go to college. Her oldest daughter managed a county ASC office (Agriculture Stabilization and Conservation). Mrs. Gerwig's strong ties to Cooperative Extension led another daughter to become a 4-H agent and one became an Extension Home Economist. Her surviving son studied Agronomy and served as Director of New Jersey Extension for 30 years. At one point, all were working in Cooperative Extension at the same time but in different states. Her husband of 49 years predeceased her by 20 years, but her community efforts continued. She received numerous awards from county, state, and national sources, but the story of her contribution to the building of the local firehouse requires special attention.

In a very rural community in West Virginia the citizens decided to build a firehouse the "old fashioned way"—they would build it themselves. The building was erected with all volunteer labor and money was raised through donations, dinners, and other events. It is still a vibrant part of the community today and is used for many group and community functions.

Mrs. Gerwig's contribution was unique—she baked and sold over 5000 loaves of banana bread, baking one loaf at a time. Her 4-H agent daughter contributed all the ingredients except the bananas (a restaurant in nearby Sutton donated those). She mixed and baked all the banana bread herself and had a regular production line arranged so that when one loaf was coming out of the oven to go on the cooling rack, she had another loaf ready to go into the oven. She prided herself on how the lines on the bread caused by the cooling rack made it easier to slice the bread evenly. Her other daughter, the Extension Home Economist, suggested ways she could streamline her production line and make more than one loaf at a time. Those recommendations were to no avail.

The firehouse kitchen was named in Pearl Gerwig's honor—a fitting tribute for her many years of dedicated community service, including over 60 years as a 4-H club leader. I am proud to share this story of my mom, a lover of 4-H for all of her adult years.

A Missouri Farm Boy in Switzerland
Dick Taylor, Missouri

I find it interesting that I was an IFYE at all. IFYE stands for International Four-H Youth Exchange. As a youth, I helped with scrap iron drives and other projects to raise money to finance the trips of the four IFYEs from our county who preceded me. While in my third year of college, county Extension specialists Virginia Norris and John Douglas sent me a message asking that I apply for an IFYE trip. Thinking it might be fun, I sent in my application with two stipulations. I wanted to go to an English speaking country and, since I had decided to apply for veterinary school that fall, I would only go if I was not accepted to graduate school.

A short time passed when I received a letter stating I had been chosen to go to Switzerland. After serious consideration I decided to put off my application to vet school for a year. This was an opportunity for me to maybe learn another language (or two) and to go to a beautiful country. When I told the state IFYE coordinator, John Burkeholder, my decision, he leaned back in his chair, put his hands behind his head and his size-13s up on his desk. Then he said, "Dick, that's a good idea! You know I play bridge with the Dean of the vet school every other Sunday night."

I am often slow in figuring things out, but it did not take me long to figure out that I was not going to get into vet school even if I did apply that year. However, the positive side was that when I got back from my IFYE experience and did apply for vet school, my acceptance was a formality. My selection interview consisted of telling about my experiences in Switzerland! The committee chairman's parents had come from Switzerland and all Dr. Weinman wanted to know was about my trip!

I do not recall learning things in Switzerland that have helped me specifically as a veterinarian except learning a little about the Swiss chemical companies. I only remember seeing one veterinarian on the farms I visited. His practice was much different than that of a mid-western general practitioner. In fact, he wore a suit and tie—much different dress than is appropriate for the type of work I do.

I did learn lots of things that have made me a better person and therefore a more successful veterinarian. I learned about diversity. On the third farm that I visited we harvested potatoes, tossing 50-pound sacks of them up onto a flatbed wagon. We went at a run, needing two of us to get the job done. On my fourth farm, each person moved a 220-pound bag of wheat into the old castle by himself. Of course, the pace there was much slower. On another farm I visited in November, I drove a tractor all day wearing just jeans and a white t-shirt while one of my fellow IFYEs reported being in an area that had significant snow in July.

The first family I stayed with had a mansion on the shore of Lake Geneva, just a few miles from Geneva. They had a large chicken operation and feed mill. My host father took me on one trip to a poor mountain area that was so iodine-deficient that most of the people were cretins. That same family took me on a vacation to their wonderful chalet next to St. Bernard Pass.

When living with this family I was allowed to go with some of the chicken farm employees to a local dance and party. Most of those I associated with were Austrian or German, but I do vividly remember one cute little Spanish girl, Pepita. I got the idea she would like to come to America.

I learned to trust people. On my fourth farm the only person who spoke English was my bachelor host-father who spent just a few days at home while I was there. We were in the French-speaking section of the country, but most of the employees on the farm spoke Italian or Austrian. I was thankful for my French dictionary and the few times I had listened to my French tapes. Even my one semester of high school Latin helped me to understand them. I learned more about trust there than any other time of my life. I could hardly understand them so *I had* to trust them!

I learned that to be successful you need to work long and hard. A typical day with my third family helps to explain. We got up at 5:00 a.m. While one of the ladies fixed breakfast, one man milked the eight cows and the rest of us went out to bring in fresh grass to the cows. It was important to get the grass before the sun touched it or it would wither and give an off-flavor to the cheese.

Then we all would go to breakfast. After breakfast we unloaded the grass and fed the cows while one person cleaned up the barn. We then went to the field to work until midmorning when one of the ladies brought out a snack. We went back to work after the snack until noon when we ate lunch. We returned to the day's designated task until the mid-afternoon snack and then a little more routine work until it was time to go to the barn to milk and do whatever else needed to be done. Of course, we then ate again, our biggest meal of the day. After supper we went back to the field to cut grass, again after the sun went down, so we would not have an off-flavor in the cheese. Usually I got to bed by 10:00 p.m. or so.

The ladies who were not cooking or cleaning the house worked right beside the men. Actually, one mother had a young baby that even went to the field with us. While working that hard in Switzerland I gained twenty pounds but kept my thirty-two inch waist. Twenty-some odd years later, when I weighed the same as back then, my waist had grown to a "mature" thirty-six inches.

Probably the biggest thrill I got from my trip to Switzerland was finding the family of the father of one of my high school classmates. He had come to America on a Swiss soccer team twenty-some years before. When he heard from or wrote to his family it made him so homesick that he quit writing them. He had lost all contact with them, but he knew what cities they had been in the last time he had contact with them. By calling the Wuthrich families in those towns, I was able to find one of his brothers and his family. They ran a restaurant and only spoke German. He was able to resume contact with them and even went back to see them a few times.

While visiting the Wuthrich family they asked if I knew enough German to understand a Swiss joke. I thought the following joke summed up the Swiss people fairly well! A Texan came to visit and tour their farm. The tour included everything you could imagine as Swiss farms are very diversified. They all seem to have a few pigs, cows, and chickens and grow wheat, potatoes and have orchards. But every time the Swiss farmer showed the Texan something, he boasted everything was bigger and better on his Texas ranch. When the tour was over, the Texan asked if that was all. When the Swiss farmer answered "yes," the Texan said it took him three days to drive around his ranch. The Swiss farmer replied, "I, too, once had a car like that."

Like most twenty-something-year-old boys, I only sent three or four letters to my host families in the years after I got home, so I soon lost contact with all four of them. Fast forward forty years, a young city girl from thirty miles away asked me if she could go on veterinary visits with me; she was trying to decide if she wanted to become a veterinarian. She worked with me for three or four years when one day she said she would like to apply for an IFYE experience to Switzerland. She was accepted, received her departure date, but then heard nothing more! When it got to be two weeks before she was due to leave and still had not heard anything about where she was to stay or, for that matter, where to meet anyone, I took action. I fired letters to the last addresses I had for my four Swiss families. Within a week I had phone calls from two of the families. One of the host fathers, who spoke only German, met her at the train and got her to her first host family. She even spent a few weeks with one of his cousins. Now, I do not know all the details, but a couple of years ago I attended Dr. Amber McCoig's wedding at Alpine Gardens near Columbia, Missouri.

More than 50 years after my Swiss experience, I am still too involved in my veterinary practice to be willing to take time to go back to Switzerland. Christmas newsletters are now my main contact with my second favorite country. Anticipation of receiving them is another reason for me to look forward to the time we celebrate Christ's birth. When I was accepted to go to Switzerland, the beauty and mystique of it was too much to turn down. After all my experiences with it, I learned that the country's physical beauty does not begin to compare to the inner beauty of the Swiss people.

Uzbekistan Adventure
Mark Manno, Delaware

It was 1995, only six years after the fall of communism and the dissolution of the Soviet Union and here I was, a county 4-H agent from Delaware selected to travel to far off Uzbekistan with a group of eight other folks from different agencies. I was selected to teach about 4-H. The trip was sponsored by the International Republican Institute, a private organization headed by Sen. John McCain. Nothing I had ever done before could have possibly prepared me for Uzbekistan.

We landed in the capital city of Tashkent, the largest city in Central Asia. The airport was unbelievably decrepit. The only restroom had no door and was in the main hallway of the airport. We waited for what seemed forever to pass through customs until someone in our party noticed that a group of brazen French tourists passed through easily. A small roll of dead presidents presented with our passports solved that problem.

As foreigners we were only permitted to stay in the Hotel Uzbekistan. At $120 per night it must really be nice, right? We slept on army cots with wool blankets (it was over 100 degrees) and no curtains on the windows. The sun rose at 3:00 a.m. and so did the roosters. How a city of three million had roosters running around certainly befuddled me. Apparently the locals bring their livestock to town in the early morning to graze on the median strips and hotel lawns. The only computers I saw the entire ten days we were there were in the maids closets on each floor. My guess is that the maids were not really maids. I also took notice that my room was not thoroughly made up each day. I did not leave a tip.

We were bused to a youth camp in the mountains where we met a group of 60 or so young Uzbek leaders who were carefully chosen by the government to attend our workshops. They were really great people. Half were ethnic Russian and the other half were ethnic Uzbek. We each were assigned an interpreter. My first interpreter, a young Russian man, refused to interpret anything an ethnic Uzbek said. I let him go and was assigned Elina, a sweet 18-year-old ethnic Russian whose ancestors had been forcibly settled in Uzbekistan by Stalin back in the 1920s. Her mom worked for the newspaper and her work had to be screened by the government before it could be printed.

We got along great and I started my first workshop. I was explaining how 4-H worked and the role of the volunteer leader. At the break I asked Elina how she thought it was going. She frowned and said "not so good." I asked her what was wrong and she explained that in their culture, the word leader referred to someone like Stalin or Khruschev. I apparently was asking them all to become like Stalin. A few liked that idea but most did not. I made some adjustments and things eventually got much better. The concept of a volunteer completely eluded them. They could not comprehend why someone would do something for someone else for free. Under communism, volunteers were discouraged. The government did everything. The only youth group permitted was the Young Communists and they were led by paid staff.

Later on we had an opportunity to do some brainstorming. It is a pretty simple concept. You list a question on a board and everyone takes a turn throwing out responses until all ideas are exhausted. Everyone participates and there are no bad ideas. What could possibly go wrong? Apparently everything. It did not work. No one would shout out an idea unless all 20 in the group agreed it was a good idea. That was one very long brainstorming session.

The whole day I kept hearing far off thunder and expected rain, but it never came. I finally asked the camp director about it and he said not to worry. The sound was gunfire coming from nearby Afghanistan. I worried anyway. Later some local provincial government officials rolled into camp. They wanted to throw us out. After much arguing and shouting, alcohol changed hands and the problem drove away.

The Uzbek people were great and they loved 4-H. They loved the clover, the 4-H games, and pledge, which they translated into Uzbek and proudly recited at each meal. The trip really inspired me as a 4-H professional and changed my life. I returned the next year with Doug Kennedy from Virginia Wesleyan. Part of the time we were there was the 50th anniversary of the end of World War II. It was an amazing national celebration, as virtually every family in that part of the world has been intimately involved in the war, and most had lost family members. It showed me how insulated we as Americans really are from reality sometimes.

I also went to Kyrgyzstan, a country next door to Uzbekistan. It could not have been more different. Uzbekistan is desert and Kyrgyzstan has three of the five highest mountain ranges in the world. I stayed in the capital of Bishkek, again visiting local schools and teaching 4-H leadership activities. The kids were beyond amazing and their English was superb. I thought the local drivers were the worst I had ever seen. They swerve all over the road. Upon closer inspection I discovered that all the manhole covers were missing, apparently sold to China for hard cash. I stayed with a friend while in Bishkek. I swore I heard sheep bleating in the apartment above me all night, but passed it off to exhaustion or unfamiliarity with a new place. The next day, upon returning home from my day's work, I discovered the local men had slaughtered a horse in the front yard. Then they processed a couple of sheep after they had finished with the horse! Apparently, a Muslim holiday called for such a sacrifice. Clearly Bishkek is ripe for zoning laws.

Kids the world over are amazing and the 4-H idea fits into every culture. I have also made six trips to Bosnia-Herzegovina, thanks to a grant Delaware 4-H received from the State Department, and found that the 4-H idea translates well there too. I am still friends with my Uzbek interpreter, Elina. She lives in Moscow now. She left Uzbekistan while she could. There are zero opportunities there for ethnic Russians. That country is now one of the most repressive on earth with human rights violations galore. But I will never forget the warmth and hospitality the Uzbek people showed me. We really are lucky to live in a country where our freedoms are guaranteed. Most Americans have no idea what the rest of the world is really like. Just the act of reading an uncensored newspaper every day is beyond the reach of many people all over the world. Things are changing though, and the 4-H idea will surely fit everywhere.

Remembering Sarah
Joan Chong, Hawaii

Sarah once said, "I am fortunate to have received a good head on my shoulders, strong moral character, a great group of friends, and an unbelievable supportive family. *I am the one to whom much was given.* Much may be expected of me, and I may be obliged to give back. But I do not see giving as an obligation or an expectation. Giving back is a part of my nature." Sarah Rosenberg was a young woman who wanted to make a difference in others.

As her 4-H agent, I knew Sarah as a person who had a happy-go-lucky attitude and lived life to the fullest. She was fun, vivacious, spirited, loving, and a caring person whose smile would light up the room. However, when her parents first brought her to 4-H, they described her as being a strong-willed, self-centered, demanding young girl. They felt they needed a "cure" and asked if Sarah could join the Sweethearts 4-H Club. Club members were happy to have her join the club and Sarah's parents were overjoyed because they felt that, in one day, they had turned their seven-year-old "wild child" into a "sweetheart."

Working with children was Sarah's favorite way of giving back. Sarah always looked forward to assisting with "K.A.M.P" (Kindergartners Are Most Precious), the University of Hawaii at Manoa, Cooperative Extension Service, 4-H Youth Development Program's transition day camp for incoming kindergartners, and their parents. KAMP helped families to have positive experiences and eased their adjustment from preschool to kindergarten. Sarah described it this way: "At one point in K.A.M.P., the children are separated from their parents for about 30 minutes. We play fun games, read to them, and do crafts with them. This is to help them be independent without their mommies and daddies, which is exactly like kindergarten. I remember hearing one boy say, as he was crying, "I miss my mommy." I held his hand, explained to him that his mommy was right there, he would see her soon, and we would go and play with the other kids first. Slowly, the little boy stopped crying. As the day went on, the crying little boy was smiling, laughing, and having fun with his new friends. Just then, I felt complete, confident, and anxious to help more crying children become their happy, smiling, playful selves. This experience made me happy because I helped the little boy overcome his fear. I loved working with kids because they were so upbeat, eager to learn, and ready to have fun. Watching the children learn and grow during the time we spent together was magical. Working with the children at K.A.M.P. has led me to my jobs as a swimming instructor and a YMCA summer fun counselor. I now realize that I would like to pursue a career as a teacher. 4-H has helped me find my true passion in life—helping children."

Sarah exemplified the ideals of the 4-H youth development program. In her senior 4-H portfolio she stated, "Learning is impossible without sharing. If you do not share what you have learned with others, the knowledge gained will never help other people. I've learned this through 4-H." In another essay on 4-H, she wrote, "Learning how to be a leader, how to help out in my community, how to cook, sew, and bake, and how to relate to all different types of people is what 4-H has taught me. 4-H gave me a desire to make a difference in the world. 4-H has transformed me into a better person." Sarah loved 4-H and always went around saying "4-H for life!" to encourage others to join in!

On December 27, 2004, my world changed when I received an awful phone call saying that Sarah was in a horrific car accident. I could not believe what I was hearing. My mind raced with a million questions. Could what I heard be true? Will she recover? Sarah was a senior at Kealakehe High School in Kona; student-body president; all-around athlete and active 4-H'er. She was a daughter and a sister; she was a friend. The world was waiting for her to unleash her potential. How could this be happening?

My daughters and I rushed to the hospital to see if we could be of any assistance. When we arrived at the hospital I felt so helpless and I did not know what to do. My stomach was in knots. I was hoping and praying that Sarah would be all right. As family and friends started to gather, we held prayer vigils. I wanted Sarah to open her eyes and tell me that everything was okay. I wanted this bad dream to go away.

Nothing could have prepared Sarah for the head-on collision. She was on her way to work when a truck crossed the centerline and hit her. The doctors and nurses did everything they could, some even refused to go home. My heart was torn in half when I found out that Sarah had no brain activity and a decision was made to let her go. I knew in my heart this would be best for her as she was in God's hands now. Sarah fought as hard as she could, like she always did, but unfortunately this was a fight she would not win. When Sarah lost her life, it touched the lives of many people.

Seventeen-year-old Sarah was an amazing person. She was a role model, mentor, teacher, and an inspiration to others. Sarah always found a way to bring out the best in everyone and I consider myself blessed that she was a part of my life. Even as she lay in the hospital bed, she was making a difference in someone's life. Earlier in the year when she had gotten her driver's license, she specified she wanted to be an organ donor. How could someone so young have that kind of foresight and be so thoughtful and generous? Sarah's life was measured by the relationships she had and the lives she inspired. More than one thousand people attended her celebration of life.

Sarah set such an example to her 4-H friends that when they lost her they were inspired to carry on her work. They reached out and made a difference in their community, not only by participating in Sarah's favorite K.A.M.P. program but by creating special "Make a Difference for Sarah" wristbands and car magnets as a reminder for motorists to drive safely on the island's roads. Sarah's dream of "Making a Difference" lives on as she continues to touch the lives of many people.

Photo submitted by Cherl Varnadoe

Contribute in a Big Way
Katrina Castaneda, California

As a senior at UC Davis and a long-term 4-H member and volunteer, I dreamed of finding an opportunity to interact with my community in a *big* way. I started my 4-H career at the age of 10 by raising and showing guinea pigs. Prior to joining 4-H I had shown guinea pigs at the state fair. Here is where I first saw these cool young people dressed in 4-H uniforms. I remember thinking they were so poised, skillful, helpful, and willing to share what they knew. Even though showing animals can be competitive, I have always found 4-H'ers to be supportive and willing to share information and teach others. I decided then and there to join 4-H. With an avid interest in animals and a sense that veterinary school was in my future, I became involved with several 4-H animal projects. Through these projects, I learned the life skills I am now using.

As I gained experience, I expanded my leadership opportunities as a Solano County All-Star, a state ambassador, a National 4-H Conference team member, college staff member for California Focus, and collegiate representative on the California 4-H Animal Science Advisory Committee. At UC Davis I used the skills learned in 4-H to serve as a UC Davis Bonner Leader to promote higher education in Filipino communities as a BRIDGE High School Outreach Coordinator. I also had the opportunity to do research with Vet Med Extension on 4-H bio-security issues at fairs and shows; developed experiential curriculum on issues of 4-H Pre-Harvest Food Safety; coordinated SHOPS, a program that provides weekly grocery service to seniors in the Davis community; and conducted research at the Sinha Plant biology lab. In 2006 I received the Howard B. Shontz Award that is presented to a sophomore for exemplary campus leadership. I also received the 2008 Chancellor's Award for Diversity and Community for my work with the Bonner Leader Program. My recent focus has been in developing the UC Davis Arboretum Ambassador Program, an undergraduate environmental leadership program on the UC Davis campus.

I committed myself to 900 hours of community service over two years with the UC Davis Bonner Leaders Program. I participated in several student community service activities in 4-H and desired to pursue a bigger challenge. My quest led me to an interview with Betsy Faber, UC Davis Arboretum staff member. She told me about a previous Ambassador Program the Arboretum had offered as a leadership seminar on campus. Betsy suggested I expand the program and that idea was exactly the challenge I was seeking. I asked two other Bonner Leaders to join me in creating a new Arboretum Ambassador Program.

We interviewed community groups like Rotary and the Tree Davis Foundation, UC Davis student leaders, and UC Davis administrators including Vice Chancellor of Student Affairs, Dr. Fred Wood. The information we gathered enabled us to establish a program that addressed the issues and concerns of the UC Davis Arboretum, the UC Davis campus, and the greater Davis community. The information from the interviews enabled us to incorporate environmental program information from other land-grant universities across the United States. Using the California 4-H State Ambassador Program model, we created a mission and vision statement and recruiting criteria. Our goal was to enable the Arboretum to offer a program that would produce future environmental leaders who could gain knowledge in environmental issues and learn how to best translate those issues to the public while advancing their personal knowledge, skills and passion for service.

Initially, I joined 4-H to gain experience with animals and to help achieve my career goal of becoming a veterinarian. However, the greatest assets 4-H provided me were not the knowledge of animals or animal handling skills or the three golden bears I won at the state fair. Far more valuable were the life skills I developed, in particular public speaking, citizenship, and leadership. These skills have become my greatest strengths and have enabled me to take advantage of many opportunities at UC Davis. Not only have these skills enabled me to succeed in college, but have laid the foundation for me to become a better veterinarian, better leader, and better citizen.

Making a Difference
Marilyn Norman, Pennsylvania

Developing head, heart, hands, and health began for me over 60 years ago when I joined the 4-H club in our community. I did not realize then that it would become an integral part of my life.

I was 10 years old when the county home economist visited my school every other week to teach us home-making skills that included how to make a bed, polish silverware, organize dresser drawers, and about table settings and manners. We also learned mending and sewing skills. With eight younger siblings I used the sewing skills to replace lost buttons many times. I remember my first sleeveless pink floral dress with scallops and lace and how proud I was to wear it. I was shy and scared to model it at a roundup with another club, but I did it. In recent years as I have helped young members learn to sew I wonder if it was as difficult for me. My mother made many of our clothes and I was able to watch her and learn, but there are very few sewing machines in homes today. Cooking was also an important project and with it I learned about proper nutrition.

Dad enrolled the five oldest of us in the agriculture club and we all had a pig project. A group of piglets were bought and all the members were given one. The piglets' ears were notched for identification, a feeder was built from a barrel and wagon wheel, records were kept, and many of the piglets became pets over the summer. In the fall we took them to Williamsport to the livestock sale. That was my first experience receiving a check.

The county agent began teaching us other projects. Since dairying was the source of income for my dad and his brother, the three boys were allowed to take a calf project. There are many memories of helping them fit, lead, and show the cattle. We girls took gardening, flowers, and poultry projects. Besides going to meetings, the county agents came to each home at least once a summer to check on our projects and record books. The agents became our friends and role models.

Church, school, and 4-H meetings were the social events at that time. We played games and had fun at the hot dog roasts, picnics, and family days. We also broadened our experiences at county roundup, shows, day camp and achievement days, and we met young people from other parts of the county. We looked forward to achievement days as we were excused from school. We had dinner at the Penn Wells Hotel, members were recognized, and we had tours of local places including the courthouse, Corning Glass and Elkland Tannery.

My brothers could not wait to go to the district dairy shows. As we grew older we had many opportunities to meet young people from across the state. We went to Penn State 4-H Days, Kanesetake for leadership camp, and in June we attended a leadership conference that included workshops, inspirational speakers and even a presentation by Miss America.

The highlight of my 4-H experience was being chosen to represent Pennsylvania at National 4-H Congress in Chicago. What an experience for someone who had never been very far from home! In November we traveled by train, slept in the berths, and awoke to see the flat lands of the Midwest, Lake Michigan, the stockyards, and the skyscrapers of the Windy City. Extension Agent Carroll Howe directed us into the awesome Conrad Hilton Hotel and told us what the week had in store for us. We were treated like royalty. Big corporations gave gifts (I still use the Betty Crocker recipe book), hosted banquets, and provided tours. We met young people from all over the nation and learned about 4-H programs in other states. We learned about things we never knew existed. Little Rock, Arkansas, had just been integrated and we learned about segregation. Some of the southern delegates had never seen snow until that week in Chicago. Congress was well beyond anything we could have imagined.

I soon graduated from college with a degree in education and discovered I had a gift for teaching. It was natural for me to become a 4-H leader to help others learn the life skills I had found so useful. I have served as a 4-H leader for over 50 years. Club membership ranged from 50 to 90 members. A large club requires a great deal of work, organization, and time, but it is worth it when you see the young people grow into responsible citizens. Along with project work we encouraged our members to learn leadership, citizenship, and service to others. We have picked up a ton of litter along the highway, made dozens and dozens of cookies for the bloodmobile, provided programs in nursing homes, sent goodies to the troops, made Valentine cards for veterans and cleaned the local park. More than 20 former members are currently serving as club project leaders.

Sometimes I wonder why I continue leading the club when deadlines approach, paperwork is due, paint messes need to be cleaned up or candle wax needs to be scraped off the floor. But all of this is nothing compared to the excitement of an eight-year-old launching his first bottle rocket, Sarah's pride in her first sewing project, and Melissa at the craft fair with the crocheted potholders she made in 4-H. The boy who "creamed the sugar" with milk instead of butter later became the family cook when his dad died suddenly and his mother had to go to work.

With lots of hard work, many of our members have been successful at roundups, fairs, and state judging contests. I was thrilled for our 22 members that experienced National 4-H Congress and all it had to offer. I have enjoyed learning new things with the young people and learning from our mistakes. An important part of 4-H is about many people working together—enthusiastic youth, interested parents, volunteers sharing skills and helpful Extension folk. As the old adage says, "It takes a village" to equip youth to meet the challenges they will face in today's world.

The following saying was displayed in my classroom for many years: "One hundred years from now it will not matter what clothes I wore, the car I drove or the money I made. What will matter is if I made a difference in the life of a child." I know we are making a difference with our 4-H youth and that is why I have continued to be a 4-H leader all these years.

Marilyn Norman's more than 50 years of dedicated service to 4-H was recognized with her induction into the National 4-H Hall of Fame Class of 2009.

Heroes and Legends

Dorothy "Dot" Emerson
Jim Kahler, 4-H National Headquarters, and Ron Drum, National 4-H Council

To have known Dorothy Emerson was to have one's life changed in the most positive of ways! One way to get to know her was to work with her. We each had that opportunity and we both agree she changed our lives. Both of us began our professional careers in the late 1970s as a Citizenship Washington Focus (CWF) Program Assistant (PA). The one CWF session almost everyone, including the PAs, looked forward to was Dot's "You'll Be Surprised" workshop.

Dorothy instructed the PAs on how to work with youth and how to teach adults. Dorothy was always "tinkering" with her program, working with the staff to design sessions that would meet the needs of the adult programs, such as "Know America," and the many youth groups coming to National 4-H Center. In the evenings, just after dinner, she would often ask one of us, "*Would you walk with me?*" and off we'd go up and down the streets of Chevy Chase, chatting all the way. "*Tell me your love story,*" she would say, or "*What do you think will happen tomorrow?*" She was a philosopher who looked deeply into how one lived and what happened once one died. "*Do keep telling me your stories,*" she would say, "*I'll be listening!*"

As was true for many former PAs, after we each left Council and went our separate ways, we stayed in contact with Dot and looked forward to any chance to come back to National 4-H Center and continue our conversations with her. She continued her programs with youth right up to July 30, 1988—her 95th birthday. Dorothy Emerson passed away on Wednesday, January 24, 1990. She was 96 years old.

It was on July 30, 1893, when Waltham, Massachusetts, first heard the cries of baby Dorothy. Most of her formative years were spent in Lynn, Massachusetts. How proud she was, even after all the years, when she told how she graduated from Framingham State College with a Home Economics teaching certificate in 1914. "*But it was known as 'Framingham Normal School' then,*" she added, leaning forward as if it might be a secret. "*My first job was as a substitute teacher in Boston! I earned a whole $2 a day!*" she said with a smile. In 1916 at the age of 23, she began teaching home economics at Kimball Union Academy in Meriden, New Hampshire.

Dorothy has always believed that people have the ability to improve themselves. At age 25 she put her own philosophy to the test. *"I had heard about this new thing called Extension and decided I wanted to work for Extension, so I sent my resume to every state Extension office."* She clapped her hands together and continued, *"And of the 48 states, Delaware invited me for an interview!"* Soon she was appointed as the "Girls Club Agent" for Sussex County, Delaware.

Four years later, she joined the Maryland State Extension staff as "State Girls Club Agent." In 1958, she reached the mandatory retirement age, but she did not retire. *"They didn't catch up to me until 1961, three years later!"* she said almost giggling, her eyes twinkling. *"But then I had to leave, but I didn't quit!"* Accepting the title, "Consultant," she began working for the National 4-H Club Foundation, (now National 4-H Council). *"What a wonderful job! I was to travel around the United States teaching public speaking. I think the idea was that if they saw me, they might want to come to the National 4-H Center to learn more! I don't know if it worked but I visited 45 states that way!"*

Time continued to march on. As the strain of travel grew too great, Dorothy stopped traveling, but she continued providing her programs at National 4-H Center. Perhaps her greatest honor came July 30, 1983, her 90th birthday. *"The University of Maryland doesn't give honorary degrees, you know,"* she told us after receiving this honor, *"They usually only give awards to their graduates!"* However, on this occasion they surprised Dot. The University of Maryland presented their former employee with their "Alumni Award," the closest award to an honorary degree they give.

Although Dot's program theme remained virtually the same, the program's name changed a number of times through the years: "Developing Confidence," "Say It Like It Is," "Who? Me?," "You'll Be Surprised!" and finally, "We'll Be Surprised!" How it was implemented changed over the years as well. Originally, she used a most ingenious method to teach. She created approximately 30 posters, each with a word or phrase on it such as "Stumbling blocks are stepping stones," "Fail Gloriously!" and "It starts with the first step." Some posters only had letters–MYOB, KOPS, etc. Each of these cards meant something to Dorothy. MYOB meant, "Mind your own business" and KOPS was "Keep on the positive side." Placed in the order she wanted the ideas to be presented, she used these cards both as posters and note cards. Then, as she further developed her programs, she began to randomly select cards from this "idea bank" and speak from them, pulling ideas from the audience as well. She called those programs "Who! ME?"

We both experienced Dot for the first time in a similar way, by attending one of her "Who! ME?" programs. It is a tough thing for a nine-year-old, first-year 4-H member to have to travel "all that way" to hear a rather stately senior citizen speak on public speaking! She sat on a stool in the front of the room with a large black card-case near her feet. In her thick, New England accent she told us how she was going to use her "cawds" to teach us public speaking. She told about the many programs that she conducted for 4-H youth across the country and at the National 4-H Center. "Participatory theater" is how she described it, and she said that she would be asking young people from the audience to help with her presentation.

Although we each experienced this at different times in different locations, we each reacted to *that* announcement much the same! Ron hid behind the kid in front of him and Jim tried to do his school homework in the back of the room. Neither of us wanted any part of being "up there" and talking about "cawds!" Little did either of us ever imagine that one day we would not only be "up there" as part of Dot's "theater," but would actually *help* her give the presentation!

Dorothy was calling her program "You'll Be Surprised" when we became PAs in the late 70s, but she was still engaging her audiences with her "cawds" and techniques. She would describe the technique and we PAs would demonstrate:

- Mr. Lincoln: *"Pretend you are standing in front of the Lincoln statue at the Lincoln Memorial,"* she would say. Then she would ask, *"What would you say to Mr. Lincoln?"*

- Back to Back: Two youth would sit on her stool back to back and talk about speaking in front of a group. One would be negative and one would be positive. *"Always end on the positive,"* she advised.

- Do you have a pet? *"Tell us about your pet!"* she would say with obvious enthusiasm and genuine interest to a young volunteer and the young person would describe his or her pet. We would ask people in the audience to raise their hand if they could "see" a pet (had a picture of a pet in their mind), and most would. Then we would say that there were no pets in the room, but the speaker's knowledge, experiences, and beliefs helped everyone to paint a picture in their minds. *"If you talk in pictures,"* Dot would add, *"People will be looking at the pictures and not at you! So there is nothing to be afraid of in public speaking!"*

- Interviews: Dot always told her audiences that one way to help reluctant speakers feel more comfortable was to ask them questions, to interview them. She always opened the floor for questions from the participants. A question she was often asked was, "Do you have any children?" She would reply, *"Oh yes, I have thousands!"* That response would always get a reaction from the group. Of course she was referring to the thousands of young people she had mentored over her years working with 4-H.

Many people, including both of us, have taken these techniques and produced programs of our own. These programs work because her ideas work. Her ideas encourage the listener to be creative, to be self-supporting. These ideas are almost miracles. It is a wonder to see young people respond to Dot's ideas.

One of her cards was "MYOB." Dorothy originally meant that to be "Mind Your Own Business." Her definition was *"too often we think MYOB means don't be involved. But I believe our business is to BE involved with living and learning and sharing, all that our world has to offer."* During a program Ron was conducting, a girl stood up and said, *"MYOB means make your own beginnings. If you never begin, you will never know how far you can go. You have to start to finish."* It was an amazing show of imagination and creativity brought out by one of Dorothy's ideas.

She changed the program's name again in 1981, this time to "We'll Be Surprised!" When she was asked why she made this change, she said, *"Well, one evening I was doing my program. Suddenly a young woman stopped me and asked if she could speak from some of the cards. Just think of it! She wanted to do my program and thought she could do it better!"* Dorothy held her hand to her chest in mock shock, her eyes wide in feigned anger. Then she sat back in her chair, smiled, and continued, *"Of course, I said Yes! She did do better than me, and I have never spoken from the cards since! The audience does!"*

All of her life, Dorothy helped people believe in themselves. So it is not surprising that through her life's work, she still does! Dorothy Emerson was inducted into the Centennial Class of the National 4-H Hall of Fame in 2002. You can learn more about her by visiting her page at http://www.NAE4-HA. com/hof/demerson.html. Her portrait photo shows Dot seated on her stool, just as we had seen her so many times, as she began one of her sessions with, *"You'll be surprised!"*

Ann Barr, the Spirit of Alabama 4-H
Betty Gottler and Janet McCoy, Alabama

There is no one who embodies the spirit of Alabama 4-H more than Miss Ann Barr, although she is quick to point out that 4-H is more than one youth or one adult. She is shy to accept credit for the thousands of youth who benefited from her life's work, both in Alabama and throughout the United States. Her commitment to 4-H is said best by her: "I never wanted anything for myself, just for the boys and girls."

Ann Barr's commitment to 4-H went far beyond state's borders. For almost a half a century, Miss Barr unselfishly shared her breadth of knowledge, great wisdom, many skills, and kind spirit with thousands of people. She was instrumental in the development and educational programming for the Alabama 4-H Youth Development Center.

An Auburn native, Miss Barr attended the University of Montevallo and earned a degree in nutrition. She wanted to work in dietetics, but was unable to afford the fifth-year of the program.

She joined the service during World War II, serving more than two years in North Africa and Italy. During that time, Miss Barr worked with women from England and France assisting Allied Forces by deciphering coded messages and relaying secret information.

After returning to the United States Miss Barr applied for a job with the Extension System. She began her Extension career as an assistant home demonstration agent in Talladega County where her responsibilities included the 4-H program.

It was in that assignment that she realized how much she enjoyed working with young people. Life was not often easy during the early years, and she fondly tells stories of helping youth and developing 4-H clubs in rural areas—where children needed 4-H the most.

"Sears offered a program in which they would give 100 biddy chickens to youth, but the family had to own a brooder. But brooders were expensive and few families could afford one," Miss Barr recalled. "There was one child in a rural Talladega County two-room school who was insistent that his family had a brooder, but when we talked to his father they did not.

"He cried and cried because he wasn't going to be able to get the chickens. It broke my heart to see that. I thought about it and decided if I took two biddy chickens from every 100, I could give him 20 biddies. But I also knew he would not have the means to feed them. I went to the County Exchange and explained the situation. I was told of a sack of feed in the back with a hole in it, and it did have a hole when they brought it out to the car.

"I feel sure those biddies were kept warm behind the stove in the kitchen, but that was okay because it made that child so happy."

Another of her favorite stories was teaching the 4-H Pledge to youngsters. "I was in a school that previously had no 4-H program. I came in and wrote the 4-H Pledge on the chalkboard and told the children to follow my hand movements that go with the pledge as we recited it.

"I was showing them the Head, Heart, Hands, and Health. In the middle of the 4-H Pledge I saw that my skirt zipper was not fully closed and, without thinking a thing about it, I reached down and zipped the zipper on the side of my skirt—and in doing so, I looked up and all those children had followed my lead. I had to stop in the middle of the pledge and tell them that was not part of the 4-H Pledge. We proceeded and I was so embarrassed."

Miss Barr was later promoted to a state staff position and continued working with youth programs. She became the State 4-H Program Leader for Girls from 1951 to 1984.

It was during this challenging time in her career that she spent many hours listening to 4-H agents tell of their needs and returning to the state office to put their needs into action. One example of that was a request for a recreational program. Miss Barr talked her superiors into purchasing a record player and sound system and spent hours in her office learning to call a square dance and teaching herself to square dance from a manual. "I'm sure I bothered the people in the office below me because of the noise and stomping, but it was what the staff needed and I wasn't going to tell them no," she recalled.

Miss Barr worked for the state for 33 years until she retired in 1984. However, her service to 4-H was far from over. After only one week of retirement, she was contacted by National 4-H Council in Washington, D.C. and began working as a consultant. During her career she served on National 4-H

94

Congress committees 33 times and was chair six times. She also worked from 1984 to 1994 with National 4-H Council and National 4-H Congress.

Ann Barr was one of 100 people inducted into the Centennial Class of the National 4-H Hall of Fame in 2002. She was inducted into the 2005 class of the Alabama Agricultural Hall of Honor, received the American Spirit Award from the National Association of Extension 4-H Agents, and was awarded National Recognition for Outstanding Service to 4-H by the USDA. In 2009 she was included in the Alabama 4-H Wall of Fame during the state's centennial year celebrations.

As quoted in the National Partner-in-4-H Award citation, "Ann exemplifies the character, initiative, and ideals that 4-H develops in young people, and serves as an excellent role model for both young people and adults. Countless numbers of people have had tremendous educational opportunities and personal growth experiences because Ann chose Extension work as her lifelong career."

Miss Barr continues to live in Auburn and delights in telling about her 4-H career and talking with the 4-H alumni who visit her.

A Tribute to Joy Gooden Sparks
Sherry Kijowski, Delaware

My aunt, Joy Gooden Sparks, served as Delaware's State 4-H Leader from 1993 until her death in February 2009. While she didn't have children of her own, her head, heart, hands, and health all served countless kids and volunteers for over 35 years at the local, state, and national level. Her mentoring led to many young Delawareans achieving major success in their careers, including me, my sister, and my cousins. While at her memorial service, I was awed by the number of people who said, "Joy saw something in me and believed in me... Joy had a soft spot for my ornery behavior...Your aunt always found a way to laugh at my antics..." My aunt's ability to laugh, see the best in the situation, and provide an opportunity to support a future leader is a gift many wish they had, but few can replicate. I remember such an antic from one of the summers that I served as one of her state 4-H camp counselors.

It is a tradition at Delaware State 4-H Camp for all of the tribes to have their picture taken during the weeklong camp for the sake of posterity. For the camp counselors, the creation of the picture included "one-upmanship" over the previous year's counselors...even if it included most of the same people. One summer, the camp counselors decided that we should *somehow* involve the police car in the snapshot—after all, the camp is owned by the Delaware State Police, and it would be great for the police cruiser to be captured in the photo. All of the counselors were on a quest to acquire the car, the trooper's hat, and the police bullhorn. We were certain that if we could make this happen, we would live in infamy.

It was amazing that acquiring the car was so easy. All of the windows were open, the trooper's hat was on the seat, and we were able to push the car away from the building to put it in a more "picturesque" location. We were so proud of ourselves! The photo was taken with all of the counselors pretending to cuff one another, speaking into a bullhorn, and lying under the tires of the car. Meanwhile, we convinced my aunt to sit in the driver's seat of the police cruiser with the trooper's hat on her head. Her smile in the photo was like that of the Cheshire Cat. At the time I thought she was just amused by our "creative antics," but I think it was something more. Although she never admitted it, I believe she was the one who arranged the successful acquisition of a police car to make the wish of some college-age counselors a reality. After all, that is what leaders do. Leaders create the opportunity and conditions for others to succeed.

Sacagawea is credited with saying, "Plant a thought, harvest an act, harvest a habit, harvest a character. Plant a character, harvest a destiny." Joy Sparks spent her entire career planting characters and harvesting destinies. While she may not be here to see it, her legacy lives on in the countless 4-H programs she designed, enhanced, and refined. Her destiny lives on through the crazy camp counselors who have now become successful, productive adults. I like to think that a piece of my aunt lives on in the school where I am now a principal. The life lessons I learned through my 4-H experiences made me ready to be a school administrator. My faculty knows I want our school to be a place where we love to learn, where we take academic risks to challenge ourselves, and that we spend every day "making the best better." And, it should be noted that when my faculty wanted to climb into a fire engine during fire prevention week, I talked the fire chief into making that dream a reality. Thanks, Aunt Joy.

Polly Hanst, First Lady of OMC
Dan Tabler, West Virginia

When I first met Polly Hanst I was about 15 years old and attending my first Older Youth Conference at Jackson's Mill, West Virginia's legendary state 4-H camp. It was a warm day in late June and about three hundred and fifty of us were sitting in the shady grass for an afternoon assembly with Polly as the featured speaker. As she was being introduced, I wondered what this silver-haired, nicely dressed lady could possibly say to a large group of teens that would hold our attention. And, when I heard the topic was boy-girl relationships, I was even more skeptical, doubting Polly could even remember her teen years let alone any relationships with boys. Little did I know that Polly's "talks" were a long and popular tradition and I discovered she could not only hold our attention, but literally keep us spell- bound.

Polly Johnson grew-up on a farm in rural Braxton County and joined 4-H at the age of 10. A lamb was one of her first 4-H projects. At her National 4-H Hall of Fame induction in 2003, Polly told a story about riding with her dad in a buckboard to take her lamb to the county fair. That story was the inspiration for this book, but you will have to wait to hear the rest of it. After graduating from West Virginia University she became a 4-H agent in Richie County and later served as West Virginia 4-H Girls Agent. She was also one of the founders of the Older Youth Conference. She attended every year long after she had married George Hanst and raised her family in Oakland, Maryland. At some point she became known as the "First Lady of OMC." It was basically the same event as Older Youth but with the new name Older Members Conference.

I attended Older Youth for a week every summer until I had completed a year of college and was hired as a CCI (County Camp Instructor). In those days West Virginia University hired about 40 college students, provided us with a week of training, and then sent us out in pairs to help with county 4-H camps all over the state. It was a wonderful way to spend the summer. I never made much money as a CCI but the experiences and friendships were priceless. I occasionally ran into Polly and marveled at how she never seemed to age. She was always the neatly dressed lady with an ever-present twinkle in her eye and kind word on her lips. Polly was one of the most positive people I ever met. She always knew exactly what to say when someone needed their spirits lifted and when something a little more direct was needed following a youthful indiscretion. Polly was the caring mother that, at least for that week of camp, many young people had never known.

After graduating from college I was hired as the Hancock County 4-H Agent. I spent eight good years in West Virginia's northern panhandle and then had the great honor of being named the fifth and, at that time, youngest director of Jackson's Mill. I now got to see Polly more often. Every time we met she would ask about my family and how the job was going. Often she would share a story about one of my predecessors, as she had known all four: Teepi Kendrick, Uncle Charlie Hartley, Harley Cutlip, and Larry Cavendish. Harley was director when I attended state camps as a teenager and Larry was my mentor when I followed him as director. I was too young to have met Teepi and Uncle Charlie. Polly was always a great resource when I needed some Jackson's Mill history.

After seven years of full-time camp directing I needed a change. My wife Jayne, daughter Julie (the only child born to a director while at Jackson's Mill), and I moved to Delaware. I became the Sussex County 4-H Agent, the fifth West Virginian to hold the position. Two years later I accepted a similar position in neighboring Wicomico County, Maryland. There I had the opportunity to rebuild a 4-H program as I had done in Hancock County. After working for 16 years I finished my career there at the end of 2005. I did not see Polly again until she was inducted into the National 4-H Hall of Fame.

For the first several years, the National 4-H Hall of Fame ceremony was held during National 4-H Conference. At 84, Polly had good days and bad days, but on that day in April 2003 she was having a great day! Polly's hair was now white and she was in a wheelchair, but the group of teens gathered around her and hanging on her every word took me back to the day I first met her more than 40 years earlier. That evening, as the ceremony was about to begin, I had an epiphany. I was serving as the master of ceremonies and had rehearsed the script, but just then realized these 4-H treasures could best tell their own stories. I invited each laureate to share his or her 4-H experiences and the heartfelt stories they shared were truly inspiring.

When I introduced Polly and she was wheeled to the podium, she surprised everyone by standing to speak. In typical Polly fashion, she immediately had everyone's complete attention. Sharing a story that became the inspiration for this book, Polly told of riding in a buckboard with her father to the county fair to show her project lamb. The details she remembered were amazing as the story had occurred nearly 75 years earlier. As they traveled to the fair the sky grew dark and lightening flashed in the distance. Polly's dad offered to give her more money than she could win at the fair if they could turn around and go home. Polly insisted they continue so she could show her lamb to complete her 4-H project. The strong character Polly exhibited that day would serve her well the rest of her life. She was an inspiration to countless young people for nearly 70 years.

I have had the good fortune of meeting hundreds, maybe thousands, of wonderful 4-H people in more than a half century, but there was only one Polly. An old adage says a person is never really gone as long as someone remembers them. If that is true, Polly will live forever, at least in the hearts of those whose lives she so positively touched. Over the years Polly dispelled many myths about boy-girl relationships and the myth that only the good die young, as she died at the age of 100 in 2007. When Polly reached the Pearly Gates I am confident she was greeted with the words, "Well done, good and faithful servant."

Photo/Cheryl Varnadoe

Mr. Leon, a North Carolina Treasure
Travis Burke, North Carolina

It all began back in the 1950s when "Mr. Leon" realized he had an inborn fondness for agriculture and a love of animals. While Leon enjoyed the outdoors, his love of animals was his weakness. He began his 4-H work by showing market steers at a "fat stock" show in Elizabeth City, North Carolina.

One day when Leon was a young teenager he noticed a young lady having trouble handling her calf. The young lady caught his eye and Leon thought it was his chance to be a "*hero*" or a "*zero!*" He offered to assist the young lady and helped her settle her steer. A few years later, Kathleen and Leon Brickhouse were wed.

The union of those two could not have been better. After the birth of their two children in the 1960s, the next generation of livestock exhibition began. Leon and his two children would spark the interest of livestock exhibition for others in the community who did not have the means of showing and housing a steer project. Leon enjoyed cattle and sharing with other boys and girls. "Why not teach other kids what my kids enjoyed so much?" he once stated.

Leon continued helping scores of youth in the 1970s with Extension Agent Don Baker. Then in the 1980s, along came another young livestock and 4-H Extension agent, Travis Burke.

Leon and I worked together to get hundreds of youth showing sheep and hogs for over two decades. We would travel thousands of miles to locate animals and return to Mr. Leon's farm where he would provide a show ring, feed, tack room, and all the necessities for a project. What fun for a 4-H livestock exhibitor! Mr. Leon and I were quite the pair.

Many events happened on several of our trips. Some true, some questionable, and some with a sad ending. We have many stories to share, but a couple of them are priceless.

The first one was on a trip to southwest Virginia. On a cool, somewhat balmy afternoon in February, we began our journey to the beautiful mountains. When we arrived later that afternoon the weather was beautiful, the skies sunny, and the scenery was terrific. We had dinner at a local steakhouse and our general conversation was that the "weather here is just perfect for this time of year." After locating where we would pick up our sheep we turned in for the evening.

Around 8:00 p.m. we noticed the temperature had dropped about 10 degrees but gave it little thought as the sky was clear and we did not anticipate any problems returning to eastern North Carolina the following morning. When we retired for the evening, I began hearing some loud and unusual noises. I soon realized that the awful noise was Mr. Leon's loud snoring! As a young Extension agent who valued my relationship with Leon, I tossed and turned and turned and tossed until I was exhausted and finally drifted off to sleep.

Early the next morning I was again awakened by his "orchestra." Knowing I'd never get back to sleep, I decided to just get up an hour before our planned 6:00 a.m. departure. After getting dressed, I opened the door to experience an early Shenandoah Mountain morning. But I never expected what I saw.

I yelled, "Mr. Leon, we need to get the heck out of here, there's a blizzard out there!" And while the "orchestra" he was playing seemed to have lasted all night, the nine-inch snow had quietly fallen in just a few hours. That would be my luck…getting snowed-in on an overnight trip to get market lambs!

We quickly packed and slowly made our way through the blizzard to pick up our stock. When we arrived and began making our way through the farm, as you might guess, we got stuck in the snow. We had to shovel, plow, and finally get a tractor to maneuver the trailer, unhook from our truck, and reconnect up on the hill so we could return home that day. It was a close call but we finally managed to get out of the snowstorm and made our way back to the flatlands of eastern North Carolina. It was an adventure I will never forget!

Another time Mr. Leon and I traveled to Cedar Bluff, Virginia. This trip was almost to "parts unknown" in very rural southwest Virginia. Almost 500 miles away from home, Leon and I stopped at a gas station. Leon, a burly, brownish-gray haired man, went to the counter to pay. I went up to him and said, "Daddy, may I have a dollar?" He was speechless! This funny, matter-of-fact guy was speechless! For the next 10 years Leon would tell the story of how I left him speechless in southwestern Virginia. Did I mention Leon is white and I am African American?

Many more episodes of laughter and sometimes sadness would come over the next decade. All of Mr. Leon's efforts and his positive influence on the lives of hundreds of young people for nearly 50 years were recognized with his induction into the North Carolina Livestock Hall of Fame in October 2009. Mr. Leon never wanted any publicity for his many good deeds. So I decided we had to publically thank a man who had done so much for so many for so long. In December 2009, the board of commissioners conferred a resolution honoring Mr. Leon. It was a fitting tribute and a celebration of over 50 years of helping 4-H'ers! Mr. Leon Brickhouse is truly one of North Carolina's greatest treasures.

A 4-H Giant

Jessica Stewart, Oklahoma

He was called a hero, a pioneer, a warrior and a trailblazer. He had a myriad of nicknames, including Dr. Joe and Lil' Joe, and was known as the fastest, short-legged man in Oklahoma. He was Dr. Joe Hughes, the first 4-H Youth Livestock Extension Specialist at Oklahoma State University. From the time he began in 1971, until his retirement in 1999, Joe was relentless in the pursuit of quality youth development programming using animal projects across the state of Oklahoma. During his career, Joe put over 400,000 miles on his 1967 Chevrolet Impala as he drove everywhere to visit with everyone.

Joe was often called the "Energizer Bunny" because, much like the battery's pink mascot, he kept going and going. He was an innovator and was one of the earliest in the country to encourage ethical practices, sportsmanship, and quality care for youth livestock project animals. He also was instrumental in the expansion of meat science education programs beyond simple judging contests. He created the youth livestock achievement awards at state fairs, collaborated with 4-H and FFA leadership to develop ethical treatment and sportsmanship programs for youth exhibitors, and established the "Big Three" animal science field days.

There was more to Joe, though. He had a profound effect on individuals, whether 4-H members, educators, or volunteers. Joe was all about people and doing things for the kids and their parents, the Ag teachers, and educators. He did not see 4-H or FFA. He saw kids and educators, and they were all important.

If you were a 4-H member, Joe would learn your dad's name, your mom's name, your cat's name, what you showed, and something you did when you were eight years old. Then, when you were with him at a show, he would introduce you to other people and brag on you with a glowing five-minute presentation. He was very good at memorizing those things, and he genuinely wanted to remember everything. He knew everyone!

With educators and volunteers, Joe made sure each person felt appreciated and motivated. He was known for his extensive "thank you" note writing. Joe always had something for which to thank you. He was the world's best phone-caller, letter-writer, and end-of-event-thank-you person. He was an encourager.

Perhaps most importantly, he had a special way of being able to bring out one's specific talents and abilities. He was known for saying, "With your skills, talents and abilities, I'll bet you will do great in..." and then name something specific. Whether it was a 4-H member about to go into the ring, or a volunteer helping at an event, Joe always believed in people and their ability to succeed.

Of course, as competitive events go, there were winners and losers. But Joe was always able to encourage everyone no matter who it was, and he did it honestly and genuinely without hiding the fact that some may still need a bit more experience. He encouraged them to come back, and they felt good about it and worked harder the next time.

Considered a real-life model of the life skills 4-H develops in youth, Joe demonstrated exemplary citizenship and leadership, and Joe truly was an extension of the university. In fact, citizenship was never an abstract concept to Joe, but one he lived every day. After spending two years in the army (including a tour in Vietnam), Joe remained in the Army Reserves. As an active member of the Lion's Club and the Baptist church, Joe constantly worked to make his community a better place to live. You could always count on Joe to help organize others to help retirees and the elderly with daily chores, lawn mowing, and other tasks he saw as being needed in the community.

Joe was the kind of leader who made others want to be on his team. He often said, "God put me at the right place at the right time and surrounded me with people who believed in the same principles of good education and life skill development. I tried to carry out programs that would teach life skills and leadership that could best be taught with animal science programs." His leadership was taken to the national level when he was involved in the development of the National Show Ring Code of Ethics, which was adopted as written by the North American Livestock Show and Rodeo Managers Association. Barbara Woods, a retired state fair show manager said of Joe, "The reason Joe played such an instrumental part in the formulation of the National Show Ring Code of Ethics was because of his genuine love and respect for the 4-H program and all that it embraces, as well as his reverence and appreciation for agriculture."

Joe lost his battle with pancreatic cancer in the spring of 2009. He fought with all the energy and dignity that characterized his life and career. At the end,

Joe regretted having to leave behind his lovely wife, Lynn, but looked forward to his final prize. Joe's legacy lives on through the "Big Three" animal science field days and the fond memories that Oklahoma 4-H alumni, educators, and volunteers have of him. Perhaps Wayne Shearhart, Joe's right-hand-man for more than 25 years, said it best: "There's people with grandkids still showin' so he must have done something right."

Dr. Joe Hughes' outstanding contribution to 4-H was recognized with his induction into the National 4-H Hall of Fame Class of 2009. Oklahoma State 4-H Leader Charles Cox and Oklahoma 4-H Foundation staff member Jim Rutledge contributed to this story.

Let Her Retire!
Jim Rutledge, Oregon

Alberta Johnston spent 40 years as an Extension professional. She began her career as an Extension agent in Wyoming. From there she became a home economics specialist in Montana and eventually spent many years as the Deputy Director of the Oregon Cooperative Extension Service. About a year after she retired, Extension Director Ernie Smith asked her to fill in as the acting Executive Director for the Oregon 4-H Foundation. He informed her that this volunteer job would last about six months until they could hire a permanent replacement. That was in 1990. In the year 2010, Alberta is still waiting for someone to be hired as the permanent replacement for the Executive Director!

What started out as a temporary assignment became a passion for Alberta. For twenty years she maintained regular hours, every morning from a little before 8:00 a.m. until noon. Alberta always got to work a little early to make sure she did not have to fight the traffic and so she could get a parking spot close to the back door of the Extension building. Monday through Friday (except for Thursday during bridge season), Alberta was on the job. When there was an important meeting that had to be held in the afternoon, or an all-day function at the 4-H Center, she was there—even on a Thursday. In addition, she was, and still is, one of the most faithful and generous donors to the 4-H Foundation. She never accepted any kind of reimbursement for her out-of-pocket expenses for the many meetings she attended. In fact, if there were refreshments, she probably brought those too. For years she leased whatever was the standard Buick sedan, and she would usually insist that her traveling partner do the driving. It was not a problem being Alberta's chauffeur as she also liked to eat at the best restaurant in the area, and if you were driving she would take you along and buy your lunch.

Over the years Alberta has coached, mentored, trained, and put up with a number of state 4-H program leaders and directors of development for the Foundation. Through it all she has maintained her sense of humor and style. She would say that she was not the fundraiser for the Foundation, but her ability to build lasting relationships with those she met has certainly led to some very large gifts being made to the 4-H Foundation. For many years, as Deputy Administrator for Extension, she met with county advisory committees and key community leaders. At one time she had been involved directly or indirectly in the hiring of most of the county educators in the state, so she had many friends she could call on for information or support. When she became the Executive Director of the Oregon 4-H Foundation she called on some of these folks to serve on the Board of Directors and, consequently, some then became major donors. One recruit eventually gave over a million dollars to the Oregon 4-H Foundation. Others gave mature timber, commercial buildings, or support for scholarships and leadership programs. The bottom-line was that everyone knew how much Alberta had given of herself, and it was hard for anyone to say no to Alberta.

While she would say she never personally asked for a gift, she was certainly the reason many large gifts came to the Oregon 4-H Foundation. During her tenure, the average annual contributions went from about a quarter million to over one million dollars. Over the past three years, contribution income ran from one million up to three million dollars a year. In 2010 the Oregon 4-H Education and Conference Center went from a collection of rustic cabins to a facility with many new cottages, a renovated dining hall, a new office/education building, and a brand new activity center. The Center is now worth at least four million dollars. Endowment funds grew from less than $400,000 to almost five million dollars during Alberta's tenure.

For 20 years Alberta handled all the board communications, newsletters, recruiting, and relationships with the Oregon State University Foundation and the 4-H program area, and has done it with style and grace. After 20 years as a "volunteer" she finally asked the board to find a new executive director. I think it is about time they let Alberta Johnston finally retire from this six-month assignment. After all she has done, she deserves it!

Alberta Johnson's dedication to 4-H was recognized with her induction into the National 4-H Hall of Fame Class of 2004.

Thelma Pickens and Jack Burton, West Virginia 4-H Legends
Sally Howard, West Virginia

It is impossible to think of 4-H in Webster County, West Virginia, without the somewhat connected names of Thelma Pickens and Jack Burton. Both were agents there for more than forty years. To those of us in the 4-H program, they *were* 4-H. They were agents 24 hours a day, seven days a week. Miss Pickens was the "assigned" agent in charge of 4-H and Mr. Burton was the agriculture agent.

When I was in 4-H from 1954 to 1965, there were about 40 clubs in rural Webster County. There were not many summer activities for kids; no soccer or ball leagues, very little employment, and most families did not take vacations. But there was 4-H. Camp was a huge part of 4-H then, as it is today. Spending five and a half days and five nights at Camp Caesar was the thing to do each summer. The third week of July was camp week. It was after the miner's vacations, in the middle of the summer between school terms, before football practices, and was warm. (If you have ever been to Camp Caesar, you understand the importance of warm.)

Mr. Burton was the "Big Chief" in 4-H camp and was responsible for council circle. He believed in fun, but with decorum and respect. Miss Pickens was responsible for things like assemblies, vespers, and classes. They "wrote the book" on volunteer responsibilities in camp. There was an adult in charge of assemblies and his or her job was to chair a team of youth who planned them. There were skits based on the daily themes, an educational component, and, of course, time for bed check reports, announcements, and singing. Webster County 4-H Camp did a lot of singing. Vespers was organized the same way with an adult and a group of youth who planned the meditations. Again, skits, thoughts, and music composed the program. Campers were invited to participate in both and you *had* to attend the practice. Camp classes were learning times. Instructors were from local businesses such as Monongahela Power and the West Virginia Department of Natural Resources.

In the regular 4-H program there were traditional club meetings. Miss Pickens attended nearly every club meeting and if she could not, Mr. Burton did. There were times they both attended, especially if the club was having a problem or if there was something in both areas (4-H and agriculture) to be addressed by the agents. Club meetings were conducted with parliamentary procedure and with all the "components" of any typical meeting. Fun and games were held indoors during bad weather and outside when possible. As part of the project requirements, members had to do two demonstrations or presentations during the year. To get 30 to 40 kids to give two presentations meant there were several at each club meeting. 4-H club meetings were the place to learn how to get up in front of a group and speak. Kids participated in reading poems, making motions, and business discussion. That was just something expected and most everyone complied.

Webster County had a reputation for winning demonstrations in area and state competitions. That was due, in great part, to Miss Pickens. 4-H youth were encouraged to present in the club and on the county level by their parents and/or their leader. Their parents, leader, and the agent then coached winning demonstrators in the county contest and area competition. The kids practiced, and practiced, and practiced. Miss Pickens met with them frequently to help them hone their demonstration skills. Mr. Burton often sat in on practice sessions to help with demonstration skills, eye contact, and dialogue. They asked questions at the end to be sure the kids knew their topic and were prepared for questions they might be asked at the state and national competitions. Because of this, many Webster County youth had the opportunity to go to Jackson's Mill for state level competition, then on to national competitions, and experiences well beyond our rural county. 4-H helped us to develop in the four-fold way and to look beyond ourselves, our county, and our comfort zones to seek new heights.

County fair was a major production. There was always a theme to the 4-H section of the fair and elaborate decorations carried out that theme. The dining hall was filled with exhibits and the livestock exhibits in the barns were plentiful. Going into the barns and seeing the wide variety of animals was an education. Entering what seemed a magical area of the dining hall with all the decorations made the youth feel special and proud to see their exhibits displayed. Following the fair was the achievement banquet that featured a special meal served in the Camp Caesar dining hall. Participants got dressed up and were recognized for achievement where top scorers received pins appropriate to their projects. Those pins were revered and proudly worn to show accomplishments. Miss Pickens and Mr. Burton also "popped their buttons" as they saw the fruits of their labors and over time, how their youth had "increased in wisdom and stature and in favor with God and man." (Luke 2:52). That was the bible verse we said as part of the opening of every 4-H club meeting along with the pledges. Miss Pickens and Mr. Burton never "yelled" at the kids for not doing something they should have done. They did not have to raise their voices because the kids respected them and wanted to work hard and do the right things to make them proud. No one wanted to besmirch the name of 4-H.

In talking with contemporaries of those wonderful years, the question might be asked what contributed to a person's success in life. The frequent answer is "4-H, Thelma Pickens and Jack Burton." They helped 4-H'ers dig deeper, work harder, and achieve more. They worked with adults in our communities to be leaders of clubs, to teach classes at camp, and to support the 4-H program. They encouraged those past the 4-H age to give back to the program, to help others, and to continue to support the 4-H program.

Webster County 4-H "Pin-Wearers" formed a county organization to support the 4-H program. We do this in memory of our positive role models, Miss Pickens and Mr. Burton.

Watch the Children and the Elderly

Ron Drum, National 4-H Council

"Remember, if you want to fit in, watch the children and watch the elderly; then do what they do!"

I was sitting in an orientation preparing for my "Great African Adventure" as an IFYE-YDP (International Four-H Youth Exchange–Youth Development Project) delegate to Botswana. Kathleen Flom was giving us "helpful hints" on how to be successful in our assigned countries. In just a few days it would be January 1980, and I would be boarding a plane, heading off to a place about as far away from home as I could get—and I was just a little scared. "Why would I watch little children?" I wondered. As if reading my mind, Kathleen supplied the answer in her typical, down-to-earth logic, "The elderly always practice good social graces, and the little children are always having their social graces corrected!"

During my first visit to a village, I watched how the children and the elderly ate their meals. I ate likewise, using my hands as they did, laying aside the fork and knife I had been given. Sure enough, one of the young men of the village came to me after the meal and through a big smile said, "You will do fine here in our country. You eat like a Motswana!"

Kathleen was, by her very nature, a teacher. The day after she died of natural causes at the Hebrew Home of Greater Washington in Rockville, Maryland, December 12, 2005, Don Floyd, President and CEO of the National 4-H Council, said:

> It is with a great deal of sadness I let you know that Kathleen Flom passed away yesterday morning in her sleep. Some of us were privileged to know her as the first lady of the National 4-H Center. For years after she retired from a long career in Extension and 4-H, she worked here at the Center and provided tours, guest support, and just made the Center special. She was here early and left late. As the day would wear on she would pull up a chair to rest. What a treat it was to pull up a chair next to her and listen to her stories about 4-H. Many times I would be searching for an answer and would ask her advice. She never told me what to do but instead would tell me a story, and in the story was the answer. If

you never met Kathleen you still know her because she is forever a part of our National 4-H Council values and culture; she helped build them and she helped make the National 4-H Center a special place.

It was this way with everyone. There was nothing more special than to pull up a chair beside Kathleen Flom to listen, to learn, and to enjoy the moment.

Kathleen Solveig Flom was born in 1913. Growing up in Belview, Minnesota, she was an active 4-H member. She actually won two Minnesota grand championships, earning two trips to the National 4-H Congress in Chicago in one year. She went on to earn her Bachelor of Science degree in Home Economics from the University of Minnesota in 1942. She launched her career as a Minnesota Cooperative Extension Service County Home Economist and 4-H Agent and it only took her 18 months to receive her first promotion to the position of Assistant State 4-H Leader. She held that position for the next 11 years.

In 1954, Kathleen moved to the Washington D.C. area and joined the staff of the National 4-H Foundation (now known as National 4-H Council) where she served as the Regional Program Leader for Europe and Far East for the International Farm Youth Exchange (later changed to International Four-H Youth Exchange). In 1959, she played a major role in the opening of the then new National 4-H Center, National 4-H Council's headquarters in Chevy Chase, Maryland. One of the highlights of her life was serving as host to President Eisenhower at the Center's official opening. She often told the story of running out at the last moment to purchase a good pair of scissors for the ribbon-cutting ceremony. Those scissors are now on display in a special room in National 4-H Center's J.C. Penney Hall, a room called "Kathleen's Corner," dedicated to her in 1997.

Kathleen spent 1960-1962 as a home economist with the British government working in the East African nation of Uganda. Returning to Washington in 1963, Kathleen became a consultant for International Programs for Women Leaders, and with the Extension Service, USDA. It was not long, however, before her skills became vital to the expanding international programs of the National 4-H Foundation. In 1965, she became National 4-H Foundation's Assistant Leader for 4-H International Programs. She was promoted in 1971 to Assistant Manager and Home Economist for the National 4-H Center and she served in that position until her retirement in 1979. In 1973, she coordinated an International Extension 4-H Travel Seminar to Botswana, Kenya, and Swaziland.

Did I say "until her retirement?" Well, technically it is true that she retired, but after she "retired" she continued to serve full-time at the National 4-H Center until 1999 as a Special Projects Consultant, delighting numerous visitors with her comprehensive knowledge of 4-H and the Center. You could ask Kathleen almost any question concerning a gift received by the National 4-H Center—a painting or a tree or a vase—and she would not only tell you when it was received but where it was located on campus! It was Kathleen who made sure the grandfather clock in the J.C. Penney Hall lobby was moved forward or back in the spring and fall at 2:00 a.m. each year!

If you knew Kathleen, you wanted her to be part of what you were doing. Kathleen was a board member of the International Home Economics Services (IHES), Inc., a member of the American Home Economics Association, the Society for International Development, Phi Upsilon Omicron (National Home Economics Honorary), Epsilon Sigma Phi (National Extension Honorary), Clovia (4-H sorority), the UN Association, and she was also made an honorary life member of the IFYE Association of the USA.

She received many honors through the years. Just since 1990, in addition to having a room dedicated to her at the National 4-H Center, she was nationally recognized with a Partner in 4-H Award by National 4-H Headquarters, USDA. In 1998, as part of the 50th anniversary celebration of 4-H International Programs, the 4-H International Exchange alumni honored her during the World IFYE Conference in Washington, D.C. And in 2002, she was inducted into the Centennial Class of the National 4-H Hall of Fame by the National Association of Extension 4-H Agents.

This suggestion would have embarrassed her, but remember, if you want to be successful, be like Kathleen Solveig Flom.

Mel Thompson, former director of International Relations, National 4-H Council, contributed to this story.

4-H Horticulture Judging - Photo/Edwin Remsberg

Volunteers,
the Heart of 4-H

The Heavenly Gate
Ken Culp, III, Ohio

A leader knocked at the heavenly gate
with face both worn and old,
and stood before the man of faith
to seek admission into the fold.

"What have you done," Saint Peter asked,
"to gain admission here?"
"I've spent a lifetime," the old one said,
"as a 4-H volunteer."

"I've attended meetings and signed up kids
and made calls into the night,
hemmed up skirts and shortened sleeves
until the dress fit right.

I've encouraged kids and cheered them on
and watched them grow each day,
broke steers and lambs, washed cotton tails,
led games in which all could play.

We hauled kids to camp, sold candy,
completed record books galore,
fed my family fast food dinners
until they begged 'No more!'

I've sampled yeast rolls and coffee cakes
'til nothing without flour tasted right,
and learned to peel from posters
stickers and labels which looked a fright!

I hauled in my trunk enough record books
for each and every child,
transformed my dining room into a place
where posters just grew wild!

My 'fridge and calendar were covered
with places, dates, and times,
for meetings, trips, and activities,
many of which were not sublime.

I borrowed a camper for the fair
and lived there night and day,
I coached new agents and took them in
and helped them learn our ways.

I wiped up noses and dried up tears,
offered a shoulder upon which to cry,
gave advice or held my tongue
and encouraged my kids to try.

I put thousands of miles upon my car
seems we were always on the run,
but looking back upon all those years,
my, but did we have fun!

Not all those days were happy ones
the good things just take time.
But were I to do it all again,
I'd be the first in line!

No payment now do I request,
my reward has all been won,
shy smiles, hugs, and thank-you notes,
good memories and times of fun.

I've left a legacy behind on earth
in the lives of those I've touched,
my only hope is that someone else
will step forward to do as much.

Our youth deserve the very best
that we can hope to give,
my only regret I now must say,
is I have but one life to live."

The heavenly gates swung open wide;
Saint Peter rang the bell.
"Come in and choose your wings, my child,
you've served your master well."

Debbie Clonan
Nancy Veal, Alaska

4-H leader Debbie Clonan always found time for community service projects. In 2003 she gathered a group of young people together, including her daughters Carol and Katie, and they started the Sensational Sterling SuperStars 4-H Club. Members were involved mostly in animal, gardening, and craft projects; however, they always had time for community service. The first few years they started small with recycling projects and playground clean-ups.

Then in 2005, the kids were a little older and chose to begin a bigger service project. They formed a team for the American Cancer Society's Relay For Life. The relay is a fun-filled overnight event designed to celebrate cancer survivorship and to raise money for research and programs of the American Cancer Society. During the event, teams of people gather and take turns walking or running laps. Each team tries to keep at least one team member on the track at all times. Relay For Life represents the hope that those lost to cancer will never be forgotten; that those who face cancer will be supported; and that one day cancer will be eliminated. The kids raised money by asking their friends and families for donations. During the Relay they walked for miles and realized their efforts had a real positive effect on their community. Before the first Relay was finished, the team was planning for the following year.

That December the fight against cancer became more personal when Debbie was diagnosed with breast cancer. Due to her treatment, she asked Connie Ferguson to become the leader of The Sensational Sterling SuperStars. Debbie stayed as involved as she could with the group. During a stressful time, 4-H gave her kids something positive to do.

The next year (2006) the team came through with flying colors, rallying behind Debbie as she battled cancer. They worked hard and were the top fundraisers bringing in over $7,400 dollars for a great cause. Instead of being satisfied with that, they immediately set a goal to raise $10,000 the following year.

In 2007, with Debbie's treatment completed and feeling great, they dove into fundraising with renewed energy. The club held a raffle for several items, including a beautiful handmade, spruce log, loveseat-sized porch rocker; and they also sewed jean purses and quilts to sell at silent auctions and at various events. Once again, this great group of kids were the top fundraisers. With huge amounts of help from family and friends, they exceeded their goal and raised more than $12,000! During the closing ceremony, awards were given out and a final lap was done by all the teams. Seeing the Clonan family and club members with arms around each other as they walked around the track together, swelled a person's heart with thanksgiving. Who knows what this great group will do in the future!

Debbie Clonan passed away in January 2009. Cancer; however, did not define her life. She was a writer, a craftsman, a loving wife and devoted mother. She was a "get'er done" creative 4-H leader who made sure her members learned great life skills and had fun doing it!

Debbie was on the front line in every activity she undertook. In her battle with cancer, she networked with people from around the world to comfort, mentor and find solutions. Her life made so much difference to so many people, there were no pink roses left in Alaska following her memorial service. She reached people around the world with encouragement and hope. Her club went back to Relay for Life in 2009, and in Debbie's honor raised more funds to fight the scourge of cancer.

Mary Ruth McKinney
Jane Miller, Illinois

Mary Ruth McKinney, a 4-H leader from Neoga, Illinois, led the Work and Play 4-H Club for 61 years. I was a co-leader with her for 23 years and have many happy memories of her leading our Cumberland County youth.

One former 4-H member, now in her seventies, remembers Mary Ruth when she was leader of the Victory Co-Eds, primarily a girl's club devoted to home economics projects. Mary Ruth, a young mother, did not take after her mother who was petite, genteel, and an "everything in its place individual." Mary Ruth was more boisterous and did not follow the "rules of Emily Post," but showed the girls how they could "multi-task" with cooking, sewing, and helping on the farm. Winona Carrell Saathoff, another former member, recalled Mary Ruth taking a genuine interest in each 4-H'er, their projects, and instilling the drive "to make the best better." Many of her 4-H'ers became nurses, administrators, pharmacists, teachers, politicians, florists, computer programmers, lawyers, farmers and more. She was a good role model for thousands of folks from Cumberland County, the United States, and the world, as she knew people from many places. Mary Ruth and her husband hosted an exchange student from Australia, entitling her to be considered a worldwide role model.

Mary Ruth had no daughters and felt her two sons should know how to take care of themselves. She encouraged her sons to take cooking and sewing projects in the early 60s, which was almost unthinkable for boys then. Can you picture a tall, gangly boy modeling a vest he had sewn or giving a foods demonstration?

Share-the-Fun activities could also be called "share-the-work" by leaders, but the 4-H'ers enjoyed showing their talents in skits and dances. The Work and Play 4-H Club was a co-ed club with members ranging in age from 10 to 19. Vernon Miller, my husband, recalled one of the skits in the early 1960s. Vernon was short, rather portly and dressed in a pink ballerina costume complete with tutu. Mary Ruth's son, Bill McKinney, with his slim 6'3" frame and long hairy legs, wore a complementary blue ballerina tutu outfit. It was quite a sight as they danced and twirled across the stage!

Mary Ruth had two items she never went anywhere without—her purse and her cameras. Usually she had a camera in her purse and another around her neck. She never carried a small purse, but one that could hold "everything that has a purpose." One year at the Cumberland County 4-H Fair there was a nest of ground wasps near the goat pens. I was stung and my arm began to swell like a balloon. Mary Ruth said, "I've got just the thing," pulling some meat tenderizer from her purse.

Making posters for 4-H events is another example of where Mary Ruth's purse often came to the rescue. A 4-H'er would ask for tape or glue sticks and Mary Ruth would produce the item from her purse. If a rubber band was needed, there were always several around her checkbook or billfold. Other items in her purse included t-shirts discarded by 4-H'ers during the day, a first-aid kit, a sewing kit and anything else that might be needed.

Mary Ruth took thousands of pictures of her 4-H'ers during her more than six decades of club leadership. She made sure members had a photo of their participation in all kinds of events that included meetings, project shows, Share-the-Fun, showing animals, judging contests, food demonstrations, hands-on workshops, achievement programs, lemon shake-up stands, National 4-H Week activities, and state events such as state fair, leadership conferences, and the University of Illinois open house.

The Cumberland County Fair is always the "last hurrah" of the summer because it occurs the last full week in August. The fairgrounds are located in a river bottom and it can be very muddy when August rains come. And it always seemed like Mondays of fair week always brought rain. One year, three days of rain resulted in a "pig pen" with 4-H'ers in muddy clothing everywhere. So Mary Ruth and I gathered up the dirty blue jeans and took a "truck load" to the local laundry-mat so all our 4-H'ers would have clean, dry clothing for livestock shows.

Mary Ruth encouraged her 4-H'ers to be involved in community concerns and needs. These projects included Angel Tree that provided needy people with winter clothing and items for Christmas; military packages; helping families who had house fires; The American Cancer Society, March of Dimes, Crippled Children, and raising money for "Million $ for 4-H."

Boys and girls were taught to show respect to both county fair judges and their project animals. The rule was *"No hats in the show ring."* If someone forgot, Mary Ruth was at the fence reaching for the offending hat whether judging had started or not.

In the summer of 2008, Mary Ruth's health deteriorated and during the Cumberland County Fair she passed away. When she died, 4-H animals were in the show ring—a place where she had spent so many years helping her own children and grandchildren and leading three generations of 4-H'ers. Mary Ruth may no longer be with us but her presence lingers on. Her booming voice encouraging young 4-H'ers showing their first animal, snapping a picture as a child went by with his or her animal and her many other thoughtful acts will long be remembered. Mary Ruth made a huge difference in the lives of countless Cumberland County 4-H'ers and their families, and her 4-H spirit will live in our hearts forever.

My Mentor, Myra Meeker
Susan Parr, Washington

The following was written for the Pierce County 4-H Leaders' Banquet held on October 3, 2008. I was honored to share a few words about Myra Meeker prior to the presentation of her Diamond 4-H Leader pin recognizing her for 40 years of dedicated service.

"I get upset every time I open the *News Tribune* or the *Pierce County Herald* and see a close-up picture of someone's dog or cat with a write-up about how wonderful their pet is! Don't get me wrong, I like pets as much as anyone but I don't understand how newspapers can use that valuable space for an animal and refuse to print articles submitted to the papers about all the good things that 4-H clubs are doing!

Back in the late 1960s, when Erna Bens was the Farm Editor for the *News Tribune,* I read an article submitted by the club reporter of Valley 4-H Club listing the newly elected officers of the club, with Myra Meeker as the main club leader. If anyone was interested in the Valley 4-H Club, they could contact her at LENOX 7-0130. As a newlywed who had moved into a fixer-upper house on Lidford Road, I recognized the names of some of the club officers as kids from Riverside Elementary School, where I had been substitute teaching. As a 10-year 4-H member in Oregon I had attended National 4-H Congress, National 4-H Conference, and the IFYE Exchange to the Philippines. I was ready to be involved in 4-H again.

I called Myra Meeker and discovered she lived on my road. She made an appointment to meet with me and discuss Valley 4-H. She even wanted to see some of my knitting when I volunteered to be a knitting project leader for the club. I soon found out what a dedicated leader Myra was.

Every year Valley 4-H Club put on a community 4-H fair at Riverside Grange Hall. Valley 4-H Club had purchased six acres of property behind the Grange by collecting newspapers and recycling them through the years. The property had some animal pens that could be used for large animals. There were rotating trophies for the large animal project winners. Valley 4-H members (including two Meeker daughters) made and sold sandwiches in the Grange Hall kitchen and did whatever else was needed. This fair was usually held the first Saturday in May, which sometimes coincided with Myra's birthday. I remember seeing her carry buckets of water from the Grange Hall to the animals out back. One winter a storm demolished the animal pens, so we decided to confine the fair to small animals and indoor exhibits. By that time I had become more active in the club and introduced judging contests for foods, clothing, needlework, arts, gardening, etc. It was a great practice fair for everyone.

Seeing that the 4-H property behind Riverside Grange was becoming a liability rather than an asset, Myra and I were instrumental in setting up a Valley 4-H Club Advisory Board that administered the sale of that property through the newly formed Washington 4-H Foundation. Interest from the proceeds of that sale is used annually by the club for scholarships and camperships for its members. Trudy Wargo, Jean Waldherr, Bob and Myra Meeker, and I have served on that advisory board now for over 30 years. Other former Valley 4-H Club members and parents, as well as Myra's granddaughter, Jessica Dunton (a Valley 4-H alum), are now on the board.

Through the years Myra gradually relinquished club leadership responsibilities to me, but she remains the guiding light who is always behind the scenes of Valley 4-H Club activities. I remember when a member wanted to have a beef project. Myra had me go with her for a home visit to discuss the responsibilities of the project with the family to ensure the animal would have adequate pasture and shelter.

Thirty-four years ago Myra suggested that we should have an annual Valley 4-H Achievement Potluck dinner in November. We continue that tradition to this day. Our club has outgrown Riverside Grange Hall, and we now fill Waller Road Grange Hall each November as we distribute end-of-the-year awards to members and leaders, and present new members with their membership cards and project materials.

Myra's rule of no gum chewing during meetings still stands.

A few years ago when a group of 4-H'ers were making jam and jelly in my kitchen, my electric stove died. I called Myra and asked if we could continue in her kitchen. We loaded the canner, produce, and equipment into my car and went to her kitchen and finished our food preservation!

To this day Myra remains my mentor. She is actively interested in the Valley 4-H Club and helps judge the members' record books annually. Whenever I get a new idea to try with the club, I ask her advice because I value her wisdom. I am sure sometimes she has the feeling that Valley 4-H Club is a runaway freight train, but change can be good, and she recognizes that.

It is often Myra who calls to remind me it is time to begin planning for the garage sale. Or, she will read something in the county newsletter and call and ask how can we be involved. She will often bring me yarn, fabric, canning jars, or produce to be used by our club members.

Because a 4-H news reporter wrote an article about his club back in the 1960s that was published in the paper, I became involved in Pierce County 4-H, and a great friendship and mentorship was formed between Myra Meeker and me. Tonight we recognize Myra for 40 years of faithful volunteer service to Pierce County 4-H."

4-H Blooms!
Betty Ann Yoder, Illinois

Cindy came to our 4-H meetings the first year that eight-year-olds were eligible to become members. A friend of mine, who was also a 4-H leader, and I were not sure about starting kids at the young age of eight. She said, "If they cannot reach the top of the stove, how can we teach them to cook?" As Cindy's first year in our club progressed, she would sit at the meetings leaning on her mother, not actively participating in much even though she had an older sister who was already a member. It appeared to me that she was not really sure she wanted to be a part of this thing called 4-H.

At each meeting, talks and demonstrations were scheduled. At the end of the meeting the club president would ask, "Are there any others to be given today?" I knew Cindy's talk had been scheduled early in the year, but she never let on she was ready to give it at any of the meetings.

The end of the year came. I said, "Cindy, to count this year as a 4-H member you will have to give your talk today." I looked in her big eyes and saw such fear. Then, I said, "Cindy, let's you and me go into the kitchen!" Our club was very fortunate to meet in the small township building. It was carpeted, had a small kitchen, and plenty of nice tables and chairs. Cindy and I went into the kitchen, and closed the door. I said, "Okay, let's hear your talk!" She quietly took a crumpled piece of paper from the pocket of her little pink shorts and proceeded to read to me "How to Make Jell-O!" I put my arm around her as we came out of the kitchen. I told her mother she had given a really great talk! Cindy's mom gave me a wink and a big smile. She later told me that Cindy had that talk in her pocket at every meeting and just could not get up the nerve to go to the front of the room.

Cindy bloomed in 4-H after that, and in her senior year of high school she went on to be one of the best presidents our club ever had. We had members from five different schools and one of our main goals was to see these girls bond. Cindy was friendly and helpful to each and every member, no matter their age. Her sense of humor brought much fun to our meetings over the years. At one of our club overnights we scheduled talks and demonstrations at midnight. Since she was from a dairying family, she showed us how to clean a milking machine. Before she was finished we were all rolling on the floor with laughter as we lounged in our sleeping bags!

Today Cindy is a dental hygienist and I am told she talks a lot to put patients at ease. She has an eight-year-old son ready to join 4-H. I learned a child's age does not really matter if they are interested in joining 4-H. I later became a Cloverbuds club leader (children ages five to seven), when my grandchildren were that age. That is where the idea of 4-H gets planted. Kids bloom when they are planted in a 4-H garden!

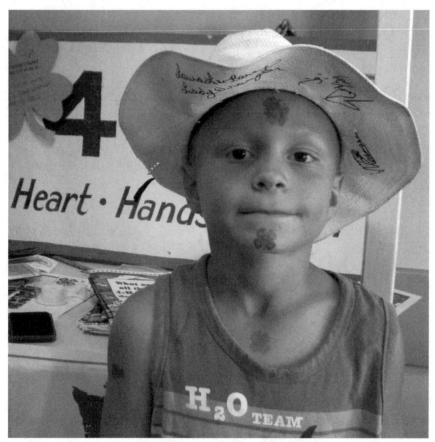

Clover All Over! - Photo/Diane Russo

Full Circle
Kathy Janik, Illinois

It is only about seven-eighths of an inch in size and a half-inch at the widest point. The gold color is still shiny and the small green 4-H clover proudly stands out. The word "Bread" is in tiny letters, and a loaf of bread and several rolls complete the little medal that has been in my jewelry box for about 40 years. The monetary value is surely insignificant, but the emotional value is priceless! The bread medal that I won so many years ago holds numerous memories for me of my 4-H work, as well as my family.

As a child, my mother was a 4-H member. She met my father through her best friend whom she had met in her 4-H club. My grandmother always told us stories about the wonderful 4-H Halloween parties they held at their home. My mother's wedding picture shows her in a beautiful wedding gown she made herself—a product of her years in 4-H. So, naturally, my mother became a 4-H leader and started a club for my older sister and me. It was called "The Gretchens" and was located in Belleville, Illinois.

4-H was such a huge program in our county that it was a real challenge to win a spot at the state fair or to receive an awards medal. The competition was intense. I can remember how excited my mother and sister were when my sister went to the state fair in sewing one year.

I enrolled in a lot of great projects, but breads and cereals was one in which I really wanted to excel. My grandparents and I were very close and my grandmother was a fantastic bread baker. My dad, who was a fireman, was also a great cook and I really wanted to impress them all. I walked to downtown Belleville to a local store and found a perfect set of crockery bowls for baking bread. The largest bowl was big enough to make seven loaves of bread! It was a warm Saturday morning and I set about baking my first loaf. My 4-H project book had a great recipe for basic white bread and I thought I should start with it. I measured, poured, stirred, and kneaded. I had helped my grandmother bake bread before, but this was my first time working alone and I was anxious and very nervous. But that bread dough rose nice and high and I punched it down and formed my first two loaves of bread. I placed them in their pans, covered them with a clean towel, and placed them on top of the refrigerator to rise for the last time before baking. All seemed to be proceeding without a hitch.

Then my sister and I received a call from my father. He was not only a fireman, but also a land surveyor, and he was in charge of a conference his surveyor's organization was hosting in Belleville. He needed me and my sister to babysit for some of the people at the conference and we would get to do it at the hotel swimming pool! We grabbed our swimsuits and headed out the door. It was only supposed to be for a couple hours and my bread would need that much time to rise, so no problem! Many, many hours later when we finally were able to return home, I raced inside to check on my bread. It had risen just as it should, but after such a long time, it had fallen and looked rather sad. I hated to see all that work and ingredients go to waste so I decided to bake the loaves anyway. Guess what? The bread started rising again when I put the loaves in the oven. They looked great but I was too tired to wait for the bread to cool. I left it on the counter and went to bed thinking I had done a great job.

The next morning I was really looking forward to a mouth-watering piece of fresh, homemade bread, but when I stepped into the kitchen there was a surprise waiting for me. My father had left me a note and a broken knife stuck in one of the loaves. Apparently the bread that had looked so nice was as hard as a brick! All that raising and falling is not good for bread, but I did not know that at the time. I kept practicing my baking that summer and became an excellent bread baker, but my dad never missed an opportunity to tease me about my first loaf of bread. When I filled out my record book that year and actually won the Bread Award, my dad laughed really hard. He always said that if the judges had only known about my first loaf of bread and what it had done to his knife, they might have reconsidered that award!

That medal became my proudest memory of 4-H and it epitomized how trial and error and hard work could make all the difference. I continue to make bread to this day, still using the bowls that I bought when I was 14 years old. I taught my children how to bake bread along with other skills I had learned in 4-H such as sewing, knitting, and arts and crafts. When my children joined 4-H as members of the Turkey Hill Busy Bees in Freeburg, Illinois, we expanded those projects to include computers, animals, and gardening. My eldest son found he loved the cooking projects. We were not too surprised when he decided to move to Oregon to attend the culinary institute and became a chef. He credits his 4-H talks with giving him the courage to teach cooking classes at the St. Louis Kitchen Conservatory and to keep his cool when he was filmed for a morning television show while a chef at a restaurant in St. Louis. Our daughter's love of animals and the projects she took in 4-H inspired her to get her degree in biology. She currently is working on her master's degree in Conservation Biology at Eastern Tennessee University. She says 4-H prepared her to study wolves at the St. Louis Zoo and for her current study of salamanders in the mountains of Tennessee. She always thanked me for "making" her give talks and demonstrations while in 4-H. She thought it made all the difference for her in class presentations and now in teaching as a part of her graduate work.

I thought I was done after so many years in 4-H as a member, a parent, and club leader. Then we started all over again with our youngest when we adopted. He was our first Cloverbud and I became the Cloverbud leader. Now that he is older I have become co-leader for his club, the Turkey Hill Busy Bees. He has enjoyed foods projects and giving food demonstrations since he joined 4-H. This past year he enrolled in breads and cereals and I thought again of my bread medal and that first doomed loaf of bread! Thankfully he did much better on his first loaf; but I believe failing so dramatically with my first loaf of bread makes it more memorable and that medal much more special. Each time I pull it out of my jewelry box I am flooded with memories of 4-H meetings at my house with my sister and mother, my dad teasing and laughing (but always eating my bread), and how very proud I felt when I received that medal. It is so very tiny, but so very powerful and I cannot help but smile and feel proud of my family and their 4-H work over all these years. What a powerful impact 4-H has made in our lives—and for me it is all wrapped up in one little gold medal that I will cherish all of my life!

The Visit to See My Friend
Ken Culp, III, Kentucky

I drove into town one day last week
to run some errands and see a friend,
went to the bank and hardware store,
mailed a package we had to send.

Took care of business that afternoon,
I paid some bills and ordered feed;
picked up parts for the four wheel drive,
ordered fertilizer, herbicide and seed.

I put off doing that afternoon
the visit to see my friend.
For the visit that day which I would make
would be final; would mark the end.

I'd met this friend many years ago
when I'd been nine years old.
I'd joined the local 4-H Club
and tried that night to be brave and bold.

We'd walked inside and stood apart,
my hand in Dad's clasped tight;
I'd wanted to join in the big kid's fun,
but was filled that eve with fright.

From across the room a face did smile;
and hummed a tune which came my way.
The face squatted down in front of me
asked my name, "Would you like to stay?"

With a look up at Dad's slow smile,
I loosened my hand from his;
placed it into this new friend's palm
and a relationship began to fizz.

The Visit to See My Friend

We spent many hours, this friend and I,
working together and having fun;
finished projects, exhibits and record books,
built a float, wrote a speech, ate on the run.

The happy times we shared those years
stretched out it seemed on end.
We went to camps and fairs, took trips;
I gave speeches, wrote scholarships to send.

My friend encouraged me to try new things,
to stretch, to dream, to grow.
I learned to speak without knocking knees,
raised an animal and learned how to show.

I served as a 4-H club officer,
learned leadership skills galore;
and when I'd held most every office
found out there was still more in store.

I served as area delegate,
was appointed then to state!
Served as a Teen Camp Counselor
and learned not to be late!

At eighteen I went off to college
and helped staff Cloverville;
taught a class at Senior Conference,
my experiences took pages to fill.

My parents stood beside me,
guided me in different ways;
but my friend went an extra mile
gave encouragement, kind words, bright days.

When I married, my friend was there;
That smiling face drew near
to share that happiest of days,
with family and friends so dear.

My first-born child turned nine last year,
the pattern was now complete.
Drove to the meeting one cloudy night
to a smiling face on shaky feet.

I watched my child unfold last year
the bud opened, began to bloom;
and guiding her along the way
was a smiling face which hummed a tune.

How can I thank a friend like that?
How do I say goodbye?
But pausing before the casket now,
the time has come again to try.

For all of those times you encouraged us,
dispensed advice along the way;
challenged each of us to stretch and grow
by brightening so many days.

We thank-you now this one last time
for all that you have done.
No earthly gift will e'er repay
your time, your help, our fun.

If Heaven has a floor of glass,
if you look down you'll see
a brand new 4-H volunteer,
and that volunteer will be me.

The legacy which you have left
must be honored on in time.
The only way to thank you now
is to give your service back in-kind.

So thank you now, my cherished friend,
for input and contributions great.
I'll say goodbye this one last time
and remember our days of late.

Your life was bright and beautiful.
You touched 4-H great and small.
You were so wise and wonderful.
May our Lord God bless us all.

What Ever Happened to Clarence Walker?
Jeff Goodwin, Colorado

When I think of examples of how 4-H volunteers can have a positive effect on the lives of young people, I think of Gerald Tate. Gerald was a 4-H volunteer leader from McLean, Texas, when I was a county Extension agent in Gray County in the mid 1980s.

Gerald was one of those great 4-H volunteers who worked with FFA kids just as much as 4-H kids. He was a joy to be around and to work with. While the vast majority of 4-H volunteers *are* great to work with, there are a few who stand head and shoulders above the rest. Gerald was one of those great ones.

I witnessed first-hand how Gerald's involvement in the 4-H and FFA programs was important in the lives of young people. It was at the McLean Community Youth Livestock Show in March of 1987. One of the young people that Gerald was helping with his FFA swine project was a high-school-aged youngster by the name of Clarence Walker.

Clarence was challenged with his lot in life more than most can imagine. He had a learning disability that would not allow him to gain the normal education that most of us take for granted; however, he could function just fine in everyday life. In addition, Clarence was from a large family with extremely limited financial resources. His family's financial situation was apparent as his "dressed up" attire included the basic rope for a belt, highlighted by an old pair of tennis shoes that looked as if they had just been devoured by a weed-whacker.

With the financial aspects of Clarence's swine project arranged for by Gerald Tate, the last item of attention was to get Clarence a wardrobe upgrade for the big swine show. Gerald took care of that by buying Clarence a brand-new pair of boots. Nothing fancy, just a good pair of nice looking work boots.

Clarence was so proud of those new boots that on the day of the big show he wore his "weed-whacker" shoes all day prior to the time he was to enter the arena. He did not want to get his new boots dirty. All day he clutched his new boots next to his chest. Just before he went into the arena, he put his new boots on. He did fine that day in the swine show, but he was proudest of his new boots.

About two weeks after the big swine show, Gerald Tate died of a heart attack in the middle of the night. It was a sad day indeed for all of Gerald's friends at his funeral—sad for everyone but Clarence Walker. You see, at the graveside service and among the hundreds of people in attendance, there was Clarence Walker standing there with a big smile on his face. He looked happy. After the service I worked my way over to Clarence and asked him what he was smiling about. Why was he so happy? Clarence responded that he was happy he had known Gerald Tate. He was happy that Gerald had helped him with his swine project. Most of all, he was happy because of Gerald's generosity and unselfishness, he was standing here at this man's funeral in a new pair of (slightly used) boots.

Nearly twenty years later, I did some looking into the life of Clarence Walker. He enjoys full-time employment with United Supermarkets in Amarillo, Texas. He is married and living a productive and happy life. It's people like Gerald Tate that helped make Clarence Walker successful in life.

Dr. Jeff Goodwin, Ph.D. currently serves as the Colorado State 4-H Program Leader.

Drawing by Maria Barga

Camp, Romance, and Family

Camp Romance
Bill and Wendy Harmon, Illinois

Bill's Story: During my junior year at the University of Illinois I was employed as the summer youth assistant with Christian County Extension. As an agriculture education major, it seemed like a good job that might help me in my future career. Little did I know what it would lead me to instead.

One of my duties included accompanying the delegation of 4-H campers to 4-H Memorial Camp at Monticello, Illinois. I had never attended 4-H camp when I was a member, but had gone to Scout and church camps many times, so I thought I knew what to expect. I remember one of the older 4-H leaders telling the group during the opening meeting that he had met his wife years before at camp. As a 20-year-old, I thought that sounded pretty corny.

That week at camp, I met a young staff member named Wendy. She worked with the Kaskaskia "tribe" of 4-H'ers during games and other group events. We often sat across from each other during meals, which lead to some awkward flirting between us. I later found out that Wendy thought I was winking at her, but I was probably suffering from allergies. At the end of the week we agreed to write to each other. I wrote a few times that summer. But when school resumed that fall, I lost interest in writing.

The next summer I returned as the summer assistant. I again went to camp as a counselor with no concerns, until one of the camp staff greeted me and said Wendy wanted to see me. It took me a few moments to realize whom she was talking about, and then I became a little nervous. Wendy's first words were, "Why didn't you write me anymore?" accompanied by a punch in the shoulder. I was reminded of my transgressions throughout the week.

We started dating later that summer, and continued throughout my graduate school year and first teaching job. She eventually forgave me for ignoring her. I visited her at camp the next summer, when she had been promoted to camp nurse. I proposed during Sunday brunch in 1992 by having a magician working the restaurant pull the ring out of her ear. The family sitting near us exclaimed, "That's not a ring, is it?"

We were married in 1993. One of Wendy's best camp staff friends was her matron of honor. Her toast described our camp story to the guests, who enjoyed a good laugh. Today Wendy and I have two children, ages 13 and 8. Our son enjoys 4-H camp, and our daughter is looking forward to her first visit there this summer. They have heard this story, and our son has asked, "what if you and Mom did not meet again the second year?" I told him he would not be here and I know my life would not be as happy had 4-H camp not given me two chances at love.

Wendy's Version: As a youth I had attended 4-H Memorial Camp many times and had set a goal of someday working as camp staff. As it turned out, I got my wish starting the summer of 1987 when I applied as a college student and was accepted as a lifeguard at the waterfront area.

At the time I was already involved in a long-term relationship and had no intention of meeting anyone special at camp. However, that year a young man name Bill volunteered as a counselor with campers from his county for one week. He was unlike anyone I had ever dated before because he was a farm boy with red hair and freckles and was in a fraternity.

The camp at that time divided the campers and counselors into Indian tribes to hold competitions with each other. Bill was assigned to the tribe I was working with and so we spent a lot of time together working with the kids that week and getting to know each other a little. He would also come down to the waterfront area where I worked as a lifeguard. At the end of the week we agreed to write each other. Well, I followed through on my promise and wrote him two or three times, but never heard back from him.

Fast-forward to the next summer when I again worked on the camp staff and he again chose to volunteer as a counselor with his county. Another staffer at camp was from his county and knew he was coming. She agreed to be a greeter at the camp entrance where the buses and campers checked in. She met the bus from his county and teased him that I was at the camp again and was mad at him for blowing me off for a year. He later told me he was scared to death to run into me again. I found out much later that the guys at his fraternity had discouraged him from writing me and he listened to them.

During this camp week we again engaged in friendly flirting and hanging around each other. At the end of camp I was not going to count on him writing me, so I made plans to meet him at the Christian County Fair being held the following weekend. I drove down and it was at that fair we had our first kiss. We began dating that summer and after three years he finally proposed. We have been married for 17 years and have two children who both enjoy attending 4-H Memorial Camp themselves. Who knows, maybe they too will meet the love of their life there one day!

4-H Creates More Than Just Life-Long Friendships
Laura McKenzie, West Virginia

One of the things I have noticed over the years is the strong bonds of friendship created through 4-H. Very often these bonds surpass your average relationships.

My entire family on my father's side was involved in 4-H. When you stereotype the traditional farm family, you will find my aunts and uncles in Princeton, West Virginia. The McPherson children had to walk two miles over a mountain from an old farmhouse to catch the bus to school, grew all their own food, and so on. When I was nine years old, my dad found a 4-H club outside of Fairmont. He would drive us to the meetings with the neighbors up the street. There were big meetings and little meetings. We once held the whole meeting in our neighbor's car because all four officers were in attendance!

My very favorite 4-H activity was Marion County Camp. My first year I was lucky enough to have my dad come to camp daily to teach a class on forestry. I can still see him pulling up in his state vehicle and getting out of the car in his uniform. I attended county camp every year. At age 17 I had one of the most rewarding experiences of my life as chief of the mighty Mingo tribe. It was an amazing week! My tribe won the spirit stick for the second year in a row, and I had the lead in my class performance at camp.

For the first time ever we had three VCAs (volunteer camping assistants) in camp instead of two, which turned out to be the biggest blessing of my life. Funny, I do not remember the name of the two in charge, but the third, well; he spent a lot of extra time with the campers. Tony McKenzie was a 22-year-old engineering student from West Virginia University who had special permission to come to camp.

The next year I saw Tony at the last council circle (campfire) and was rewarded with the usual "hello 4-H friend" bear hug! Then, as a student at WVU, I ran into him once or twice on campus. I remember the day he dropped off his master's thesis at the Wise Library where I worked. I found out a few years later that he had seen my photo on the cover of the campus newspaper advertising the show the theatre department was performing my junior year.

He saw the picture and said, "I know her. I better go see her show in case I run into her sometime." He convinced a buddy to go with him to the show where he chose a performance scheduled specifically for the students in the law department. The show was sold out, but Tony waited to see if any seats were available. He and his friend got the only two tickets left that night.

About eight years later, Tony was available in the summers to be on the staff of state camps. The Older Members Conference (OMC) that year was doing something called secret pals. Staff members drew names of campers and became secret pals, writing them little notes, and giving little gifts and such. Tony had to draw about five or six names before he got the name of a camper he did not know, Andi McPherson.

The Saturday morning before they left camp, the pals met and ate breakfast with their partners. Tony was certain he knew of someone with the same last name as Andi and quizzed her about her relatives, thinking he might know one of them. She said, "You might know my sister, Laura McPherson." He replied astonished, "Laura McPherson, the actress!"

Andi called to let me know she met someone I might remember from my camping days. Then she arranged to have him come to Camp Mar-Mac in Marion County where I was helping for a few days. Tony first saw me from across the center of camp as he was leaving the dining hall. You have to know him personally to understand the statement he made to himself, "I'm going to date that girl!" Well, he flirted with me shamelessly all through council circle that night as we sat in the Big Foot (counselors) tribe.

We dated, which was no small feat, as I lived in Pittsburgh at the time and he lived in Morgantown, West Virginia. We married in 1997, went to Disney World for our honeymoon, then to OMC to be on the staff. One night we were invited to sit on Council Rock (place of honor), one of the most memorable experiences I have ever had! We were additionally recognized during council circle by a 15 minute serenade with the entire camp singing every toe tapping, couples song ever sung at a council circle! What could ever top that?!

I found out later that summer that Maggie, Tony's mother, had grown up in Mercer County. To be specific, she remembered attending Mercer County Camp with my aunts and uncles. Maggie even remembered going to my Granny's house for meetings. The farmhouse no longer stands in the valley, just the memories. Incredible, but true. It must have been fate.

Tony and I now have two 4-H'ers of our own (and two more who will become 4-H'ers when they are old enough). They attend the 4-H club organized by two other 4-H born couples, one whose mother camped with my dad in Mercer County. Since then, we have had the good fortune of serving on the state camp staff with our own children in attendance…but those events have stories all their own.

Personally, I prefer to hear the story I just shared rather than telling it. I never tire of hearing Tony tell it and am near tears every time. I can also correct him because he changes many of the details, but the basic plot is always the same!

What 4-H and Camp Shaw Mean to Me
Deb Augsburg Needham, Illinois

My name is Deb Augsburg Needham, and I can honestly say that my 4-H and Camp Shaw experiences have played an enormous part in building the person I am today. I started by learning to cook and sew, speak in public, being a leader in our 4-H Federation, and as a counselor at Camp Shaw in Illinois.

I clearly remember begging to be allowed to join 4-H when I was seven years old or so. My mom had been a 4-H'er and a Camp Shaw camper. I could not wait to learn to cook! My first 4-H leader, Doris Finnestad in Kendall County, took pity on me and let me be a "junior member" in the Stitch 'n Stir club when I was eight. I could not show at the fair, but at least I could start cooking!

Once I got to be a real member, I could not get enough. I practiced hard to get my cooking projects perfect before the fair. Some were highly popular with my family, especially oatmeal cookies and Rice Krispie bars. They could have done without the baking powder biscuits, but they were always supportive! I also loved learning to sew and was supported by Charlene, our sewing leader. My mom was a wonderful basic seamstress, but Charlene helped us with the harder jobs. Buttonholes were my biggest nightmare! Eventually, I made it to the state fair with my sewing project. Public speaking contests and cooking demonstrations gave me the confidence to speak in front of a group.

The great love I developed from 4-H was for Camp Shaw-waw-nas-see, located in Manteno, Illinois. Once I finally got into 4-H (legally), the next question was "When can I go to camp?" My mother attended Camp Shaw as a girl and had great memories of her time there. She saved a charm bracelet that spells out Camp Shaw-waw-nas-see and loans it to me only for *very* special occasions. Finally, it was decided I could go to camp the summer I turned 10.

So it began. At that time campers checked in early Monday morning, so I pulled Mom out of bed as early as I could. It was crucial I get a top bunk next to my girlfriend Diane! Most years we arrived at camp before the poor staff members had finished breakfast.

I loved *everything* about camp. Swimming was my favorite activity, but I also loved hiking to Chief Shaw's grave, rock-hops, night hikes, and leatherwork.

I loved the songs, the milk-drinking contests, trotting, the Indian ceremony, and the dance. We always cried during the closing ceremony after the dance, and sang our hearts out to "shake the chandeliers" in the dining hall after lunch on Friday. By the time our parents came to pick us up, our voices were nearly gone (but we sang in the car on the way home anyway). The next summer could never come fast enough. I am lucky to still be in contact with some of my camp friends from our early days. Nonnie and I were campers together and she now sends her daughters to Camp Shaw!

When I was about 15, my friend Beth and I were allowed to be "junior counselors." At that time, counties camped together for a week and provided their own counselors. Beth and I had come to camp for so long, worked at open houses, and made camp presentations that they let us start "working" at camp early. We could not have a cabin of our own but we were on our way! Around that time I also got involved with teen camp and the Sagamore council. One experience I will never forget is the year that PMA (Positive Mental Attitude) was our theme. To build our confidence, we were awakened during the night and told that two of our teen campers (one of whom was Verla, who later became my college roommate, and our friend Dan) were "lost" in the woods and we had to search for them. There was a police car at camp and the experience was very realistic. Once the activity was over (and I finished crying with Verla since she was safe), we felt we had accomplished something really important.

During my late high school years I spent lots of weeks at camp as a volunteer counselor. I would get home from camp on Friday night, do laundry, and generally get a call on Saturday confirming they needed me back on Sunday night! I had the opportunity to work in all of the program areas and always loved working with the campers, other counselors, and program staff.

Once I graduated from college and started working at Arthur Andersen (now Accenture), I worked my way back to Camp Shaw helping as a counselor. After my sons were born, I could not *wait* for them to be old enough to take to family camp and eventually to regular camp. As my sons attended camp each summer, it was wonderful to see them enjoying many of the same experiences I had! They begged to get to camp early (to get that coveted top bunk) and sang themselves hoarse on the way home. My two sisters (who also attended camp and worked as counselors) have remained involved as well. My sister Alice sends her sons to camp, and Linda has attended many family camps and helped with lots of work days, open houses, and fund raising events.

About the time my sons started to attend camp, I was privileged to join the board of directors for the Northern Illinois 4-H Camp Association (which owns and operates Camp Shaw). I have been working on the board for several years, serving as president and treasurer. While it is a great deal of work, I enjoy every minute of it including leading tours at open house, painting cabins, checking in campers, updating the camp website (www.campshaw. org) and any of the other "millions" of jobs that need to be done. I work with a wonderful group of board members who are all just as dedicated to the success of Camp Shaw as I am. We have currently kicked off a building campaign to renovate and repair many of our structures. Most of them are original from when the camp was opened over 60 years ago, so many need some work. There is always something challenging to do! Please visit the camp website to learn how you can help.

My greatest joy comes from working with the staff at Camp Shaw. While of course I love the campers, I truly enjoy working with the staff. I love seeing our staff learn to lead, solve frustrating situations, and think on their feet. I enjoy helping them work through problems they encounter in their work. I love seeing how proud they are to have moved into staff roles. Many of them are long-term campers who, like me, could not *wait* to be on the staff. I have been privileged to get to know many of them well, and have watched them move from Camp Shaw to college and later successful careers. I strongly believe working at camp gives them an experience they cannot get anywhere else.

This past summer I had the great joy of having my sons work at Camp Shaw. Cam is a wonderful counselor, patient, and all about the campers. John completed the first session of the Counselor in Training (CIT) program, and also volunteered in the kitchen. It is wonderful to see them grow and develop doing something we all love!

So that is my story. I hope to continue working with the board for years to come, participating in the songs and skits around the campfire, and dancing at the camp dances until…who knows? I am so grateful to 4-H and to Camp Shaw for the big part they played in making me the person I am today.

Bacon and Eggs in a Sack
Mary Jo Boots, Minnesota

Recently, Henry and I were going through the receiving line at the funeral of a former 4-H parent. Her son, now in his 50s, said, "Oh, I remember the camping trips, and the bacon and eggs in a sack." At the same funeral, we ran into two other 4-H'ers of the same era, and both said something about the 4-H camping trips. That is always the way it is when we see former 4-H members.

Henry and I were newlyweds in 1956 when we were asked to be adult leaders of the 4-H club he grew up in—the Redwood County Four Leaf Clovers. In the 25 plus years we were leaders, the club grew to more than 60 members. We found ourselves looking for ways to develop leadership and a sense of working together among the older club members. Enjoying tent camping ourselves, we decided taking them on a weekend camping trip would not only help achieve these goals, but would also teach camping skills and an appreciation of the natural world. It sounded like fun and soon became a club tradition.

We would drive in several cars to one of our beautiful Minnesota State Park group camping sites where we would pitch our tents. We cooked all our meals over a campfire and would hike, fish and play softball. We had scavenger hunts and other activities to help the campers learn to identify the birds, flowers, and trees they were seeing. At night, we would sit around the campfire, make s'mores, sing, and tell stories.

The first year we camped together I introduced the campers to cooking their breakfast of bacon and eggs in a paper sack. We took a medium-sized brown paper bag, laid three or four slices of bacon to cover the bottom of the sack, and dropped a couple of raw eggs carefully on top of the bacon. Then we folded the top over, put a stick through the bag, and held it over the campfire to cook. The campers were all convinced the whole thing would go up in flames; but I do not remember losing a single one because they listened to our warning to stay well above the hot coals. This breakfast took real patience to fix, but the campers would be rewarded at the end with a delicious meal.

On every camping trip we took after that, the experienced campers would insist the "newbies" had to fix their bacon and eggs in a paper sack, and it became sort of an initiation ritual. Many others chose to do it again, while a few used a frying pan. As our three children came along, they too went on our annual camping trips as toddlers, and then 4-H members in their own right.

To this day, every time we see one of our former club members, they invariably bring up the camping trips and bacon and eggs in a sack, so we know the trips served their purpose of fun, fellowship, and skill building. We did not know then that we were also making memories!

A Bearable Story

Eleanor Drum, Pennsylvania

I became a 4-H volunteer in 1967 by default when my children needed a 4-H entomology project leader and no one else would volunteer. My husband, Harry, had already been volunteering as a 4-H beekeeping project leader, having started in 1966. We made quite a team, Harry, me, and 4-H. In 1972, we organized our own club the members called the Sugarloaf Valley 4-H Club.

I thought our teamwork might end in December 1984. I was diagnosed with colon cancer and we spent all of 1985 fighting that disease. But we kept the club going. By the end of that year the doctors were calling me a "miracle." The cancer was in remission and by January 1986 I was feeling the best I had in some time. That changed again in February.

This time it was Harry's turn. While at work during a snowstorm he slipped and fell, resulting in a very badly broken right knee. He put up a good fight, but complications from the break and subsequent surgery ended his life just six weeks after his fall. That was more than I thought I could handle. I gave up the club and spiraled down emotionally. Try as I might to turn myself around, my spirits just continued to sink lower and lower.

Then one day the county 4-H newsletter came in the mail. In it was a cry for help. They were building their 4-H camp program and seemed to need everything including nurses, cooks, counselors, special sessions leaders—everything! One special session was the nature program. Now that is something I could help with. I am a bird watcher. The boys did wildlife 4-H projects. I love to go camping. So I called the 4-H agent and told her to count me in.

Our county 4-H camp is a part of the Hickory Run State Park. I piled all sorts of nature stuff and books in my car and headed into the mountains. When I arrived, they showed me around camp and then took me to the Nature Hut, a small cabin off by itself where I would spend most of my time. After a bit of cleaning I unloaded my car and got ready for the campers.

Monday and Tuesday went very well. Having great teen leaders to help and interested young people to teach took my mind off of me and my troubles, for a little while at least. Wednesday started very busy, just like the others, but the afternoon was quiet. The campers were off doing other activities and I found myself alone in that little cabin.

I busied myself with cleaning and preparing but soon was just standing alone, looking out the window and beginning to feel sorry for myself again. That is when I noticed the blueberries. Bushes and bushes covered with berries spread everywhere. Harry and I used to love going blueberry picking, so I decided that is how I would fill my afternoon. I grabbed a pail and headed out the door.

The sun felt so good, bird songs filled the air, and the berries were delicious! I was eating more than I was picking. Suddenly I noticed the birds had stopped singing. Everything had grown very quiet; everything, that is, except for one bush. I could hear a lot of activity behind that bush but I never questioned what it might be. I continued picking berries and thinking of Harry and my plans for Thursday's program.

Then, as I moved to a section with more berries, I stepped backwards and bumped into something. As I turned around I realized what I had bumped into was a full-grown black bear. There he was (I assumed it was a male as I could not see any cubs about), standing on his hind legs reaching up to get another mouthful of berries. We were inches apart, staring at each other. I gasped and then gulped. It was all I could do not to turn and run, but I knew if I did that, it might encourage him to attack.

Slowly I backed away, all the time thinking how I could get around that bear so I could get back into the Nature Hut! After a few seconds the bear turned back to the berry bush and began eating again. I took a deep breath and began to move slowly in the direction of the hut—all the time praying, "God be with me and keep that bear eating!" Well, he must have been *very* hungry because he took no further notice of me and just kept taking great mouthfuls of berries and having a very pleasant time.

I, on the other hand, was shaking so badly it is a wonder I was moving at all. But moving I was, directly for that Nature Hut door! I sneaked along the side of the hut and around to the corner and then, finally, my hand was on the knob and I was *in*!

Now how to get back out! I knew suppertime was approaching and if I did not get down there, 4-H'ers would come looking for me and that was the last thing I wanted. That bear was still outside, grunting, and huffing, and eating. I wanted him to eat only berries that day!

So, still shaking and still praying, I decided to sneak out once again and head toward the mess hall. Well, I knew I could not go past that bear again, but thought the trail circled back around so I headed out that way, the long way around. What I did not know was that while the trail I was on did double back around, it was right back to that bear!

As I sneaked around the bend, there I was, face-to-face with that bear again! He was chewing a mouthful of berries while staring at me staring at him, surrounded by berries, and I thought to myself, "Oh Lord, this is it. I'm a goner!" But that old bear just dropped to all fours, turned his back on me, and grabbed another mouthful of berries.

That was enough. I began running, crashing through bushes and making more noise than a freight train. "Eleanor! Eleanor!" I heard called repeatedly, and I headed toward the sound. "Where have you been? What are you doing? We've been looking for you!" I told them where I had been and all about the bear.

"You should never have been up there by yourself! That bear comes to eat there whenever no one is around. We do not let anyone stay up there alone!"

But I survived. It was the third time I told myself that in less than a year. Suddenly my troubles seemed far smaller than they had before. I had *survived!* It turned out to be a great summer.

Funny how meeting a bear at 4-H camp can help make the things that happen to you in life seem just a little bit more "bearable."

Love at First Sight
Amy Zeintek, Ohio

As a 13-year-old, I was frantic to finish getting my animal ready and myself dressed on time for my calf show. As I walked past the steer barn I was taken aback by a brown-haired, blue-eyed, five foot seven inch, very handsome young man. I stopped and looked a while and thought to myself, "I'm going to marry him someday." What would he have thought of me, an awkward young teenager with a crush on him?

Two years passed. The summer I was 15, I got invited to be a Fulton County 4-H camp counselor. I was so excited to be in a leadership position, and knew it was an opportunity I would not forget. That handsome young man I had noticed a couple years before was also a counselor. Both of us had grown a little, and I had shed some of my preteen looks and had blossomed into a young lady that might be noticed by guys my age. Through group activities and talks, I was sure that farm boy was the one for me.

At camp that summer my nerves were a wreck. I wanted him to notice me as someone more than just a fellow counselor, and throughout that week he did! We had lots of fun on the high ropes course and at the dances. We probably paid more attention to each other than our campers. Camp ended with a sick feeling in my stomach that told me what I thought might have been love was just a teenage fling. When it was time to leave I made a point of hugging him goodbye. To my surprise, he quickly responded to my hug with a little kiss.

A week later he called and wondered if I remembered him. How could I forget? We have been together for 15 years and have shared many memories and 4-H experiences. I told him on July 6, 2002, our wedding day, that I had known for as long as I could remember that we were going to be together forever. We have been married eight years now and have two beautiful daughters. At least in my case, love at first sight is real.

An earlier version of this story was published in Farmland News, Archbold, Ohio

Love at First Sight - Photo submitted by Amy Zeintek

Hearts Meet Through 4-H
Sarah Jackson Hill, Missouri

For many 4-H members, being selected to attend National 4-H Congress is the highlight of their 4-H career. For Sarah, a petite, blonde, Missouri farm girl, that was no less true. The Missouri 4-H program had an intensive application and interview process to endure before being selected as one of 30 delegates. Sarah attended nearly every 4-H conference available and participated in as many different aspects of 4-H as possible. Being selected to attend National 4-H Congress would be the "cherry on top" of 10 successful years as a 4-H member for her.

Braeton, an ornery, handsome cowboy from Colorado, took a very different route to get to National 4-H Congress. He had signed up for the experience as just another 4-H conference—a week of girls, workshops, girls, dancing, and, of course, more girls. He expected to have a very good time; meet some cute, out-of-state girls, and leave it at that. Neither one knew this would not just be another 4-H conference for either of them. Something very special was about to come into their lives.

It was the day after Thanksgiving, 2003. National 4-H Congress was just kicking off and a huge ballroom was abuzz with 1500 young people from all across the U.S. These were the premier 4-H members in their respective states, the cream of the 4-H crop. They were ready for a fun week of workshops, making new friends, community service projects, dances, and more. The event started with a pin swap. Sarah descended the stairs into the ballroom with an envelope of Missouri pins in hand. She immediately drifted over to a group of 4-H'ers standing off to the side of the room. They were from Colorado, but did not have any pins to trade since their luggage was late. Braeton was not with the group; he and his friend Danny were off talking to folks from other states. Sarah chatted briefly and left, with the promise to trade pins later.

She knew exactly when the Colorado 4-H'ers' pins arrived because two lines of girls formed, each eagerly wanting to trade pins with Braeton and Danny. Sarah made a quick decision which line to get into, based on which young man was better looking. She got at the end of Braeton's line and patiently waited her turn to trade. When it was her turn to swap, she had no pin to trade with him as she had already traded all of hers away, she told him with a smile. Braeton gave her a Colorado 4-H pin anyway, and she went on her way.

Another Missouri 4-H delegate, Sky, was passing out bumper stickers from his hometown during the pin swap. He jokingly told everyone to put the stickers on their "bumper," or backside. When Braeton and Danny received their bumper stickers, they did not hesitate to do as Sky told them and affixed the bumper stickers to their Wrangler-clad rear ends.

After dinner Sarah and her friend Kat were sitting in the lobby area talking about the day. As with most teenage girls, the subject of boys came up and Kat complained that she could never meet or flirt with guys. Sarah, now feeling a bit brazen, confidently told Kat that flirting was easy! It was so easy that Sarah would choose a guy out of the crowd and show Kat how flirting was done. She turned and looked out over the crowd of chatting and laughing young people. A black cowboy hat, Wranglers, and cowboy boots caught her eye. She leaned over to Kat and told her that the guy in the cowboy hat was the guy she was going to demonstrate her flirting skills with. Sarah did not realize she had picked Braeton out of the crowd, the same Colorado cowboy she had briefly met earlier.

The evening progressed, and Sarah and Kat were talking with a large group of about twenty 4-H members from different states. Braeton and Danny had somehow worked their way over to the same group and were talking to other people. Sarah noticed the cowboy she had picked out of the crowd was nearby and made up her mind to find a way to talk and flirt with him, just as she had promised Kat. As soon as Braeton was close enough to be within hearing range, she giggled to Kat "Those silly guys have bumper stickers on their bumpers!" Two seconds later Braeton whirled around and made a clever comment in return, and shoved out his hand in introduction. Sarah smiled, shook his hand, and introduced herself. A few minutes of conversation later, Braeton sat down next to Sarah and they talked some more. He soon had to leave for supper, but asked the number of her room so that he could call her later. As he headed toward the banquet room, Sarah thought to herself, "What a nice guy. I hope I get to talk to him again."

As curfew approached, Sarah and her friends made their way to their room on the eighth floor, all wound up and laughing. The hotel was arranged so that the rooms were on the outside with an open atrium in the center that provided a view of the rooms across the hotel and down to the lobby. As Sarah walked, she recognized the Colorado group on the seventh floor. What a coincidence! Maybe she would get to talk to Braeton again.

Sarah went out on the balcony in front of her room to visit with some friends and noticed that the Colorado folks were also out on their balcony. Very faintly, she overheard one of them say to Braeton, "Hey, hey! There she is!" A few minutes later he appeared from the stairwell door, which was only a few doors down from their room. They talked some more, comparing families, 4-H programs and experiences, hometowns, schools, and more. They both discovered they had a love of showing animals, reading, and dancing. Shortly before curfew, he bid her good night.

The next day, after a long day of workshops and fun, the first dance was underway. With so many 4-H members it was next to impossible to find anyone, but Sarah really wanted to dance with Braeton. She told herself that if she found him somewhere throughout the course of the night, she would ask him to dance, and if not, then she would dance with other guys and have fun anyway. A conga line started and Sarah quickly jumped in with her friends. She spotted Braeton in the crowd as the line wove around. She got his attention and he joined the line behind her. After the song was over Sarah turned around and, to her surprise, Braeton wrapped her up in a huge bear hug. She asked him to dance, and they fast danced, swing danced and slow danced to every song for the rest of the evening.

For the next few days they spent every spare moment together, spent every night talking on the hotel room phone, only getting three hours of sleep each night. Anytime they walked anywhere together Braeton held Sarah's hand, causing a chorus of "Aw!" from the Colorado 4-H'ers. Sarah blushed and giggled from the teasing the Missouri 4-H'ers gave her, but neither seemed deterred. At other 4-H conferences Braeton had usually kept several girls on the string, but for some reason this time was different—Sarah was the only girl he wanted to hang out with.

The day before they were to leave, Braeton and Sarah were walking down the stairwell between their floors so she could get a jacket for a tour. They were holding hands, and came to a landing. Just as Sarah was about to take the next step, Braeton pulled her close and kissed her with all the sweetness and innocence of a budding 4-H love. She blushed, laughed, and they continued on their way.

All too soon the departure day arrived. Braeton and Sarah traded phone numbers, email addresses, and promises to keep in touch. Sarah did not know if he really would call her or not, but was delighted to get an email from him the day after they got home. That weekend they shared the first of many epic phone conversations, and their friendship grew deeper with every exchange.

Six months later Sarah boarded a plane for the very first time to fly to Colorado to be Braeton's date for the senior prom. As college students their friendship remained as strong as ever. Each time a relationship did not work out for one of them, they would call the other for comfort and support. When either had a reason to celebrate or had good news, they called the other person to share. They shared three and a half years of friendship and caring over the miles, and a handful of scattered visits.

Sarah had just broken up with a boyfriend she had been with for a year and called Braeton late one evening for some tearful venting. He told her what she had been waiting all that time to hear. Whenever she was ready to date again he wanted to be the guy she dated. A couple months later Braeton flew to see her in Wisconsin, where Sarah had a summer internship. Thus began their official relationship, built on a simple 4-H friendship.

On August 8, 2009, Braeton and Sarah were married, nearly six years after they had met. Their wedding favors were green 4-H ribbons, a small nod to the youth organization that had such a profound impact on both their lives. While Braeton attended graduate school at the University of Wyoming, Sarah got a job as a 4-H educator, inspiring other young people to achieve their dreams and encouraging 4-H members to attend National 4-H Congress. Sarah and Braeton's National 4-H Congress experience had changed the course of both of their lives for the better.

Iowa 4-H Love Stories
Compiled by the Iowa 4-H Foundation

To celebrate Valentine's Day 2009, the Iowa 4-H Foundation asked folks to share their 4-H love stories. You will find some of those stories below.

"My wife and I met during the summer of 2003 at the Iowa 4-H Center. We became close friends while on the summer camp staff. The miles between us during college only made our hearts grow fonder and we began dating that fall. We spent two more summers on camp staff making many more friends and memories. We had an outside wedding on October 14, 2006, in the grassy area just east of Linden Lodge at the 4-H Center, with the reception following inside. Three flags flew that day: Northwest Missouri State University, Iowa State University, and the 4-H flag. Our colleges kept us apart but 4-H brought us together. Some of our wedding photos have been placed on the Iowa 4-H Center website." – *David and Betsy Stephens, Humboldt, Iowa*

"It was February 1969 and Page County was sending senior 4-H'ers to Winter Camp, about three hours away at the Iowa 4-H Center. I went to high school in Clarinda, but in the same car was a very cute farm boy who lived only five miles up the road on Highway 71. This cute boy went to school at Villisca, so we had never met. Winter Camp was an awesome experience, complete with a night hike led by Howie to the Des Moines River. It was lots of fun going to the river, but all uphill in deep snow going back to the old Oak Lodge. It was a memorable hike for everyone who tagged along.

Those farm kids married in September 1971 and took a short 'honeymoon' to Cedar Lodge at the 4-H camp. The new groom was on leave between USN boot camp/basic training and was heading out to sea during the Vietnam War. The bride was attending nurses training, so time was short.

Fast-forward to 2008, we have three 4-H children of our own and hundreds of 4-H members from the Clarinda Classics 4-H Club. We still love 4-H and the Iowa 4-H Center. We planned numerous Winter Camps at Camp Aldersgate near Villisca, and Howie still led a Night Hike each year—a tradition and favorite of the next generation of campers. When our children began dating, one of my first questions was "Are they in 4-H?" There is nothing like 4-H love. Thanks for this opportunity to share our 4-H love story." – *Howie and Janelle Stephens, Ames, Iowa*

"Carol and I were 4-H'ers in the same county and were on county council together for a year or so, but had no real connection. We were at a dance around Christmas time of her senior year and we danced some. I asked her to a Valentine church youth group party and then our invitations to each other's proms followed. That summer at the county fair I was the experienced beef showman and she was a novice, so I helped her fluff out the tail switch; that was the thing to do in those days.

That was 41 years ago. Our four children were active 4-H members and we were and still are leaders. A few years ago I decorated a five-gallon bucket for a flower exhibit for fair board members with a smiley face and wrote, "I met my wife through 4-H and won a prize. 4-H was good to me." – *Dudley McDowell, rural Sheldon*

"The 1991 National 4-H Congress, held in Chicago, holds a special place in our hearts. Neither of us knew this trip would lead us to a lifetime partner and friend. Allison was Iowa's 1991 State 4-H Horse Project winner and I was the 1991 4-H Sheep Project Winner. We did not know each other before traveling to Chicago for Congress. However, as the week went on we found ourselves spending more and more time together on the trip. After returning home there were many letters, phone calls, and dates. Since we lived a little over two hours apart (Allison lived in Lime Springs and I lived in Gladbrook) our favorite meeting spot was in Waterloo. I attended Allison's senior prom in 1992. We chose different colleges to attend with Allison going to Iowa State University and me to Simpson College. We continued to see each other throughout college. I finally proposed to Allison in November 1995 and we were married on December 28, 1996. We recently celebrated our 11th wedding anniversary.

Allison is a microbiologist for Fort Dodge Animal Health and I work for Iowa State University Extension as a 4-H Youth Field Specialist/State 4-H Coordinator for Safety and Education in Shooting Sports (SESS). We live in Eagle Grove, Iowa, and have two children. Our daughter Shea is five and our son Quinn is two. We both have fond memories of our 4-H experiences and look forward to becoming 4-H parents. We hope our children will acquire all the life skills we developed by being involved in 4-H." – *Bryan Whaley (nine-year member of the Tama County Wolfcreek Whirlwind) and Allison (Steen) Whaley (nine-year member of the Howard County Howard Center Stars and Flying Hoofs)*

"We were active in rival 4-H clubs while growing up in Mills County. We have many wonderful memories showing cattle and hogs against each other. One of Dan's first memories of me was during the annual county fair water fight. I was pelted with a bucket full of water and manure and then slipped and rolled down a hill. We were more rivals than friends growing up. However, it was at Iowa State that our love blossomed. We dated for seven years and on June 2, 2007, we were married in Des Moines. We continue to stay active in the 4-H program and love to share friendly banter about our old 4-H club rivalry. Thanks for the opportunity to share our story!" – *Stephanie and Dan Pollock*

"I met my wife Julie when we were both in 4-H in Jones County. The year was 1973 and we both were in the county group called Builders. Julie belonged to the Olin Ship Ahoys and I belonged to the Oxford Livewires (Oxford Junction). The thing I remember most was going on a trip to Dubuque and going out to dinner as a group with dancing afterwards. Julie and I danced for the first time that night. That was the first time we really talked and started getting to know each other. We started to date shortly after that. I graduated in '73 and she in '74. We were married in April 1975. We have been dancing together since that first date. Dancing country and ballroom is just one of the things we love to do together. We have since moved from Jones County to Mahaska County, but continue to live in the country. 4-H holds many memories for us. It has been an important part of our family for three generations." – *Brad Flory and Julie (Jones) Flory*

"Ah, yes, a 4-H love story. This is a joy to relate. Going to the Winneshiek County Fair was the highlight of the whole summer. I was going to be a senior in high school when I met the most handsome young man at the county fair. My friend and I were walking through the hog barn when we met a couple of boys. I knew one of the boys, and he introduced me to his friend. *Wow!* He made a great first impression! We had never seen each other because we went to different schools. He asked if I wanted to ride on the Tilt-a-Whirl. That night at the fair was the start of a dream romance that has lasted for 62 years.

But wait, I am getting ahead of myself. At the time, there were girl 4-H county presidents and boy 4-H county presidents. Ironically *we* held those two offices, so naturally we needed to get together to plan the 4-H party. Ted's farming and a year as state FFA president followed. I taught two years at a country school.

This 4-H romance became a permanent love story with a wedding in 1948. We have had many years of sharing dreams and raising five wonderful children. I might add that we have a beautiful 4-H love story that has become even more precious as we think about that first meeting at the fair. Do I believe in love at first sight? Yes!" – *Phyllis and K. Ted Green*

My 4-H Family
Pat Bunge, Illinois

We are a 4-H family but I did not particularly plan for that to happen. My siblings and I had been members of a 4-H club where we grew up, but there was not a whole lot happening in the neighborhood in those days. Hard work, some hard times, and a few of the well-known associated legends represented the arduous nature of *our* childhood. The reality was that the four children of our family did indeed share a room in a very small home. We three sisters shared a bed with me, the youngest, sleeping in the middle. Our lone brother had the privilege of having his own bed and then eventually his own small room. Hand-me-down clothes, mostly made by my grandmother, were worn without question and with gratitude. A black and white TV was seldom turned on until after the evening meal. But there were lots of 4-H activities.

We lived in the house my father built with his own hands. Nearby was the farm my grandparents owned where they raised corn and soybeans, ubiquitous to the Midwest. For a "little extra" Grandma ran an egg and fresh poultry business. My father worked at his parent's place, two towns over, where they owned a dairy. The 4-H club was the center of our world in a community that was changing from an agricultural-based lifestyle to suburban sprawl. It was the 1960s and that 4-H club provided our social network in a not-so-affluent but deeply rich community. Through 4-H we learned to dance and gain social skills. We played sports and learned sportsmanship. We completed 4-H projects ranging from gardening to home economics to raising a broad variety of animals, all proudly exhibited at the county fair—the highlight of our summer.

In September, at the start of each 4-H year, I remember the excitement of choosing projects and getting new project books. "School's out" meant the house was 4-H central and all horizontal surfaces became littered with photography projects, art work, and clothing items in various stages of completion. Our patient old collie dog was dragged through the rudiments of training class. Horsemanship was endlessly practiced on the one level corner of the field with a not particularly talented or good-looking horse, but perfect and beautiful in my mind.

Ours was a "hard knocks" life. Pet chickens would end up as dinner without question. We appreciated life and learned early that death is a part of it. We were scrappy kids with skinned knees and runny noses. We had chores—lots of them. If it was cold out, we were expected to pull together clothing to endure the weather and have the sense to grab an extra pair of mittens so we could swap out the wet ones. I have a terrifying memory of an unseasonably warm spring day when my older sister preceded us to school, riding her bike while we waited behind. She was to take her turn in the coveted role of crossing guard at the school. Mom, in a housedress that billowed around her as she stepped out on the porch, looked with concern at the sky. She must have realized a tornado might be coming and hastily shoved the rest of us kids into the cellar. She then ran to get my grandparent's Buick hoping to intercept my sister, who had made it to school ahead of the storm only to have the glass doors shatter over her as she held them open for the early playground arrivals scrambling inside to take cover. All was well after a frantic dash to the emergency room for a great number of stitches, which she sported with pride. I thought my mom was the bravest, most beautiful and competent person in the world—equally at home canning peaches, plucking a chicken, chasing down a twister or taking her turn as our 4-H leader!

Fast-forward to my life as a young mother. 4-H had become a fond but distant memory as I found myself making the rounds of the easily available activities in our growing, now-suburban community that included gymnastics, baseball, and Scouting. Though it all had merit, I felt something was missing. I am a farm gal at heart, though the small farm of my adult life would be considered nothing more than a big yard to a real farmer. I cling to raising a flock of chickens, indulging my love of horses, and planting a garden even as the sprawl of development closes in around me. I honestly felt like a fish out of water as I tried to fit in with other moms, "cup holders" with their favorite steaming coffee drink, nicely coifed and manicured, discussing the best choice in ballet studios or traveling soccer teams.

First an assertively parent-managed Cub Scout den, and then the news that a certain sporting activity would cost more than I made in a week left me feeling cold. I found myself thinking more and more of my 4-H past. The daily "rounds" to school and errands took us past the local Cooperative Extension Service, home of the 4-H office. Giving in to this ever-present reminder, one day I stopped to ask about 4-H.

At the first meeting I knew we were home. All three of my children were involved in one place! They fit right in, mentored by some fantastic older 4-H members, and they loved being part of the club. Many of the projects I enjoyed in my youth still had a strong presence and there was a wide variety of new subjects. Waves of nostalgia washed over me that first year as a 4-H family, as I revisited so many of the haunts of my youth. Share-the-Fun now renamed Performance Show Case and Camp Shaw-waw-nas-see (who would have thought that beautiful and amazing place would still be running!) were among the pleasant memories. For the first time as a family we took a stroll around the county fair, as my young 4-H'ers proudly pointed to their projects on display. Today's 4-H is so much more! I am proud of the community service work that has been a strong focus in my children's 4-H experience. Before long, my family began methodically making choices for deeper involvement in 4-H activities at the county, state, and even national levels. I felt the call. It was my turn to give back and spend time as a club leader.

Our house spilled over with happy 4-H friends and families. My children had now grown into well-rounded, busy adolescents. One fine, sunny day at the county fair, time stood still for me as I watched my tall, gangly teenaged daughter kindly and humbly offer to ride the rough stuff out of a horse for a tearful young 4-H'er at her first county fair. She was becoming a mentor even as she collected prizes galore and feeling on top of the world. Things have a way of coming full circle.

The years have passed in the blink of an eye. As my third child nears graduate 4-H status and 15 years as a leader are behind me, I realize that 4-H has shaped my children into the people they have become. Responsible members of a community, they step up when needed. Winners, yet knowing how to be gracious when all does not go as planned. The model of 4-H achievement has contributed to their success far beyond the club environment.

I recently once again felt a call, this time to turn over the leadership role of our club to another parent with her own upcoming members. My two adult children recently enrolled as 4-H leaders. My husband and I continue to serve as project leaders for children enthusiastic to learn about the "girls" as I call our flock of chickens. At last count I have taught over 100 youngsters how to make bread the old-fashioned way with a wooden spoon, a bowl, and elbow grease to knead the dough. Crossing paths with a young 4-H'er at the local grocery I heard her whisper, "That's the bread lady." My husband takes time to support the "woodworkers," young members who design and complete a woodworking project in our workshop. The years of 4-H horsemanship projects served as a springboard to operating a riding school at our farm, from which many of the students joined 4-H to pursue their own green dreams. As my husband and I transition to the empty nest stage, it occurs to me that my nest will only be as empty as I choose to make it. I look forward to my children, now adults, parenting and continuing our 4-H family with the next generation.

4-H Family Traditions
Zeta Nuckolls Anderson, Wyoming

4-H has spanned 59 years, nearly three generations, in our family. It started with my mom, Thea Amspoker, in 1950, continuing with me with my first year of 4-H in 1971, and down to my daughter Grace, who started as a regular 4-H member in 2009. There has been someone in our family showing livestock at the county fair every year for the past 40 years with an eight-year break between generations, when my youngest brother ended his 4-H years and my oldest niece, Brandi Brengle, started hers.

I cannot remember a time when our family was not involved in 4-H. Mom had a very memorable first year when she won the Champion Corriedale Ewe at the Wyoming State Fair. Her goal was to win sheep showmanship, which she accomplished her last year in 4-H with a little Southdown market lamb. "When you set him up he never moved," she recalls. State fair for me and my siblings was a chance to spend the week with Grandma and Granddad Amspoker since they lived near Douglas where the fair is held. It did not occur to us that you had to qualify to go to state fair because it was something we did every August.

Dad had not been in 4-H but always got away from the ranch for a few days of the fair. My siblings and I would not have gotten to do very many things or go many places if it had not been for 4-H since we lived in rural Wyoming. We would have just worked on the ranch. Instead, we were able to experience trips or camps in Jackson (Wyoming), Washington, D.C., Chicago, New Mexico, and Canada during our 4-H years.

I wanted to be in 4-H long before I was old enough to join. I had two older sisters, Nan and Dawn, and two younger brothers, Will and Sam, and we were each in 4-H for the maximum ten or eleven years. While we each took a variety of projects, we all took sheep since raising sheep was the mainstay of the ranch. Some of our fondest memories are related to getting ready for the fair. Part of our daily routine was taking care of the sheep and taking the market lambs for a walk to exercise them. The days before the fair our family would spend hours in the sheep shed fitting a multitude of sheep bred for wool production. We had one really nice pair of hand shears that were easier to use than any of the others. They were everyone's favorite so whoever got to the shed first got to use those—unless someone had hidden them.

Mom packed up the five of us and we spent the week of the fair in a pick-up camper—the six of us crammed into that little space along with several friends at mealtime. Sleeping space was at a premium and it was an obstacle course if you came in later in the evening, trying to pick your way around sleeping bodies on the floor in the dark. We had our favorite spots to camp at the fair—always near the bathrooms. Show day meant getting up at 4:00 a.m. to feed and water all the animals, card and clip all their necks before Dad got there, race back to the camper for breakfast, and put on show clothes. The sheep show was eight hours of standing in the hot sun because the show ring was outdoors, the superintendent poking fun at Corriedale sheep because he was a Columbia producer, and helping and competing against your siblings as the five of us showed against each other.

One year we created quite a spectacle when we took about 48 head of sheep to the county fair in a two-ton stock truck. We unloaded them all and herded the whole bunch to the sheep barn and started separating them into pens.

Our county agents, Milt Green, Suzette Moline, and Susan James, became invaluable mentors and friends who, along with our wonderful 4-H experiences, influenced many decisions including college choices, fields of study, and careers.

During one of my last years in 4-H I competed in the state sheep showmanship contest at the end of a long day of showing sheep. My sheep was tired and did not want to stand still. I was exhausted and just wanted the day to be over. I finally realized that the judge was paying attention to me and my competitiveness came alive. I really wanted that championship. It came down to a contest between a young man and me. I was at one side of the semi-circle of exhibitors in the show ring and he was midway around the semi-circle. As the judge turned to walk to the microphone and announce the winner the young man's sheep reared up. A murmur went through the crowd as they witnessed his loss of control over the animal. Fortunately for him, the judge did not see that and he was awarded the championship. Many strangers came up to me later and said I should have been the winner.

I have helped nieces with 4-H projects and watched them compete in their various contests; I also became a 4-H leader before I was married. My husband, Gary, had not been involved in 4-H or the county fair. He had a steep learning curve when our daughters, Grace and Faith, started showing orphan lambs in open class. Like me, Grace could not wait to be in 4-H and on her eighth birthday exclaimed that she was now old enough to be in regular 4-H. She had been told she needed to be eight to be a regular 4-H member rather than in mini-4-H, and she thought that very day her status would change!

Grace began the third generation of 4-H'ers in our family in 2009 and she had a very successful first year. Her face just beamed when she was awarded a big belt buckle for sheep showmanship, won best of shows for her cabbage and sewing, and won a trip to the state fair to model her sewing project. At the state fair that year I connected with someone from the other side of the state who was in 4-H with me, and her mother competed against my mom when they were in 4-H. Now, our daughters are carrying on the tradition.

Being in 4-H taught us the needs of livestock and how to work with them. I have a soft heart toward animals, especially lambs, because of my 4-H experiences. Grace has this same trait. In May 2009, on Mother's Day, her Grandma Nuckolls let her take home a tiny premature lamb to try to save. The lamb was so weak she could not stand and could barely suck on a bottle. A few days later we discovered Daisy was blind. A creative bottle holder enabled the lamb to feed herself when we were gone.

In the fall when we normally sell the lambs we raise, Gary and I faced a dilemma of what to do with this blind lamb. Grace came to me with tears in her eyes and said, "Think about if you had two children and one needed you because she was disabled and you could only keep one. Wouldn't you keep the one who needed your help?" She went on to say that if she could only keep one animal out of all her cats, the dog, her pony, and Daisy, she would choose to keep Daisy over all the others. I questioned her about such a declaration since she had been asking for a pony for years and had just gotten one. But she was firm in her convictions.

I emailed my friend Peggy Turbiville, an experienced 4-H leader, to ask her advice. She had such great words of wisdom, "Bless Grace for being such a kind and gentle soul. If it was me, I would let her keep the lamb. If she does nothing more than eat grass and grow fat you will have taught Grace about compassion. I am with Grace on being soft-hearted."

That evening when I relayed the day's events to Gary, I asked him how we could argue with Grace's merciful heart. We still have Daisy and of course her pal, Crystal, so she would not be lonely. Grace faithfully cares for both without complaint.

4-H has taught us all a lot of things, but maybe the most important lesson we learned was compassion.

4-H Families are Happy Families - Photo submitted by Zeta Nuckolls Anderson

4-H Is More Than You Ever Imagined–
From a Mom's Perspective
Alice Tebbe, Illinois

I did not have the opportunity to be in 4-H as I was growing up. When my husband Alan and I were dating, his youngest brother and sister were in 4-H. So, I was initiated into 4-H at fair time. I had heard stories about cooking projects that did not turn out quite right. For their meat project, his sisters made a meatloaf with each exhibiting half a loaf. One sister received a blue ribbon, and the other a red. Both were from the same loaf and the same judge! His brother showed a gallon of wheat and we all helped handpick the kernels. I certainly hope they do not do that project again!

Now, fast-forward ten years, our daughter Emily was eight. After seeing a 4-H article in the local paper, Emily and I went to the meeting. Soon, Emily was signed up for cooking projects. Her apple crisp is still a family favorite even after twenty years. Then she made a one-egg cake. Every time she baked that cake it came out different—too dry, too coarse, or it did not rise. Eventually, it turned out just right. This was her first lesson on how humidity, temperature, or different ovens can effect baking. Her cheddar cheese biscuits taste like those served at Red Lobster—really good! Then there were her hockey puck yeast biscuits. We learned that even if you follow a recipe, everything will not always taste good. Emily declined the meat project as she had heard the meatloaf story too many times.

Emily also took visual arts and knitting projects. One baby blanket was finished in the fairground's parking lot ten minutes before judging. Her main interest was citizenship; she started with our family tree. Then she studied my mom's church and Mother Jones who fought for better labor laws. Each year she would do more advanced displays on Indian tribes and interesting sites in Illinois. The Macoupin County history project was probably the most interesting, especially since we found a house that was a part of the Underground Railroad and the burial site for a soldier who fought in the Charge of the Light Brigade.

Emily was selected to attend the 2001 National 4-H Congress in Atlanta. Her favorite memory is of over 1200 people from all over the United States in the same room reciting the 4-H Pledge.

Our son, David, a year younger than Emily, joined 4-H and started with woodworking. His first project, a birdhouse, received a Young Achiever award. He was so proud of that! Then he made a small bookrack with the varnish still not dry when he handed it to the judge. The lesson: Do not procrastinate until the day before the fair when the temperature and humidity is 100 plus degrees! He made several shelves and coat racks that we use in our house.

He also took crops. Guess who showed a gallon of wheat? Guess who helped him handpick the kernels? There is nothing like going out to the field at 6:00 a.m. the morning of the general show to help your son pick the corn and bean plants he wanted to exhibit! Dave was selected for the Illinois Agriculture Youth Institute. He attended lectures and workshops on the importance of agriculture and toured the John Deere plant, ADM chemicals, and the farms at Illinois State University and the University of Illinois.

Keith was a few years younger and our club's first Cloverbud, going to the meetings and participating in all the activities. When he was old enough to join 4-H, he took cooking, citizenship, woodworking, electricity, and crops projects. Yes, we did another gallon of wheat.

Then David received a model rocket for Christmas. Keith was right there as Alan helped Dave assemble it. Finally it was launch day! It went so high we lost sight of it, and never saw it again! This was the start of Keith's love for rockets.

He started with small model rockets and each year progressed to something larger and harder. At 15, Keith was working on a detailed rocket, naturally, on the day before the show. It was finally ready to paint, but the paint came out of the can in big drops, not a fine spray. The rocket looked like it had orange polka dots on it! So off we go to the local hardware store, rocket in hand, to get some advice and more paint—stressing to the gentleman that it had to be dry that night so decals could be added. Thanks to their help, the rocket turned out fine! It is sitting downstairs, but has never been launched.

Because of his rocketry interest, Keith attended Space Camp, the Illinois Aeronautical Institute, and was a charter member of the Illinois Tech Team. In 2003 he was selected to attend the National 4-H Conference in Washington, D.C., where he had a chance to suggest possible new or revised programs and projects for 4-H to keep up with new technological advances. The highlight of the trip was spending a day on Capitol Hill and meeting Representative Lane Evans. In 2005 he attended National 4-H Congress in Atlanta. Being with so many other 4-H'ers from all over the country and our territories was a great experience.

As well as being a 4-H mom, I was a leader for eight years. I tried to keep the members interested by having guest speakers, doing crafts, and taking field trips—trying to blend something educational with something fun. We also did community service projects where we tied quilts for the ambulance service to comfort young patients, and made meals for the Ronald McDonald House. In the "Walk in My Shoes" workshop, members wore yellow tinted glasses so they could see how an elderly person with cataracts saw things and how hard it is to distinguish colors, like a blue or purple pill. Wearing gloves represented arthritic hands that could not button a shirt or take a cap off a bottle of pills. Another workshop, "Dinner is Served," focused on table manners and formal table settings. The table was set with a white linen tablecloth and napkins, my china and crystal, candles, and every fork I had. Each parent provided a course for the dinner. They had such a good time and will be beneficial to them in the future.

In the 15 years of being a 4-H mom, what did I enjoy the most? Getting those projects out of the house the morning of the general show! Yes, it was hard work and the days before the show were stressful, but it was worth every minute. My worst moment in all those years was putting Keith on that plane to Washington, D.C., the week after the bombing in Iraq started. I knew everything possible would be done to keep the kids safe. They were fine and had a ball!

It may sound like I am bragging about my kids, but I want people to realize how important 4-H is. 4-H teaches life skills—cooking, sewing, basic electricity, gardening, communication, and leadership. Keith made many friends everywhere he went and regularly hears from many of them. My kids had so many more opportunities to do things and see things because of 4-H. Experiencing special opportunities with kids just like you! Keith wrote in his story, "Things you do in 4-H and throughout your life may be stepping stones for something bigger." Keith received the William H. Danforth "I Dare You" award and a scholarship to attend the American Youth Foundation leadership camp. He liked it so much the first year, he attended all four years and even worked at the camp. His experience was an advantage for him getting a job as a supervisor for the YMCA's before/after school programs.

Dare to dream! You never know where something may lead you. Volunteering at a local hospital gives you the opportunity to see if you would like a career as a health care professional. Your small engines project may lead to a career as a diesel mechanic. You may become a chef because of your cooking skills, or a fashion designer, or an electrician! Like my kids' 4-H shirts said: "4-H–It's More Than You Ever Imagined!"

My Big 4-H Family
Carrie L. B. Lougee, New Hampshire

This year my son Chad started his first official year as a 4-H member, after three years of being a Cloverbud. He had been looking forward to doing the "big kid" projects with his older brother Ross, so this was a major milestone for him. It was a dream come true to have both my sons in 4-H under my grandmother Ruth Kimball's leadership. Chad's first year of 4-H is my grandmother's 65th year as the organizational leader of the Victory Workers 4-H Club in Pittsfield, New Hampshire! My mother was a 4-H'er, my brother, sister and I were all ten-year members, and now my sons are members of Grammie Ruth's 4-H club.

Our family's 4-H legacy is a unique one. Let me explain. For starters, Ruth Kimball is not my biological grandmother. I have always thought of her as my "special grandmother" and I have always treasured our relationship. My mother spent her childhood in the Massachusetts foster care system from the age of five after her mother died and her father was unable to care for her and three brothers. My mother was separated from her siblings when her two older brothers were sent to Pittsfield, New Hampshire, to live with relatives and her younger brother was placed in foster care.

As a boy, my uncle participated in Ruth Kimball's 4-H club. In the fall they went to the Eastern States Exposition in West Springfield, Massachusetts, with their 4-H cattle. My mother lived in the Springfield area and he would arrange to meet her at the Expo. When my uncle turned 18, he petitioned the state of Massachusetts for custody of my mother, but he needed a family for his 14-year-old sister to live with. Ruth, and her husband Lloyd, along with their six children, agreed to be that family.

While living with the Kimballs, Mom participated in 4-H along with her new "sisters" and "brothers." Ruth was patient and loving as my mother made the transition from city girl to farm girl. She thrived in school and quickly made many friends. Mom met Dad through one of her "Kimball sisters" and after high school they were married. The Kimballs have always included us as part of their family.

Everyone knows Mrs. Kimball. Her caring and patience have touched many people in our community. She can always fit another chair around her large dining table and she greets everyone with a smile. I have always admired her grace under pressure. She is the queen of improvising—a true 4-H life skill! Grammie Ruth can make a meal for 12 or 112 with the same ease, and she leads by example with her "I'll be glad to" response to any request for help. She is smart and hard working and always a lady.

I am not the only person who thinks Grammie Ruth is special. She has had hundreds of 4-H'ers over the years and many families have had three generations of 4-H'ers as members of the Victory Workers 4-H Club who share my admiration. She was the first New Hampshire 4-H Hall of Fame recipient, received Citizen of the Year honors, and has been recognized for her local, county, and state volunteer work.

My "cousins" address her as Gram, but to me she has always been Grammie Ruth. As a girl I loved spending time with her making rolls and pies or sewing. She made me feel special when she let me help her do her work. As a child it was fun; now, as an adult, I realize that those activities taught me more than just cooking and sewing—they built my confidence. When I was very young I was shy, and then I had the "awkward adolescent" years. Her gentle encouragement kept me involved with 4-H and trying new things. I loved 4-H! My favorite projects were dairy goats and fashion revue, but the club activities and projects with Grammie Ruth are some of my best memories. She has always been a great advocate of education. I learned from a young age that education meant opportunities as I watched older 4-H'ers achieve success through their club work and schoolwork. The skills I learned through 4-H have made me the person I am today. I credit Ruth Kimball for teaching me how to be successful; how to keep going when times are hard; how to look for the positive in every situation; and how to make the best better.

When I was in elementary school our class had a discussion about family heritage and our grandparents. My friend made the statement that we would not exist if it were not for our grandparents. That is when I realized that Ruth Kimball was truly my grandmother—I would not exist if it were not for her. And, thanks to Grammie Ruth, I have my own 4-H family!

Ruth Kimball's outstanding service to 4-H was recognized with her induction into the Centennial Class of the National 4-H Hall of Fame in 2002.

Kites and Kindness
Courtney Fint, West Virginia

For the past several years, I have made it my mission as a counselor at West Virginia State 4-H Camp to create meaningful and effective reflection programs for the campers. I had been inspired as a camper by reflections that were interactive, included contemporary songs, or ones that engaged multiple senses—programs that went beyond the standard readings and poems. I wanted to continue growing that trend so that more campers of all ages would look forward to the time of introspection and thoughtfulness at the end of each day. Many fellow counselors shared this attitude, and together we have created some memorable reflections. The one that sticks out in my mind above all others; however, is a kite-themed reflection. Even having planned it and done a test run earlier in the summer with a smaller group of older campers, I did not expect the effect this event would have on me.

The idea struck me while at a Patty Griffin concert with a close 4-H friend earlier in the year. Ms. Griffin performed a number called "Kite Song," which spoke of the joy, freedom, and release of flying a kite, and compared kites to dreams rising above sadness and fear. It seemed a perfect message for our 4-H campers. So when camp rolled around that summer, we cut 350 paper kites and asked each camper to anonymously write a wish, hope, or dream on his or her kite. After we gathered up all the kites, we hung them on lines between trees in a grove at Jackson's Mill, West Virginia's beautiful state camp. During these preparations, I read quite a few of the wishes, hopes, and dreams of our campers. They ranged from comic to profound. Several had a direct and honest wish for millions of dollars. (Having often wished for that myself, I could hardly fault them!) There were dreams of finding true love, success in school, and the chance to go to college. Many hoped someday to be chosen as a leader of their tribe at camp, or to become a camp counselor as an adult. Some wished for sick loved ones to get well, and many hoped for a peaceful world free from war, hunger, and hatred. The messages on some kites had meanings known only to the writer. Some simply hoped that they would be able to come back to camp the next summer. Naturally, since our pool of 350 primarily consisted of teenagers, a few of their wishes had to be censored!

We brought the camp to the grove that evening and opened with campers sharing a few poems and readings related to dreams, freedom, and kites. A camper read the lyrics to "Kite Song" and then, as we played the song on a loop, the campers milled about and read the kites. As someone who regularly gets weepy watching Hallmark commercials, I quickly realized I needed to avoid reading the kites while listening to the song, or risk making a spectacle of myself as the "overly emotional counselor." But watching from the sidelines was enough. The reality exceeded the vision that had occurred to me many months before at the concert. Each of our campers had gotten the chance to send their "kite" out there into the blue, free from judgment. And all of our campers, in reading these wishes, knew a little more about each other and the secret dreams held in each other's heart.

The message on one particular kite has remained with me since that day. While hanging the kites, I was troubled to read one upon which someone had written "I wish people would be kinder to me" in tiny letters along one edge. My heart ached to know that someone in our camp was feeling hurt and rejected. We think of camp as a place with a level of acceptance and kindness far above that of the "real world," but here was a reminder that our little utopia was not immune to life's pain and suffering. I wished fervently in that moment to know who this person was so that I could hold out a hand and offer the kindness he or she needed. I looked at the faces around me and wondered who it could be. Was it one of the obvious ones—the shy, quiet wallflower or the kid with behavioral problems? On the other hand, it could be someone unexpected—does the popular, friendly camper have problems at home? The handwriting looks more like a boy's—or does it?

Finally, after what may have been hours or days (time flows differently at camp, you know), what probably should have been immediately evident hit me suddenly—I might even describe it as an epiphany. Since I could never know who wrote "I wish people would be kinder to me," the only alternative was to treat every camper as if they could be that person. And in fact, every camper—and every human being—*is* that person. In the end, knowing the specific identity of that kite's author is not important. Every one of us has needed a kind word, and has been too afraid to express that wish directly. One can never tell by looking what pain exists inside another. What is certain, however, is that we all have the power to be kinder to each other. The small letters on that kite reminded me of that simple lesson.

A Lifetime of Memories

A 4-H First
Virginia Ward Cyr and Kay Ward Daniels, Maine

Before Thursday, October 4, 1951, owning a Hereford calf had been a remote possibility for my sister, Virginia, and me. We were 4-H members in the Hungry Hollow Hie-Hoe 4-H Club in South Paris, Maine, and that day began a three-year love affair with those beautiful animals. Actually, our father had instigated this day when he proposed (in jest, I think) if we wanted a calf, we should enter the Fryeburg Fair Calf Scramble and catch ourselves one or two. The more we thought it over, the better the idea seemed. Soon he and our 4-H agent, Mary-Abbie Kilgore, had their heads together consulting the rules. I imagine it took a little persuasion on Mrs. Kilgore's part for the Fair Association to agree to our participation. They had to admit we met their requirements—we were 15 and enrolled in a 4-H club. Nowhere did it say the entrants had to be male. They probably assumed that any reasonably sane female would have sense enough not to enter. Boy, were they ever wrong! Soon our picture appeared in the *Lewiston Daily Sun*. In fact, the cameraman caught us at West Paris High School on our noon hour. Our classmates were both amused and astounded, but we could not see what all the fuss was about. We had worked all our lives, not always under safe and calm conditions, and we knew what we were doing. We wanted a calf and soon found out that we were not the only girls who wanted one. Before the big day arrived there were five ladies entered along with six young men, one of them being Ernest Maberry from our own Hungry Hollow Hie-Hoe 4-H Club.

At last we stood in the center of the racetrack in front of the grandstands at the Fryeburg Fair, trying to ignore the watching crowd, some of them clearly amused. Our parents signed slips relieving the Fair Association of responsibility in case any of us broke our fool necks. I will admit, Daddy gave us the chance to bow out gracefully, but he *did* smile when we refused. I imagine his reputation might have suffered a little if we had bowed out, but we had no intention of quitting now! We were so close and had actually seen the ten calves milling about in the truck body that held them captive.

While the men set up the snow fence barricades to keep both the calves and kids in a central area, we were all given a six-foot length of rope and a chance to make our own halter. Newsmen, of course, were there by the bushel, some of them trying not to snicker, but we tried to ignore them.

Have you ever seen a calf scramble? If not, let me give you the basic rules. The calves, always one less than the number of contestants, were all pasture-raised, which meant they were half-wild. They were unloaded and gathered inside a circle of men as close to the center of the track as possible, while the contestants were spread out along the edges of the fence. At a signal given from the safety of the announcer's booth, the calves were scattered. The contestants were free to capture the calves by putting them on the rope halter, and then the contestant must lead them back into the center of the ring to be held until all calves are caught. Sounds simple, right? Wrong! We discovered that nothing in life is simple, especially the easy looking things.

While we were all pacing around nervously, there was a sudden blast of car horns. The men around the calves began to shout, slapping the calves with their hats, and flapping their arms to scatter the poor frightened critters. A voice blasted over the loud speaker, "Go get 'em!" I do not know who was more scared, the calves or us. We had not expected that, but we went and we "got 'em!"

Virginia was really lucky and caught her calf early and easily. The poor beastie was so terrified he wedged himself between two other calves, and before he could think or jump, she had him. Now all she had to do was get him into the center of the ring—easier said than done. She pulled on his halter but, having never had a halter on his head until that minute, he had no idea what he was supposed to do. Naturally, he braced his feet and pulled back. She coaxed, but no results. The calf was too terrified to move. She pushed—nothing. So, she went back to pulling once more. Not that Virginia was stubborn, but the calf was going to the center of the ring one way or another. It turned out to be another way. In their mad dash for freedom, a stampeding calf and kid turned Virginia's calf half way around and, seeing as he was headed in the right direction, Virginia let him go. Ernest already had his calf in the center of the ring and made a very effective brake. Big Red (though unnamed at that time) came to an abrupt halt when he found another calf in his path. Virginia put all of her energy into calming him down by scratching behind his ears before seeing how I was doing.

I was doing fine. After a chase and a few close escapes, my halter found a nice looking calf that was about as enthused about being caught as Red had been. Either I was more stubborn than Virginia, or Dom was smaller than Red, but I was making better progress than Virginia had. Soon we were together and no way were those furry little buggers going anywhere without us. When it was all finished, four of the ladies had caught steers, much to the surprise of the male counterparts. When all the dust had settled, they opened up the pen and told everyone to get the animals back to the tent where they were to be hitched until they were picked up. Can you imagine two very tired 4-H'ers and two very scared Hereford calves going down through the crowd at Fryeburg to the tent? With us girls at their heads and Daddy behind to give them a little boost, we finally made it to the tent and secured them.

When it was over Daddy and Grampa were as proud as peacocks, and our younger sister, Glory (who later entered calf scrambles), was so excited she could not stand still. Mama and Nana were smiling, but relieved to find both of us girls all in one piece. It was a wonder. After putting the calves on the scale the next day, Red weighed 394 pounds and Dom tipped the scales at 265 pounds.

The next year we both brought a steer to show and sell at the Fryeburg Fair. The following year we entered the scramble again, as we needed more fair entries. Once again we both caught calves to show and sell as steers the next year.

Being farm girls, we already knew the care and training these Herefords would need, and we had already successfully shown dairy animals. We had to learn new skills to show these larger animals, and how to clip and groom them. They soon became our pets.

Taking care of animals instills a responsibility that you carry for the rest of your life. The 4-H program teaches many other valuable skills as well. We were members of a large 4-H club. We took sewing and cooking as well as animal projects, exhibiting them at the Oxford and Fryeburg Fairs. Those life skills followed both of us through our adult lives, helping us to be successful in raising a family and holding jobs outside the home. I went on to work at the Oxford County Extension office for 29 years. Virginia worked for a long time for Robinson Manufacturing in Oxford and collected a large assortment of 4-H articles, which she shares with visitors at the 4-H Exhibit Hall each year. We are now both retired.

When Kay's daughter was old enough to join 4-H, Kay started a club named the Oxford Tigers. She led the club for a number of years, and then went on to lead the Tally-Ho Horse Club for the rest of her 4-H career. Both her son and daughter participated in the horse project and went to Eastern States Exposition on the Maine team. For a number of years my daughter Kay ran the 4-H horse show at Oxford County Fair and last year she received her 40-year leader pin. She is still involved somewhat in the 4-H program and feels 4-H had a big role in her successful life. 4-H teaches many of the skills youth will need to succeed in life and has been a successful worldwide program for many years.

Memories of National 4-H Congress
Mary Jean Craig, Idaho

Four generations of my family have been involved in 4-H. My grandmother, Catherine, was a 4-H leader; my mother, Jeanette, and her brothers and sisters were 4-H members in the 20s and 30s; and I was a member in Washington during the 50s and 60s, as well as a leader in Idaho for nearly 30 years. My sons, Andy, Jim, and Tom, were 4-H members in Idaho during the 80s and 90s and two of them have been 4-H leaders. It was through 4-H that I learned public speaking, sewing, cooking, photography, and many of the other life skills I used in my career with the Idaho Cooperative Extension System.

My mother was born in 1914, and she was an early 4-H member in Nebraska. She was a perfectionist when it came to sewing. One year, probably in the late 20s, she made a dress for the fair in a "made-over" category where she was supposed to take a used garment and make it into something else. My mother spent hours piecing the sleeve and matching the plaids on the dress she made so it would look right. When she went to the fair, she could not find her dress in the category she had entered it in. She finally found it with the new garments. It looked so good they did not believe that she had made it from another garment.

That perfectionism carried over into my mother's sewing for the rest of her life—and she passed it on to all of the 4-H members she taught to sew, including me. To this day I feel guilty if a sewing project is less than perfect, and sometimes I rip out as much as I sew. Both my brother and another former 4-H member whom she taught to sew have made similar comments about their own sewing projects recently. That desire for "making the best better" led several of us to earn trips to National 4-H Congress and at least two of us to careers in Home Economics.

I attended National 4-H Congress in 1963 as the state winner in Home Economics, sponsored by Montgomery Ward. President John F. Kennedy was assassinated on Friday, November 22, and we left for Chicago on Thursday, November 28. On the 22nd, I was supposed to go to the county Extension office during my lunch hour to have my picture taken for the local paper. About an hour before that, someone came into my English class to announce that President Kennedy had been assassinated. When I arrived at the Extension office I was told that I was a national winner and would be receiving a $500 scholarship. It was exciting news, but I felt more like crying because of the tragedy that had occurred that day. I spent the weekend getting my clothes ready for the trip (and doing some last minute sewing) while watching all of the events unfold on television. As I recall, school was dismissed on Monday, the day of the funeral.

We boarded the train for Chicago on Thursday evening, Thanksgiving Day. Among the usual conversations of young people getting acquainted was the sharing of "What were you doing when you heard about the President?" On the train, four of us became good friends as we bonded over games of pinochle, which we played most of the waking hours of that two-day trip. One of the players was Ray Crabbs, who later became vice president of National 4-H Council. The opening ceremony for National 4-H Congress that year included a memorial service for President Kennedy, and then National 4-H Congress went on as originally planned.

Montgomery Ward sponsored a dinner for all of the winners in the Home Economics program area. It was held on the top floor of the Prudential Building and we had a beautiful view looking out on the lights of Chicago. I wore the wool dress and coat that I had made for the Make It Yourself with Wool Contest that year.

As one of the national winners I was asked to give the invocation before dinner and sit at the head table, quite an experience for a girl from a little town in Washington! Each of the state winners was given a Betty Crocker Cookbook, which I still use as my main cookbook today, and a book on etiquette. After dinner we each had our pictures taken with John Barr, Chairman of the Board of Montgomery Ward, and Norman C. Mindrum, Director of the National 4-H Service Committee. That picture was later enlarged and displayed at the Montgomery Ward Store in Yakima, and I was invited to the store to be recognized.

During the week, we spent a day at the International Livestock Exposition. As the only state winner from Washington, I also got to represent the State of Washington on the floor during the opening ceremonies.

My memories for the rest of the week include: baked potatoes with chipped beef gravy at the Firestone breakfast; the Purdue Glee Club singers; Miss America; tractor races in the lobbies as we waited for the elevators, using the toy tractors given to us by International Harvester; touring the Museum of Science and Industry and the Natural History Museum; and the hard rolls with every meal. As a present to my brother for Christmas, I inscribed the hard rolls with the date and name of the banquet because he complained so much about them when he attended Congress!

Attending National 4-H Congress was truly the highlight of my 4-H career, one I was able to relive almost 20 years later when I attended National 4-H Congress as a chaperone in 1991. We still stayed at the Conrad Hilton, Miss America still came, the Purdue Glee Club singers still sang, we still had hard rolls with every meal, we still had to wait for the elevators, and we still had baked potatoes with chipped beef gravy at the meal sponsored by Firestone (although it had changed to lunch instead of breakfast). We had been told in 1963 that the reason they served baked potatoes with chipped beef gravy was because that was Mr. Firestone's favorite breakfast when he would go to the mountains.

During my 30 years with the Idaho Cooperative Extension System I had the privilege of working with and encouraging many outstanding 4-H members to apply for a trip to National 4-H Congress, including one of my sons. One of my first duties as an Extension 4-H agent in Idaho was to inform a young man that he had been selected to attend National 4-H Congress. That young man is now a good friend and my financial advisor. Later, after I took a position in the Idaho State 4-H Office, one of my assignments was to coordinate the trips to National 4-H Congress, including the selection of delegates and chaperones. In that capacity, I was able to attend Congress three times as a chaperone in three different locations–Chicago, Memphis, and Atlanta–every bit as awesome an experience as it was when I first attended as a delegate. When I became involved with the establishment of the National 4-H Hall of Fame, I was thrilled to help recognize some of those people who had made my 4-H experiences at National 4-H Congress so memorable.

1963 National 4-H Congress – Photo submitted by Mary Jean Craig

Dad's 4-H Dairy Project
Linda White, Illinois

It was a gray, rainy day in October, a good day to reminisce. Mom was going to a Home and Community Education Association lesson and I was visiting with my dad, Harold White. He had shown me some of his 4-H memorabilia before, but that day I took time to look at his project books and found a written story in each one about that 4-H year. The books date from 1932, when he was 10 years old, to 1942, the last year he could be in 4-H. Only 1933 is missing from the collection.

Dad was involved with 4-H in Effingham County, Illinois, and was a member of the Dieterich Dairy 4-H Club from 1932-1942. This club was a family effort. Grandpa served the club as a leader and Dad's siblings were also involved as club members. Once I started reading Dad's stories, I had to read them all. As he wrote in 1940, the stories describe the "steps in the ladder of 4-H life." I hope you enjoy Dad's stories as much as I did.

Dairy Project 1932: "I selected this calf because she had a straight back. Her udder was placed fairly high in the rear and carried forward. She had a good cut cup in her forehead. I started to keep records in the middle of May. I gave her equal parts of bran, corn, and oats. Also skim milk. Two weeks before the fair I added linseed oil meal and omitted the milk and gave her hay. I did not have her on pasture. At the Illinois State Fair I won 24th prize. I am going to show her at the county institute in October. I am going to continue with club work."

Dairy Project 1934: "Our club organized again and I selected a purebred calf from my father's herd. About the first of June I started brushing and taking good care of my calf. On the Friday before we went to Springfield we showed at Effingham. There I got second place. I got eight dollars. After the show at Effingham we went to Springfield and did not get anything in the class but our county got third in the county herd. I had much experience in the club and it also teaches me good sportsmanship. I expect to enter the club again next year if possible."

Dairy Project 1935: "I have found my fourth year of club work very interesting. It has helped me in making new friends and has also encouraged the spirit of cooperation. Our club had a judging team this year and I think I have received much experience from it. I think I am now more qualified to select better dairy cattle. I showed my heifer at the county show, won second place, and received seven dollars. I had one dollar trucking expense and still have a total of six dollars, which I am very proud of. I want to go to the state fair again with my calf, but I decided she was not good enough to net much profit. I appreciate the good leadership we have in our club and hope to give our club leader and fellow club members cooperation in every way possible to help make our club an outstanding club in this part of the state. I have had much fun, as well as lots of experiences in my few years of club work and I would like very much to enter a club next year."

Dairy Project 1936: "I selected the heifers I showed because I had them in the club last year. They were both pretty nice animals. About the middle of June I blanketed the heifers and kept them in the barn, feeding a balanced ration of corn, bran, soybean oil meal, and alfalfa as roughage. The ration was fixed by the Dairy Herd Improvement Association tester. The tester gave us some good advice on the care of our heifers. We prepared our heifers for the county show to be held in connection with the Farm Bureau picnic at Watson, Illinois. One of the heifers placed second with six dollars premium and the other third with a premium of five dollars, a total of eleven dollars. I was chosen to go to the State Fair. The competition was great but the heifer was not classy enough to capture a premium. We had a great time at the fair but there was one drawback—I had a good pair of pants stolen out of my tent. I am content with my proceeds of my heifer and the experience of my year's club work. August 15, 1936, we held an ice cream party for all the members and their families. The county Farm Advisor and his wife were able to spend the evening with us. This meeting was the final meeting of the year, ending the club year. I wish to continue my club work next year because I feel the work does one lots of good, gets lots of good experience, and become acquainted with his fellow club members from other counties."

Dairy Project 1937: "I have completed another successful year of club work. My project was a Jersey calf, selected from my father's herd of Jerseys. The calf was of large size at birth, clean cut head, good top line, good spring of ribs, well-developed heart girth, but a little shallow through the barrel. About the first thing of the year's activity was the 4-H tour to Urbana. The dairy judging contest was next in line. I was selected as a member of the team to represent our club and Effingham County at the state contest. Our team failed to place but the experience was worth a great lot. At the 4-H fair held at Watson my calf placed second. Four dollars was awarded as prize. This fair was held August 13. The night of August 13 we went to Springfield. My calf did not go, but I went to care for my brother's and sister's projects. I showed my sister's calf and won first prize. That was the first calf from our county to get a blue ribbon. Was I proud! Our club ended another successful year with a wiener roast, which I greatly enjoyed. Next year I hope to continue my 4-H club work because I think it is much worthwhile."

Health Activities 1938: "When our 4-H club organized last May, our local and county leader insisted that each member carry a health project and I believe it is well that they did. The main thing is to get a complete health examination. When I took the health examination I found that my tonsils were in a rather bad condition. It was not but three days until my tonsils were out. I was not in bed but four days and during that time was not at all sick. Besides knowing one's physical condition he may earn some extra credit for his 4-H project. In our club the family physician of each member gave the member a free examination and the family dentist gave free dental examinations. I am sure these acts of kindness were highly appreciated by all club members. The doctors and dentists are to be complimented on their fine spirit of cooperation."

Dairy Project 1939: "Another club year is about to close. In my estimation this has been the best year in 4-H club work since I have been a club member. The glory started last July when our club won the county dairy judging contest, with me as a member of the team. Another feather was put in our crown when we, the judging team, won "A" rating in the state dairy judging contest. There were but nine other teams that achieved this honor. When we held our county show my animals took their share of honors. Then after we came home from the state fair we realized that Effingham County still had some 4-H clubbers to be proud of. The boys had taken good enough care of the animals and stable while at the fair to receive honorable mention. There are other things that may be mentioned here, but space does not permit. It has undoubtedly been a successful club year. I shall be looking forward to the re-organization of our club next year and may next year be an even bigger and better club year!"

Dairy Project 1940: "My eighth year of club work was a continuation of the other seven. It makes another step in the ladder of 4-H Club life, and a big step, too. Besides my dairy project I carried a purebred Hampshire litter (hog) project. The dairy animals I had this year were from the herd raised on our farm, which have been built up from the other 4-H club animals. These animals were nice show animals and showed well at our county show and at the state fair. It may be said here that these animals were in the dairy exhibit that won a trophy for being the best exhibit from any county in the state. This trophy was the answer to four years of hard work to have the best exhibit. Every boy from our county worked hard for it and all are very proud of it. I hope to continue with the dairy project next year and hope to have an even better exhibit than this year."

Dairy Activities 1941: "This year adds another one to the list of dairy club membership for me. There was nothing outstanding that happened. I went to the county judging contest and was also on the county team that competed at the State Fair. The county team received an "A" rating. It had just as well been a "Z" because one team member was too young to compete at Nationals. Our dairy club had a very good showing at the county show and also helped make Effingham County a success at the state fair."

Dairy Project 1942: "This year, 1942, eliminates me as a 4-H club member. I have carried the same breed, Jerseys, for eleven years and still have my original project in the herd. Since my start in club work, I can see a great difference in the type and quality of cattle we have in our herd and hope to see a still greater improvement in the next few years due to better stock to start with, better care and management, greater production through improved sires, and a greater knowledge of dairying in general. Our club did not have many extra activities due to the lack of time and means of transportation. A special effort was made; however, to have all members show at our county show and to have the exhibits in number one condition. All exhibits were in good condition and our club made an excellent showing. There has been a good response to health activities, from which the members will benefit because of the health examinations."

Dad's accounts of traveling to the state fair are a sign of the times. A family with a stock truck would load it with the 4-H animals that were traveling to Springfield. The club members would ride in the back of the truck with their animals during the trip. When Dad first began attending the state fair as a 4-H member, the animals and members camped in tents on the fairgrounds. During his years of participation in the club, permanent dormitories and livestock buildings were built. Dad was among the 4-H members who stayed in the dormitories the first year they were open.

Dad credits the 4-H program for helping him and other local farmers with their business through education. As an adult, Dad has continued to share his 4-H principles through his volunteer work. He volunteers at Red Cross Blood Banks and has donated over 20 gallons of blood in order to help others. Dad is an active member of his church and he continues to volunteer his time with local organizations such as FISH, St. Anthony's Hospital Auxiliary, and the Cross at the Crossroads Foundation.

My brother, sister, and I were also involved in 4-H in Effingham County. Our participation, like Dad's (soon to be 88), has not been forgotten. Our family gatherings regularly include reminiscing about people associated with the family through 4-H and memories of 4-H projects and activities.

I Went Home and Cried
Glenn Busset, Kansas

Sometimes in our most introspective moments we have occasion to wonder just how successful we have been. Were our contributions important or even noticed? Have we really done anything significant with our lives? Have we done anything worthwhile for which we could be remembered, appreciated, or even cherished?

Or does our failure to accomplish the goals we set override our meager successes? Surely, all of us have, in the wakeful predawn hours of our lives, recounted our failures with all persistence of a restless tongue working under a sore tooth. Occasionally there is an unexpected and humbling surprise that levels the playing field and helps return our value system to basics. It happened to me this way in late 1945.

I had resigned from my first real job, a three-and-a-half year tenure as Extension 4-H agent in Dickinson County, Kansas, to become assistant state 4-H leader (supervising 34 counties in northwest Kansas), stationed in Manhattan. I had become so thoroughly engrossed with the work and the people in Dickinson County that I had earlier refused the offer—until a phone call from Dean Louie Williams brought on a profound reconsideration. Yes, I would move, presumably upward, in the system.

One of my most obvious duties in the county was the organization of new 4-H clubs. Eventually six new clubs were organized, three of which are still large and vigorous. One of those was the Carry Creek 4-H Club located in a remote, out of the way, farming community. Located in cutover creek bottoms in extreme southeast Dickinson County, it was not exactly the county's most prosperous area. So I spent perhaps a bit more time helping the club get established, training and reinforcing the leadership, and calling on the new officers in their homes.

One such stop was the Martinitz farm, not impressive by any count, but the parents were cooperative and anxious that their six children would have the advantages of 4-H membership. I think that it was in the third year of the club when the 15-year-old daughter Arline was elected president. She responded with enthusiasm to suggestions for her duties and the help I could give by letter, visits, and monthly club meetings. It was a long haul from Abilene to the Carry Creek schoolhouse. The dirt roads were more dirt than roads as I traveled on worn tires with a C-ration gasoline card. Occasionally, I would accept the family's invitation and have supper with them.

Now we leap forward and it is November 1945. I am in Manhattan organizing the 4-H record judging, preparing for the three-day job of the state screening committee. Here the 4-H record books, containing the cumulative accomplishments of 4-H members who have been recommended for various awards, are judged.

As I catalogued the record books by projects and activities to assist the committee, I came across Arline Martinitz's record book. Quickly I turned to the narrative, which to me was always the most interesting and sometimes valuable account of a 4-H member's progress toward accomplishing maturity. It was a familiar story, until I reached the final paragraph.

There, added to the standard narrative, was this short statement:

"Today at school (Chapman High) I was having lunch with my friend (a Harmony Hustlers 4-H member) when she suddenly said, "Mr. Busset is gone!" When I asked her what she meant, she said, "He has resigned and moved to Manhattan.""

"I didn't know what to say to her or to think. When I got home, I went to my room and cried."

Maybe Arline was affected by the unexpectedness of the announcement. I do not know why she cried, but standing there in that empty file room where other awards would be made, I slowly realized that I had received my unexpected purple ribbon, my reward—to have been deeply appreciated.

Now as I write of something that happened more than 60 years ago and look back into that tangled web of things called memory, I wonder why I get a lump in my throat. Maybe because I was young and naive then, it took awhile to understand that I could not have received a greater compliment.

Dr. Glenn Busset served as Kansas State 4-H Leader from 1966 to 1981. He was recognized for his outstanding contributions to 4-H with his induction into the National 4-H Hall of Fame Class of 2005.

Betsy Was a Winner
Martha Bozeman-Griffith, Louisiana

When I was in fifth grade and nine or ten years old, my mother bought me a registered female Durock Jersey piglet for a 4-H project. She had very bright eyes and a shiny red coat like a brand new penny. I named her Betsy and she became a very beloved pet. We built a large pen for her with hog wire nailed to pine trees and a shed filled with pine straw, which was especially nice for her in the cold winter and also when she had her two litters of piglets. She used the pine trees to rub against and massage her dry skin.

I fed and watered her twice a day. She had a very nutritious diet of what was called "shorts and chops" with a handful of minerals added. Shorts were made up of a substance somewhat like coarse wheat flour, and chops were dried corn kernels. I would mix them together with water. I would prepare her morning feed at night, especially on school days to save time. She liked her food soft and a little sour. She had a trough for food and one for water. We did not have electricity so I drew her water from a well in our yard. I had to ease the bucket very slowly because if she heard the action she would get very anxious and try to break out of her pen. Sometimes she succeeded. Then she would come running to meet me and often she would knock me down to get her food. I would struggle with the bucket to get her back into the pen and mend the fence as she ate. I have had a recurring dream through the years in which the school bus is coming around the bend in the road and I have not finished feeding my pigs!

Betsy had a large hole in the ground which I would fill with water on hot days for her to wallow in. Pigs need to lie in water because they do not perspire, and not because they like to get muddy. I bathed Betsy at least once a month. I brushed her shiny red coat often.

The following fall, in 1946, I entered Betsy in the state fair, which is still held in Shreveport, Louisiana. The day of the judging was a very exciting and memorable day for me. I hardly slept the night before. I had a very dear aunt and uncle, Aunt Rainie and Uncle Corley Walker, who lived in Shreveport and came to watch me "show" Betsy. They were like second parents to my siblings and me. They did not have any children of their own. Aunt Rainie was my Daddy's sister. She came to the show all dressed up in heels, hat and gloves. One would never guess that she too grew up in the country.

Each pig was in its own pen, which was about 10 feet by 12 feet. For the showing, I had to demonstrate my control of Betsy and the judges made notes about each of us. Using a small stick to prod her, I would maneuver her into different positions, or get her to sit down or stand. We went home with a first place, blue ribbon for my showmanship, and a second place, red ribbon for Betsy. She did not get first place because she was a little too fat. Well, she got much fatter! In the next few years she grew to be over 600 pounds!

Over the next two years I had Betsy bred twice, and in both litters there were 13 piglets. Each time I kept one piglet for show. I sold the others for $5 each and saved the money. Speaking for myself, there is no cuter sight than watching 13 baby pigs squealing and fighting to control a teat! In each litter there was a runt, and it would usually have to take what was left. Each time, the runt grew up to be one of the finest pigs.

Pigs were auctioned off at the fair. Businessmen would bid on them and pay much more than would be paid on the common market. I sold my other show pigs, and along with money from selling piglets I had acquired about $300.

Our home had burned twice in the early 1940s. We lost everything. Our grandparents had given us some old furniture, such as iron beds, tables and a stove, but we needed some living room furniture. I wanted to use my money to buy a couch and chairs, and that is what I did.

Mother took me to the only furniture store in the small town near us, which was Johnny Murray's Furniture and Appliance Store in Pleasant Hill, Louisiana. I chose a bright, royal blue couch and chair set, and a wine-colored, platform rocker. When we got home with our purchase, my older, artistic sister blew her stack! "Mother, why did you let her buy such gaudy furniture?" Mother simply said, "It was her money!"

In retrospect, I think my purchase was wise. We all had a place to sit. To satisfy Mary's taste, we would have been able to buy only one chair at a more expensive store! Eventually, the old heavy couch and the platform rocker were either hauled off to the dump or sold in a garage sale. We did, however, keep the heavy blue chair, and had it recovered several times. It came to be called the "pig" chair. We still have it in the garage of our vacation home and it is in surprisingly good condition. I may have it recovered again for old time's sake.

Occasionally, I see Johnny Murray at the Pleasant Hill Methodist Church. He always has a laugh with me about my purchase at his store with my pig money. Actually, it was mother's money considering all the pig food she had bought.

Betsy got to be a problem breaking out of her pen. Mother needed some money and I insisted that selling her was okay. By that time I had other interests. I have often joked and said I switched my interest from pigs to boys. Anyway, Mother got $100 for Betsy and told me she sold her as a brood sow, a "little white lie" she confessed to me years later. I should have been suspicious when Betsy was taken away in a huge Oscar Meyer truck! I do not know what happened to those ribbons, but I do know that winning them and making my big purchases with my 4-H pig money were both positive, defining moments in my life.

Make Me, Me
June McAuliffe, Minnesota

The children were grouped on the floor, not knowing what to anticipate. Their eyes moved from the face of one stranger to the next. The strangers returned their quizzical looks with warm smiles and words of welcome. The music played.

The children were mentally challenged, 24 in number; they needed, and searched for, respect and acceptance just as much as every other child in the world.

They each received a green leaf from the 4-H strangers who were quickly becoming friends.

"Let's look at each leaf and see if we can find two leaves exactly alike." A scramble for comparison by a few resulted in curiosity toward "why" by most. "Do you think there are two leaves exactly alike?" One young man became the spokesman and, despite the stifling motions from his classroom teacher, continued to answer for all. "Each leaf is special just as each grain of sand and flake of snow is special."

"Look at your thumb print that you put on your name tag. Yes, it is indeed special. What does your nametag say? That is right! "I am a very special person." No one else is quite like you because your experiences have been different. You have different feelings and your artwork will be special as you are special. Art is another way to talk about how you feel. We are here because we love art and want to share a day of art with you. The large pictures of children we have around the room are other friends of ours who love art, too. Let's begin to have some fun, explore, and discover together!"

The questioning children moved to the other room to find five tables. 4-H leaders invited the children to participate in any of the five, non-threatening experiences. Choices were handled very well. Some folded paper and dipped the corners of the small paper packages into dye. The discovery was obvious by the screams of excitement when the brilliant colors were revealed after the paper was unfolded. Others moved quickly to the ink table to paint by blowing the variety of colored inks with a straw. There were more pleasurable sounds of success and the room looked and sounded like a huge party. The diazo paper turned blue but left the white silhouettes of the leaves and butterflies, as if by magic. The smell of the ammonia brought strong reaction. The blotto prints offered still another experience of surprise with tempera paint. Crayons and watercolors were controlled with confidence. As one table was explored and conquered, another was waiting with friendly leaders to encourage at each stop. First names were used freely.

The hour of confidence building passed quickly and it was time to hear a story and pantomime the characters. One boy's only language was pantomime since he was mute. Mural painting was accepted as a challenge. It was the first experience with such huge space and big brushes. No child competed for space and each seemed to be in his own world. If they had known there would be more paper and paint tomorrow and each day after, would they have obliterated their first fresh paintings for the sake of continuing the experience? Some identified their pictures; others were just absorbed in the actions.

After lunch and rest for all, more dramatic exercise and poetry preceded puppet making. The children were largely unable to make their own puppets, but were assured their job would be to bring life to the head being dipped in hot wax. While they painted features and glued hair, they were encouraged to talk about their new creation: "What is its name?" "Is he happy?" "What does she like best?" Puppet gloves went over each hand and, with the head attached to the longest finger, a new life with unique character was born. "I, too, am a special person." A puppet show resulted as each group of four or five responded to questions from the audience and a choir of puppets came into being singing "Jingle Bells."

Everyone became big fat music balloons and danced around the room to music with varied tempos. Balloons led to a circus book and posters of clown faces.

Back in the art room they found mirrors on all tables. There were make-up sticks and clown white for the grand finale—clown faces for everyone! After carousel music and a circus parade of clowns, everyone got ready to catch the bus—all but one. He stood looking at his face in every possible contortion until all the boxes were packed and the mirror was the last piece to be placed in the university truck.

Each child, in his own unique manner, had stories to tell to all who would listen at home that night. One father was greeted at the door by a son made up as a clown. All the work was hung until the parents could come in to see, and then hopefully, each piece went home to be hung on the refrigerator door. Is it all right to lay order and rules aside for one day just to celebrate life?

To become what I can;
To be now what I am;
To be present where I am;
To be aware of who I am and who you are.
To reach out for my potential.
To find fulfillment in a blade of grass or a certain smile or a simple touch
Because another has enabled me to be,
I became all these things… And even more.
Author Unknown

My Dresser Scarf
Lois Redman, Missouri

I made a dresser scarf for my 4-H improvement project when I was about 12 years old. I thought I had done a great job and was sure I would get a blue ribbon on it at the fair. There were no purple ribbons in my time. I waited for the judging to get finished that day at the fair, but it was getting late and I needed to get home to do my chores. So I sneaked under the rope and went over to see my scarf, and there was a red ribbon. I was shocked, why did the judge do that? She was still judging across the gym. I just walked over to her and asked her if she would come over and tell me what was wrong with my scarf. I could just see horns sticking out the top of her head. She said she would be glad to. The horns went down a little.

The judge said I had done a great job on my embroidery. The color selection was nice, and the fabric was really good, but she said there were three things that bothered her. First, I had used a lot of French knots. They were not very tight and after some washes they would be standing up. Second, I had used a large black stitch around the edge, and it would probably break while ironing. Third, I did not do a very good job of putting the lace on the edges. The judge still made me feel really good about my scarf and encouraged me to do other 4-H projects. The horns on her head turned into a halo.

I liked that scarf so much I used it for more than 30 years! Guess what happened. The French knots are standing up, the black stitching around the edge is broken in several places, and you should see how the lace looks now. Exactly what that judge said would happen really did happen.

Some years later I decided I wanted to become a county home demonstration agent just like that judge who talked to me about my dresser scarf. That dream came true and far exceeded my expectations.

After I had spent a year in Washington, D.C., on a National 4-H Fellowship, some years working as a 4-H specialist in Oregon, a year's sabbatical in Sweden, and had toured India, Nepal, and Sri Lanka with other 4-H specialists to see 4-H work there, my stepmother said to me, "Lois, you are only 42 years old and you have already lived a lifetime of experiences." Yes, I really had, but the wonderful experiences did not stop there. They kept on happening throughout my career and just look at what is happening this very moment—I am telling a story about how a 4-H learning experience helped me become who I am. Thanks to all of those who helped me to make my best better so I could help others do the same.

Lois Redman shared this story, using the actual dresser scarf as a visual aid, at her induction into the National 4-H Hall of Fame Class of 2009.

Making 4-H Memories
Nico Janik, Illinois

My name is Nico Janik and I am almost 13 years old. I am a fifth-year member of the Turkey Hill Busy Bees of Freesburg, Illinois. One day this past summer, my dad drove my 4-H best friend Jacob and me to the Illinois State Fair in Springfield. Dad dropped us off at registration and went looking for a good parking spot. Jacob registered his computer project while I registered for the fashion revue. You read that correctly, and please do not laugh at me for being in the fashion revue. I was the only boy amongst a big bunch of girls! Yippee!

I went to my project area and listened carefully to the instructions. When it was time to change for revue practice, the lady in charge said, "Everybody go behind those curtains and change your clothes." And I did. My parents had told me to listen to whatever they told me and do it. It caused a ruckus since I was the only boy among all those girls. They quickly made a change in plans. One mother was really mad I went into the dressing area, but I was just following directions!

Mom was worried I would be angry that I had to spend all day with the girls practicing for the fashion revue, but I really enjoyed it. There were a couple hundred people watching us. I did not get nervous, and in my opinion it was awesome. It was great when everyone applauded for us.

I made and modeled a bathrobe. The material had a print of Garfield, a 4-H mascot, and there were blocks of fabric with Head, Heart, Hands, and Health. It was really colorful, soft, and comfy. It took a lot of effort to make, but was well worth it.

I took sewing as a 4-H project because I am a re-enactor portraying the French from the mid-1750s Illinois country. I portray a flag bearer for the Ft. De Chartres French Marines. If I had lived then, I would have had to know how to sew since even the young had to mend their own torn clothes. If you were good at sewing in those days, you could make a good living. Sewing skills would come in handy even if you were injured and could not work at other jobs.

I enjoy a lot of 4-H projects. Foods demonstrations are not my strongest area, but I learned a lot giving them. I love visual arts because I get to express my feelings, especially when I get to take pictures of anything I want. I like fishing even though it is not one of the easiest projects. I made two cool woodworking projects, including a flower box and a great bench, and learned woodworking is a hard project. Theatre Arts is also one of my favorites. I really enjoyed being in *A Christmas Carol* and as a "scare re-enactor" at the Historical Haunting.

There are just so many 4-H projects I have enjoyed and each one has its own special memories. I believe the Illinois State Fair 4-H Fashion Revue will be something I remember for a very long time.

4-H, Always In Style – Photo/Edwin Remsberg

Little Girl, Big Horse
Susan Dudasik, Idaho

Wooden poles scattered in every direction as the little rider, perched on the back of a big, fat white horse, tried to guide the horse backwards through the tightly spaced ground poles of the trail class "back through" obstacle. Unsuccessful at that, the girl steered her horse to the next obstacle, a mailbox. But the horse wanted no part of that obstacle either and stepped away from the mailbox just as the girl tried to open it. By now it was obvious that this pair was not really ready to be showing in the 4-H Trail Class I was judging. I could not help but feel sorry for the rider, who was about nine years old, as she valiantly attempted to get her horse over, through, or around the various obstacles on the course. After demolishing nine of the ten obstacles, the determined girl took a deep breath and headed her horse for the last one, a wooden bridge. You could hear a surprised gasp from the audience as the horse dropped its head and calmly walked across the bridge. As the judge, I too was stunned as I wrote a big perfect score of 10 in the "bridge obstacle" box on the score sheet next to a line of one and two points for the other obstacles.

That was not to be the only surprise from this young rider. As she approached me, she had tears rolling down her face and the biggest smile I had ever seen. She was also hugging and petting her horse. This was unusual. I expected her to be upset, not smiling. So I asked her what she thought of her performance and, since we use the Danish system of judging, what color ribbon she thought she should receive. I will never forget her response. "I know you have to give me a white ribbon and that's OK. We worked all summer on crossing that bridge and today we did it!" The statement was followed by a smile of pride and more hugs for her horse.

I have been involved with horses and competitive events for over 30 years and on that summer day in 1999 I saw real sportsmanship in action. That young rider was not concerned about how all the other riders did. She was judging herself against a self-set standard and was excited because she had set a goal and worked hard to achieve it.

Over the years I have competed in numerous trail classes, but I will never forget the lesson I learned from that young 4-H'er and her horse. I no longer approach an event as something I must win or at least earn a ribbon. Instead,

I have learned to set a standard for my mule and myself, and we strive to meet that standard. Since adapting this policy, I have had more fun and success in competitive events than I have ever had before, when all I was concerned about was winning ribbons and impressing judges. I credit this new outlook to a little 4-H girl and her horse who, despite demolishing a whole trail course, was excited because she had achieved the goal she had worked so hard to accomplish.

4-H Made It All Possible
Melanie Duncan, Georgia

When I was in the eighth grade, my younger sister Amanda joined my 4-H adventure. My Daddy (Spencer) farmed, Momma (Lois) taught at the local school, and my sister and I grew up on a farm surrounded by animals. Since fourth grade I knew I wanted to become a veterinarian. 4-H provided many experiences with animals and helped me build my college fund.

In January 1983, Amanda and I both entered the county hog show with many strong contenders, but I was confident I would do well. Momma and Daddy took me aside just before the show began and gave me "the speech," as I have come to think of it. They told me that since I was older and had more experience showing hogs, I was absolutely, positively *not* to rub in Amanda's face any ribbons and prizes I might win. They made it clear I was not to taunt, tease, bedevil, or upset her since 4-H was about the experience and, while winning was great, it was not what was most important in showing hogs. I said something along the lines of, "Uh-huh, yes ma'am, yes sir, okay, whatever, can I go show my hogs now?" and off I went secure in the knowledge that I would end the day a winner.

Showmanship was not my best class with hogs; I handled my steers much better. I struggled through the weight classes and managed to end the day with a ribbon in one of the classes, but I do not remember what place. What I do remember are the actions of my sweet, innocent, baby sister Amanda who I was not to taunt, tease, bedevil, or upset by rubbing in her face any prizes and ribbons I might win.

Unfortunately, Momma and Daddy did not think to give Amanda "the speech." She won first place in her hog's weight class—and since her hog was born and raised on our farm, she was eligible to compete in the homegrown class—and she walked off with the blue ribbon for the homegrown grand champion! When all of the weight class winners were called back to the ring to pick the show's overall grand champion, there was Amanda and her hog. No, she did not win grand champion, but she did win reserve grand champion. And, yes, she did rub the fact that she had won in her older, more experienced sister's face!

I spent eight years in 4-H, from fifth through 12th grades, showing hogs and steers each year. I was lucky to have parents who were actively involved in 4-H with me, and to have a little sister to share the experience with for five of those years before I graduated from high school.

The money I earned from 4-H shows went into a college fund, which was later used to purchase a foundation herd of purebred Black Angus cattle—with the help of money from Amanda's college fund and Daddy too. Triple D Angus Farm (named for three Duncans—Amanda, Daddy, and me), would not have existed without 4-H. Amanda and I both went to college, earning a bachelor's and master's degree in psychology and library science respectively (physics was my downfall on the veterinary science track, so I switched to my other obsession—books), thanks to 4-H and the many opportunities we had in the program.

We were very fortunate to have had some excellent role models, and if you are reading this—Mr. Richard, Mrs. Jane, and Mr. Don (4-H agents)—you and 4-H made a positive difference in my life by encouraging me to explore my interest in animals and introducing me to other 4-H'ers from around Grady County. You taught by example, and your support lifted me out of my comfort zone and gave me the courage to try new things, like livestock judging, when I was nervous and unsure.

Mom's Passion
Kassi Grooms, New Mexico

She was a ten-year 4-H member herself, attended National 4-H Congress twice, once as a national winner. She was a club leader for more than 20 years and was active at the county and state level and received recognition for her work in the 4-H program. She has touched the lives of countless youth in our county and state and yet, when recently asked about her most memorable experience in 4-H, tells the following story. "It was my first year in 4-H and I was at the fair. I had my steer tied to my pigs' pen so I could watch them and brush him at the same time. A group of schoolchildren came by who were about my age–9 or so–and one of them pointed to my steer and said, 'Wow–look at that big pig!' I was stunned. I could not believe there were kids out there who could not tell the difference between a pig and a cow!"

So that explains why, for as long as I can remember, it has been my mother's passion to introduce as many kids as possible to our 4-H animals and our country way of life. One year our 4-H club celebrated Dr. Seuss Day at the childcare center by reading "Mr. Brown Can Moo-Can You?" and we brought a week-old baby calf for the preschoolers to pet and feed with a bottle. Or the time when the post office called my mom's office to report there was a box that was chirping that needed to be picked up because she had ordered day-old chicks for the kids in her 4-H summer camp to feed and take care of for the week. Then there was the time she was trying to explain about what 4-H'ers had to do to get their animals ready for show and I had 42 first and second graders helping me wash my dairy heifer and my sheep. That was quite an experience for all concerned. But my mom would just smile and say "You just gave these kids a memory that will last them a lifetime–isn't that what 4-H is all about?"

One of the most memorable experiences was when the 4-H club was helping with the Preschool Pet Day one summer. We could not get the pickup started so Mom loaded us four kids, two rabbits, a duck, a chicken, two goats and a turkey into her little red hatchback car and off we went. Other than people pointing and smiling as they drove past us as we tootled down the highway, the day was quite successful. The kids had a blast, as always, playing with the animals. And then it happened–we were on our way home when we had a flat tire and the spare was underneath the goats, turkey, and the duck. So here I am on the side of the road, holding two goats and trying to keep the turkey from being run over while they changed the tire. People pointed at us as they drove by, and even worse, my friends waved and laughed. Several people stopped, not to help, but to take pictures and watch the fiasco. At the age of 13 it was one of the only times I really wished I was not my mother's daughter. But when all was said and done and we were back on the road, Mom just smiled and said, "We made another 4-H memory today!"

As we grew older, Mom's crusades continued. As PTO president, she set up a literacy program where if the students read 1000 hours collectively, the school principal would kiss my brother's dairy heifer. They did—and she did—and that 4-H memory appeared on the front page of our local newspaper. Mary may have had a little lamb, but at our school it has become a tradition to have our 4-H goats, cows, and ducks at school the day of registration to celebrate the beginning of a new school year. And just today, Mom called me all in a thither to say she needed me to start asking around if anyone had a llama for sale because she had been reading the preschoolers the story "Is Your Mama a Llama?" and one of the kids had called the llama—*oh no*—a *cow*! Is there a 4-H llama project? If there is, I see one in our future.

As I have grown up, farmland has turned into houses as I have listened to people talk about urban development and the need for more expansion. Today 4-H is reaching more and more youth, which is a good thing, but with less and less of them living on farms. I am beginning to see why my mom is so adamant about sharing our culture and making sure the generations to come understand the importance of agriculture, even if it is just recognizing the difference between a pig, a cow and a llama. I realize today, just as she did years ago, that 4-H is the avenue to continue sharing that word. So when I heard my mom ask my nephew, who is in his first year of 4-H, if she could use his pig to take to the toddler room next week to celebrate National Pig Day. He said, "Sure!" followed by, "And I'll skip school to come help you!" I just smiled and knew that the 4-H legacy of preserving agriculture through education would continue—at least in this 4-H family.

Alpaca and Llama are 4-H Projects too! – Photo/Edwin Remsberg

Lessons Learned

Lessons Learned in 4-H
Jan Seitz, Delaware

I have numerous mementoes from my 10 years in 4-H; items that have increased in value over the years. But the one item that has come to mean the most, and the only recognition from my 4-H experience that I have framed for my office, is the third place white ribbon I received for my first sewing project—a hoop skirt.

Why, you ask, would I choose to display a third place ribbon for all to see, rather than one of the many blue or red ribbons I still have in my possession? As Associate Dean for Extension and Outreach and Director of Cooperative Extension at the University of Delaware, why would I not be embarrassed to have others know of my substandard performance?

Well, the answer to these questions is simple: my white ribbon represents one of the richest learning experiences I've had in 4-H.

You see, we did not have electricity the summer I announced I wanted to sign up for my first sewing project (the Ohio Rural Electric Association was having difficulty connecting with homes located a substantial distance from town) and no one in my family had ever used a sewing machine.

Fortunately my grandmother had an antique treadle machine someone had given her. When she heard what I wanted to do, Grandma agreed to offer it to me for this effort.

I still remember the day Mom and I went to town (always a big deal) to purchase material for my skirt—pink with lavender flowers. What fun I had making my selections!

The real excitement came a few days later when Mom, Grandma, and I sat down to learn how to work the treadle machine…how we laughed and celebrated as we got it to sew in a straight line. There we were, three generations working and learning together *and* enjoying each other's company.

I later recall the pride I felt as I modeled the finished skirt for these two special ladies and how proud we were of "our" accomplishment. Then, of course, it was on to the county fair.

After proudly displaying my skirt in the junior 4-H building, I must tell you that my heart literally sank as the sewing judge began to point out the many imperfections she found in my garment: uneven stitches, tension not adjusted properly, and so on. I vividly remember the painful moment when she pinned the white ribbon on my skirt for all to see.

Back home that evening I shared my bitter disappointment (and yes, a few tears) with my family and announced that under no circumstances was I going to participate in the county fashion show the next day. What followed was one of the many nurturing, life-impacting lessons my mom was known to deliver on such occasions.

"Janice Ann," she admonished (she always called me that when she wanted to make a point), "I want you to put aside your disappointment and think about what you learned from this experience." She then went on to tick off the many things she felt I had gleaned from my first sewing project: (1) making choices/decisions (e.g., material, thread, button, matching hair ribbons, headband, socks, etc.); (2) tackling something I had never tried before; (3) asking for help and working with others; and (4) having fun in the process.

She also emphasized her hope that from this experience I had learned that I did not always have to be perfect; that there is both pride and joy in trying one's best; and that my best is all anyone could ever ask of me.

To make a long story short, I did participate in the fashion show the next day and after modeling my skirt and all of its carefully chosen trimmings, the county agent asked me to comment on what I had learned from my project.

As I responded, I found myself repeating the very things Mom had so eloquently shared with me the night before (which of course I had not totally bought into at that point). Our county agent beamed and commented to all those in the audience that I had helped everyone focus on what is really important about the 4-H experience and the judging of projects: that it is not the color of the ribbon/award received, but what was learned in the process.

Epilogue:

In her later years before her death in 2003, my mother resided in an assisted-living facility in Van Wert, Ohio. At times she had trouble remembering what she planned to do that day, let alone next week. However, what she did remember and loved to talk about were the things we did together when I was young.

And, you guessed it—one of her favorite stories was the fun she and Grandma had helping me with my hoop-skirt project.

When I assumed my previous position of Assistant Dean and Director of Illinois 4-H, Mom dug out the many remembrances from my 4-H experience that she had kept for me over the years: pins, medals, ribbons, certificates, mementoes from camp, newsletter articles, etc. Much to our disappointment, my white ribbon was nowhere to be found. Fortunately it resurfaced again several months later when we moved Mom's remaining possessions out of her home. I am sure you can imagine the excitement we both felt upon finding this token of a special time we had together.

My friends, as the years have passed I have come to realize that the lessons I learned from my hoop-skirt project, and of course from my mother, helped me to develop important skills that have served me well over the years, both personally and professionally.

It goes without saying that my white ribbon is a constant reminder of why I do what I do; put simply, "to help our youth learn skills for living."

Moreover, I have learned from literally hundreds of longtime 4-H alumni that the reflections of my 4-H experience are not unique. I have rarely encountered a 4-H alum who has talked about the number or color of ribbons, pins, medals, trophies received, or contests won. Instead, their reflections, like mine, focus around the friendships/experiences they made while participating in 4-H at fairs, camp, club meetings, and other activities. They especially remember the important lessons learned and the many memorable and fun times they had.

Janice A. Seitz, PhD, currently serves as Associate Dean, Extension and Outreach and Director, Cooperative Extension, University of Delaware.

The Timid Orator
Meghan Kenny, Alabama

The girl was a timid equestrian. She loved her horses more than anything, and had been riding since she was seven years old. Today, she was forced to be more than just a little girl with a riding helmet.

This quaking contestant at the Alabama State 4-H Horse Show had volunteered herself for public speaking. Under the coercion of her peers, she had been diabolically convinced to enter the individual demonstration contest at the state horse show. After the morning's hippology contest; treacherous enough with numbers, letters, diagrams, and feed samples, she felt less than worthy of the competition.

She nervously watched her competitors give their presentations. She had prepared her own presentation for the show: "How to Make Homemade Horse Treats," complete with recipe books named for her horse, General Beauregard Jackson Pickett Burnside III.

The 12-year-old stepped anxiously in front of the small audience and cleared her throat. Her hands shook and her voice trembled, but she managed to get through the motions of her presentation. She smiled at the right places and magically revealed pre-made samples of her favorite horse treats, Beau Bits and Marty's Munchies.

Her confidence slowly grew as the interminable five-minute presentation came to a close. She finally ended with a flourish, and silently relished the fact that her presentation was over.

She had been the final demonstrator and the judges were now deciding the placing for the class. She had cleaned up her peanut butter and apple cores and was sitting anxiously in a plastic chair, waiting with her friends for the results.

She imagined herself not winning, humiliating her club, and disgracing horses everywhere. They called fifth place, fourth, third… they still had not called her name. *No ribbons for me*, she thought, silently chastising herself for her less-than-worthy presentation. Suddenly they called first place, Meghan Kenny.

She felt her feet rise and walked to the center of the humble room, with a big, beautiful blue ribbon. She smiled, and almost fainted walking back to her seat. She had won her first award in public speaking.

Since that time, the little girl has grown into a young woman. With everything going on in her life, she still finds time to teach the younger kids about public speaking. She teaches in the club and the community, and now stands in front of groups of thousands with inspirational or informational messages for her peers, associates, or as a guest speaker. Her nerves are still omnipresent every time she steps on a stage or in front of a small audience at school, and each time she remembers her very first speech, her very first success, and her very first great oration.

Meghan Kenny is currently studying zoo archaeology at Washington University in St. Louis, Missouri. As this book was going to print, Meghan is on a "dig" in Turkmenistan identifying ancient animal bones, an interest that began with her love of horses and serving on the 4-H Hippology Team. Her 4-H public speaking led to Meghan competing in the National Forensics League's oratory finals and being named Washington University's 2010 Orator of the Year. She is obviously no longer a timid orator and it all began with 4-H.

Overcoming barriers with 4-H – Photo/Edwin Remsberg

What 4-H Has Done For Me
Guin Mikols, Arizona

I have to admit, I initially joined 4-H entirely because of the animals. Little did I know, at ten years old, how much this program would become a major part of my life, and just how much it would come to mean to me. I truly believe that without 4-H, I would not be the person I am today.

Although 4-H helped me all along the way, it was not until high school when I felt the real impact. During my freshman year of high school, 4-H was one of the places I could really express my true self without feeling any pressure. The social support of being around peers with similar interests helped me build the self-esteem I needed. In class I was usually shy. At 4-H meetings I would share my opinions and my sense of humor. I was elected secretary and later president of my club. This helped me realize that I was actually outgoing and 4-H nurtured this. Even so, I still dreaded the required demonstration every year.

However, with each passing year, demonstrations became easier and easier. I now realize that without this experience I would not have been able to excel at public speaking and college speeches, another gift I owe to 4-H. My fifth year of 4-H was definitely a highlight. That was the year I was blessed by being chosen as a LaPohave 4-H Camp counselor and given the responsibility of being camp co-director. That opportunity helped me develop my leadership skills. LaPohave 4-H Camp also helped me realize I have a gift for working with children.

That year I was also a teen leader in the poultry and pigeon project. I helped to teach younger 4-H'ers from various clubs about the projects and how to show their animals. Teaching younger members helped me discover my passion for teaching. I continued to be a camp counselor and teen leader throughout my 4-H career.

Every year I attended the Mohave County Fair and the Colorado River Small Stock Show. These were very important events in my life. Showing at these events taught me that a person must be a good loser as well as a graceful winner, a life skill I have often used. Overall, these experiences and competitions have helped me become a better person.

I cannot begin to describe how much 4-H has meant to me. It has become a part of me. Through 4-H I have learned leadership, commitment, acceptance of people, integrity, fairness, self-esteem, and even a sense of self. I hope one day to become a 4-H leader and pass on to others what my 4-H leaders have given me. I know my 4-H experiences have helped me in college and will continue to help me excel throughout my life.

The Rest of My Life
Abbey Hilty, Colorado

It was a bitter cold evening in March 2004. There was a stale wind about the old parking lot as the evening light glistened over silver-flaked snow. I walked into a weather-beaten church that was full of complete strangers. I had no way of knowing that this moment and every one after it would change my aspirations and the course of my life forever. Every curious stare pierced my skin. It felt like I was being prosecuted under a bright light, rendering me speechless and incoherent. To my relief, from the corner of the room came a calming voice that said, "Would you like to take a seat? You can sit anywhere you like." I sat down and all I kept thinking was "What have I gotten myself into?" When asked, I stated my name and age as if it was really important for anyone to know how old I was.

When I entered 4-H I was just another shy, quiet, and introverted kid, headed down the same path as everybody else. I would have never thought of straying off the path, or taking a chance. Now, nearly four years later, I find myself looking for the unbeaten path and take every chance I can get, even if it is a little precarious. Throughout the past four years I have been led to try things I have never done, and have become somewhat of a risk taker.

My friends in my 4-H group have helped me overcome my fears, and have aided me in my decision to go to college. The annual State 4-H Conference is held at Colorado State University every year, and this led me to discover my desire to attend CSU. Because of 4-H, I worked very hard academically so I would be able to attend "the best school in the state," the place where dreams come true. However, getting good grades was never very easy for me. While I was in high school, I was told if I did not change my ways I could never fulfill my dreams. From that day on, every day has been a battle to win the fight of school and life. Through my participation in 4-H, I have been able to improve my life and myself.

I am very grateful to 4-H because through it I was given my horses, my lifestyle, and my love for livestock. I began with an old, experienced gelding. He taught me to trust him and to ride. He has been a steady influence in my life, the constant that helps me to never stop learning. That gelding, like my life, has had some rough turns and a few bumps along the way. Yet through perseverance and a little fight, we seem to have pulled through and are looking at greener pastures ahead. After my gelding was seriously hurt, he became ill and his future—and mine in riding—was in doubt.

Then on my birthday in 2006 came a storm of a horse. I was supposed to train this mare, which was destined for slaughter, and have her ready to show in three months. If you have not guessed, this mare would prove to be one of the biggest challenges of my life. We took her because she was free and we were desperate to find a horse. She came at the worst possible time. I was struggling in school and did not really need another problem. In reality, she helped me. Because of my dedication to her, I was actually improving at school. I found this horse was teaching me as much as I was teaching her. She came from a very disturbing past, and had "suitcases" of issues. The lessons she taught me are ones I will never forget. I learned to put the past behind me and move forward because life is worth living and there are many things each day that make living so great. Who knew that a rundown, beaten horse could turn into a championship-level competition machine? Just as she has moved forward in her life, I feel I am moving forward in mine and into my next stage—college. Every day I find that I truly am ready and, no matter what, I will always have a stable foundation to look back on and lean on from time to time.

Prince is a name of royalty, a name you do not expect to hear every day—well, at least not with horses. Then again, my life has not been what you would call predictable. I found Prince, a young, green gelding, late in 2006. I came upon him mostly by accident, with no intentions of getting another horse, at least not one like him. He was what is called a "blank canvas." I could make him into any dream I could imagine. Without a doubt, he came at a time when I was unclear and very confused about where I was going and what I was going to do. Just as I was painting his future, he taught me that I can paint my own future. I can control my own destiny. Through Prince I found my true calling, so to speak. I learned where I needed to go to college and what I am to do with my life. All of which I am able to control and make my canvas the colors of the dreams I have had for so long. I will always remember, whether I need a shoulder to lean on, a friend to learn with, or a canvas ready for painting, I will be welcomed home, no matter how far away I end up.

There is a saying that I have pretty much come to live by, "Don't Sell Your Saddle" and it has a lot of very deep meaning for me. "Don't Sell Your Saddle, don't give up on dreams. Take time to see 'em through. There is no magic recipe. Hard work is what makes 'em come true. Even when you are struggling, your friends will stick like glue. Don't ever sell your saddle, your dreams won't give up on you."

I think I am ready for college. I have my tools and knowledge packed and ready to go. I have left my struggles behind me and I am ready to look forward. I am done struggling with academics, and with the life that I feel has barely started. I am ready to get out there into the real world. I am just an eager kid looking for a platform to launch my dreams, and I believe that CSU is that platform. It is the platform for greater education, a place for me to begin the second chapter in my life, and start this one off on the right foot. Being in 4-H has most definitely prepared me for life in college. I have become more self-governing, better informed, and more strong-minded in beginning my own life, and breaking away from my hometown ties.

Since I first walked into that room in 2004, the events of my life have been more or less sporadic. I finally laid out on the table everything I have ever learned, and looking back I feel very satisfied with what I have accomplished; but also feel there is a lot of room left for more learning. With the help of my peers and my horses, my struggles have been short-lived. Somehow I have always found a way to overcome obstacles through helpful friends; there is no better place than 4-H for friends and for learning.

It was a bitter cold evening in January 2007. There was a familiar wind about that beaten down parking lot as the light sparkled over the winter snow. I walked into the musty old church, into of group of friends laughing and cracking jokes. I sat down at the head of the table as the president of my club and asked a shy young girl her name and how old she was, as if it really mattered why I wanted to know. This would be one of the last meetings with my group; after that I would never see most of them again, besides the occasional visits to ring rides and to the families. I knew I would miss them very dearly, and I will never forget that this moment and every one before this one that changed my life forever.

My friends led me to horses, and my horses led me to my 4-H club. That club and the events that ensued inadvertently led me to college. Hopefully, this great institution can lead me to places I have only dreamed about. That will involuntarily lead me full circle to my friends who will stick like glue and will never give up on me. As long as hard work and some elbow grease can see me through, I will always have my dreams and remember the times I have had. Hopefully, I can look back in four years at what I have accomplished, and use those skills to help drive me out of school and into the workforce. There is only one way to do it all, and that would be the next chapter—into college and the rest of my life.

Horse Bowl, Hippology, and Hard Work
Barbara Flores, Illinois

Some memories do not fade. I remember so clearly trying to find the home of a Dr. Barbara Frampton one dark evening. I had read in the 4-H newsletter that 4-H horse bowl practices were being held at her home that year. It took stopping at a couple of houses before we found her house in the dark. I wondered what "horse bowl" practice would be like. What would my eight-year-old, Elizabeth, learn? The 4-H newsletter did not give much information; it was the word "horse" that caught my eye. Well, we found the house and met junior coach Ginger Tuomey and senior coach Mary Ann Arenson. Dr. Frampton, a veterinarian, was the leader of a 4-H club that met about 20 miles from our house. These folks were to add so much to our 4-H experience.

Our fate was sealed at that first meeting. From 1994 until 2002, studying for the horse bowl and hippology (horse science) competition became a ritual. Each fall, study began for the regional competition which was held in late winter, followed by the state competition in April. That was great fun, but here is where we were really hooked: we learned that there was an Eastern Nationals competition for the top senior-level horse bowl team from each state, as well as for the top four hippology individual contest winners. Our goal was fixed.

During the next eight years my girls (Rebecca, a year younger than Elizabeth, joined the following year) learned an incredible amount about horses and horsemanship. My husband and I count the knowledge gained and experience our girls received from horse bowl and hippology as among the most fun, educational, and exciting things they have ever done. When they started we had two ponies, a Shetland named Tootsie and a registered Welsh pony named Gabriel. We did not know much about horses. And then Calpurnia, a small Tobiano that we loved so much, came along accompanied by Iris, a small, white (I learned she wasn't really white although she looked white) mule who was a "piece of work" (to put it charitably). They were our first four charter members of a herd that grew to eleven—including two saddlebreds, one thoroughbred, an Oldenburg, a Quarter Horse, one crossbreed, and a grade pony. Writing this now is bittersweet, as we have lost our original four horses.

But back to horse bowl. The material my girls studied was a biology lesson—not just about horses, but about all mammals including us humans. It was taught in terms of the anatomy and physiology of the horse. As Rebecca once said, "Everything was so much more interesting when it had to do with horses." She could care less what enzymes were working in her sister Liz's intestines, but what was happening in her horse's gut, now that was really important! They learned about all systems of the body: reproductive, digestive, skeletal, muscular, and respiratory. They learned about breeds and breeding, training, Western and English tack and riding, parasites, pasture management, vital signs, diseases, symptoms, and prevention. Oh, and the part about nutrition was terrific. They learned the importance of vitamins and minerals in the diet, and how crucial to health they were. It was the best way to get a kid to care about good nutrition!

I homeschooled the kids, and horse bowl and hippology were ideal for so many reasons. They were part of a team, they were learning terrific information that we were all interested in, we were becoming informed horse owners, and the competition was exhilarating. The "kids from Winnebago County" became a force to be reckoned with. Ginger (the junior coach) took the girls through junior horse bowl and gave them a terrific foundation of knowledge. The junior team took first place at the state competition in 2000 and 2001. It seemed so sudden—they were now old enough for senior horse bowl. The desire to qualify for Eastern National 4-H Horse Roundup was so strong. Now it was senior coach Mary Ann's turn to work her magic. The kids loved studying, and weekly practices were intense. After only one year as seniors they made it, taking first place at state and then heading to Eastern Nationals. The scary part was that there was only one shot at nationals to "show your stuff."

Senior material was really tough and the four girls on the team worked so hard to be their best. Mary Ann made practices both tough and fun. First was a contest at Quarter Horse Congress, a huge horse show in Columbus, Ohio. The team took fifth place there out of 21 teams. It was good, but not good enough. Three weeks later they were off to Louisville, Kentucky, for 4-H Eastern Nationals. The team of four, Liz, Becca, Marie, and Jackie, studied and studied some more—and it paid off. During a round of horse bowl, Rebecca questioned a judge's decision. She was sure she had just read something that conflicted with the judge's opinion on a question. A copy of the source, a glossary from an Equus magazine, was checked. It was a few long minutes while I wondered if my little girl had it right. Thank goodness she did! However; the judges were so kind that I know, had she been mistaken, they would have treated her with great respect for her bravery in challenging the information. During another round, Liz, who worked at a saddle shop, insisted that some bits could have a plastic mouthpiece. She lost that one, but argued forcefully. In fact, every time I enter a tack shop I have to smile when I see a plastic mouthpiece. The judges had to go by what was in the study materials, but they heard her out with patience. I was so proud of Liz for speaking out so well. The judges were terrific to my daughters and to all the teams and participants.

That day the competition seemed to have lasted an eternity, yet it was over in a flash and they had taken first place. We were absolutely jubilant! To this day, it is a source of much pride and pleasure.

Rebecca is now in her first year of veterinary school and is reminded so often of how much she learned during those horse bowl years. Liz is a psychology major and continues her love of animals through animal behavior studies. Our thanks begin with Dr. Frampton, opening her home for practice that first year, as well as her strong support over the years, and coaches Ginger Tuomey and Mary Ann Arensen (and her dear, patient husband, Alan). These good people volunteered their time through the 4-H program, part of the Cooperative Extension Service of the University of Illinois. The Illinois horse program was led by Dr. Kevin Kline and later by specialist Deb Hagstrom. All of this was established by the Smith-Lever Act of 1914 to disseminate knowledge. Man, did it work!

Please, Don't Make Me Go!

Shannon Cleary, Illinois

My mother and my three older sisters were all 4-H members from very early on. I grew up in a primarily rural area and had little choice but to follow in their footsteps. Whether I liked it or not, I too would be a 4-H'er. I recall the first meeting I ever went to. At the age of eight, I could barely even mutter the word "present" when the roll was called. I was resentful about having to be in 4-H in the first place, and being forced to follow in my sister's footsteps was enough to make me want to run back home! Not to mention the fact that I had to sit by people I had never even met before! But the worst part of all was realizing I would soon be required to give a talk or demonstration to the entire club. Considering my paralyzing shyness, it seemed impossible. I had no intention of speaking in front of people, and I was far too stubborn to even try. A lot of the people in my club told me that when I first joined, older members or adults would say "Hi Shannon," or "How are you today, Shannon?" and I guess my only reply was to hide behind my mother's leg. For the most part, that is the only place I felt comfortable. I was too introverted to talk to anyone outside of my own family and did not foresee my shy ways changing anytime soon.

My main concern was having to leave my comfort zone. I started getting nervous about my talk and demonstration that was supposed to happen in a couple of months. Because of my anxiousness, I decided to start preparing a little early. I managed to take notes on other speakers, do a little research, and get a feel for what the club leaders were looking for. I began to prepare myself more and more. Finally, when the time came, I actually gave my public demonstration with little difficulty. Soon, I started feeling less insecure and more comfortable with the people around me.

As I became more at ease, I signed up to get involved in a couple of new events here and there. Becoming more involved opened up opportunities for me to explore and develop new interests, and I gradually became more willing to participate. I started out signing up to volunteer my time at the local nursing home. Every month a family had to "adopt" a nursing home resident, and even though it sounded kind of boring at the time, I actually *liked* it. It felt surprisingly good to talk to someone outside of my comfort zone. And the look on the resident's face after enjoying some company was enough to make me feel satisfied. I was also able to express my creativity in 4-H fair projects. My mom would sign me up for projects like "woodworking" or "visual arts" and I was excited about throwing myself into something new again. When fair time came around, I was able to talk to the judges comfortably about the various projects of which I was so proud.

With the passing of time, instead of dreading meetings like I had in the beginning, it was almost as if I looked forward to them. I always felt a little excited and privileged to work on some of the community tasks that I was able to at my age. 4-H was an escape for me, it was not another room filled with strict rules and adults. The youth were the foundation, and our opinions were encouraged and welcomed on a regular basis.

I credit 4-H for my talents and abilities today. The international program not only helped me to open up, but it was in 4-H where I developed my leadership abilities. The program creates so many opportunities for youth to get involved and help. Instead of taking a back seat, I would dive in and help get projects going. I signed up to work on committees such as "June is Dairy Month," and I went from brainstorming ideas to doing public service announcements for local radio stations, setting up dairy displays at libraries, and volunteering my time to serve dairy products at blood drives. I was constantly learning how to convey my ideas to other group members and my communication skills were improving at a rapid rate. I was even able to work closely with adults and, in the end, lead my committee to produce satisfactory results. One success led to another, and soon I was running for club office and taking advantage of every chance I could to get involved. I felt I was an important part of something, and went from being barely able to speak in public to becoming the person other members looked to for advice and direction.

In my high school years I was accepted on the county's Federation Board. Within this organization I met a lot of teens my age that shared common interests. We helped to organize different events and volunteered our time to improving 4-H activities. I also attended our 4-H camp to become a counselor-in-training. I was the recipient of the "I Dare You" award and, 11 years later, I am still an active member. I try to give back to the 4-H program as much as I can because I feel 4-H gave me so many positive traits for my future. Becoming a leader of my club gave me the ability to set goals, work through problems, and always work towards success. I have utilized traits from 4-H in my everyday life as well as my schoolwork. I understand what it takes to be successful, and that the process is not always easy. I credit 4-H for teaching me the basics on how to learn and lead to my fullest potential.

There is no doubt, however, that the most rewarding aspect of my 4-H years has been helping others. Our club has always stressed community service, and as a group we try to impact the community by giving back and helping those in need. We would collect canned goods for local food pantries, and clean up the local parks and schools. The feeling of helping, and wanting to help, is something I cannot even begin to describe. 4-H has given me the foundation to be a good citizen, show compassion for my community, and has taught me that whenever I am able to lend a helping hand, I need to do it—without giving it a second thought.

Through my experiences as a member of the Ashkum Go-Getters 4-H Club, I have learned leadership, communication skills, and the importance of community service. Being a leader of my 4-H club has had a profound impact on my personal development. Not only did I change my introverted ways and become a stronger person, but I learned that what is most important is not being able to lead, but leading to *serve*.

What 4-H Offered Me
Laura Gregory, California

Anyone who has been a part of the 4-H program can attest to its significance in youth development. But sometimes the most important effects of the program are those that are not immediately seen. 4-H members learn skills that they will carry with them throughout their lives. In addition, youth develop aspects of their character in 4-H. They are given a positive environment in which they learn to be respectful, responsible, honest, and caring individuals. In this environment youth can obtain the self-confidence needed to lead a group or simply to try new things. It was 4-H that gave me the self-confidence that I needed to stretch my comfort limits in college, work, and in the Peace Corps.

I was a 4-H member in California for nine years and involved in a variety of projects. In high school I focused on citizenship, community service, and photography. During college I had the opportunity to serve on the California Focus staff for two summers. I am grateful to the 4-H program and the volunteer leaders that gave me an environment in which I could thrive. A sense of giving back to the community and believing that one person can make a difference was instilled in me.

In May 2006 I began my Peace Corps service in Panama. I wanted to help a community in a very grassroots and hands-on way. After an interview, I was slated as an agricultural volunteer because of my 4-H experience. Looking back, it is ironic that the 4-H experience they thought was relevant (three years of raising pigs) was not the 4-H experience I relied on to be a successful Peace Corps volunteer.

My work in Peace Corps was small-scale, working with families and community organizations. My primary project was working on agri-business techniques with an association of farmers who farm rice patties. I taught basic accounting, English classes, HIV/AIDS awareness and prevention, and first aid. I also taught them how to make mud stoves, create a business plan, and basic organic farming techniques. When new aqueducts were installed with chlorinators and filters, I helped them form committees that were responsible for maintaining clean drinking water. I noticed the women were interested in my cooking, so we formed a women's group to learn something new every

Saturday. Overall, as many volunteers know, I learned more from the people I was there to help than they learned from me.

In Peace Corps I relied on the skills I learned early on in 4-H—only this time I was in the position of a volunteer leader. I encouraged people to try new things and to understand that just because something fails does not mean that the person is a failure. I facilitated discussions instead of telling them what to do. I encouraged them to take on leadership positions and boosted self-confidence with positive reinforcement whenever possible. I wanted them to make their own mistakes and learn from them. If I had never seen these roles modeled by adult 4-H volunteers, I do not think I would have applied for the Peace Corps in the first place.

Laura Gregory extended her Peace Corp service for a third year to serve as a Regional Coordinator in Panama and has recently returned to California.

Life Lessons Learned in 4-H
Lynn Garland, Maryland

"Why are you in 4-H?" This question was often asked as I grew up in Beltsville, Maryland, when the closest thing to a farm-type activity was our large vegetable garden. Mom became our leader and our 4-H club met in the dining room for meetings, crafts, and sewing, and in the kitchen for cooking. She had started in 4-H (and enjoyed 4-H glee club) with 4-H Club Agents Dorothy Emerson and Ethel Regan. When I joined 4-H at age seven, little did I know the impacts 4-H would have, the skills and knowledge I would learn, the wonderful people I would meet, and the amazing opportunities I would have.

Life lessons learned and practiced through 4-H were many. "If in doubt, rip it out" was our 4-H sewing slogan. Learning quality standards, assessing workmanship, making improvements, and being happy with one's creations applies not only to sewing, but throughout life.

4-H provided me with wonderful role models. As a young 4-H'er learning to sew, I wished I could sew and model, and be as nice as Carolyn Buck, the "star" of our county fashion revue. 4-H encouraged us to develop our talents and keep excelling. Staying with 4-H and assuming greater responsibilities, I realized younger members were looking up to me. "Be and Do Your Best" became the goal as you learned what and how you did things made a difference, not only to yourself but to others. Volunteers and 4-H agents, like Ella Smart, became second moms and dads.

Many hands laboring together made work light and more fun. From food booths and fair displays, to camp programs and state fair floats, we learned to get along with others of different ages, backgrounds, opinions, talent sets, and personalities. The optimism our 4-H leaders possessed was amazing, even when we came up with an outhouse float theme with moonshiners and revenuers. At the big bang, the outhouse fell apart revealing a person sitting in the outhouse who pulled down a shade, "Don't wait until it's too late to join 4-H!" What a challenge to get that working, yet what fun for our county teen club.

Giving 4-H demonstrations started with "Tutti Fruity Punch and Whacky

Cakes" and continued until communication skills were fine-tuned. Demonstrations were presented at meetings where others observed and offered suggestions. I will always remember Roberta making slash marks for every "take and put" I said in my foods presentations. At competitions we even asked Mom and Dad to watch others so that we would not see their faces when we did things differently. When we posted supply lists on the front door or refrigerator, I never realized the life-long skill of creating "to do" lists was in development.

Demonstrations taught me to think quickly and cope with the unexpected. I remember a pimento jar that I forgot to pre-loosen. During the demo, when the top just would not budge, I quickly asked a 4-H dad to assist—ad-libbing that cooking is more fun when others help. Before my district level "Pressing Pointers" demonstration, our 4-H agent said that the school would have an ironing board, which would be helpful to us as it would save space in Dad's station wagon. While demonstrating the tailor's clapper, the ironing board collapsed. I had been coached in continuing the presentation and making the best of situations. I picked up the ironing board, found the iron, press cloth, and wool blazer, and somehow managed to keep talking. For state fair, we brought our own ironing board.

In 4-H I learned to work under the pressure of a deadline, and to turn mistakes into successes. Regardless of how early you started, there were always last minute crunches before fashion revue as the club shared one sewing machine. The day before judging, Mom and Dad went grocery shopping. All I had to finish on my wool suit were the shirt's buttonholes. With the buttonhole attachment secured, all the buttonholes came out perfectly. Unfortunately, as I was cutting open one buttonhole, I cut all the way through the stitching and beyond. *Whoops*, my shirt was ruined! Tears came next. Then I remembered when it comes to obstacles, find a way to go over, around, under, or through. I found extra fabric, cut and stitched a band for the blouse front and then made new buttonholes on top of the former ones. With a sigh of relief, my suit was completed. Mom and Dad were proud of my problem solving and amazingly the judges did not discover the error.

Sometimes 4-H nudges you out of your comfort zone. At 4-H camp, our tribe needed another shooter to qualify for awards. As the Cherokee Chief, I had been teaching crafts and had not even visited the rifle range. Our team pleaded that all I needed to do was barely hit the target to qualify in the top group. We raced to the range, surprising the range director. He taught me to shoot safely since I was a rookie. He gave me three bullets; one hit the bulls-eye, one 1/8 inch above the first bullet and the other 1/8 inch below. My nickname became Annie Oakley and our tribe won. If you think you can, you can, but good luck helps!

Another wonderful opportunity through 4-H occurred when Pat Stabler, Carroll County's 4-H agent, asked me to be O'Chief for their first county camp held at the Western Maryland 4-H Camp. What a special experience! Later, as a college junior, I was selected for a University of Maryland Cooperative Extension summer internship working with Pat and her 4-H program. That opportunity cemented my desire to pursue an Extension career.

4-H opened the doors of opportunity and gave me the confidence to say, "I'll be glad to." My first long-distance train ride was to National 4-H Congress in Chicago. My first plane ride was to Schenectady, New York, to the Farm-City Youth Conference. Together with our family's camping trips to different states, I got the travel bug. Chaperoning state and national 4-H trips and organizing our 4-H travel trips to Great Britain enabled me to share special travel moments with 4-H youth.

In my freshman year at the University of Maryland, the entire state 4-H staff, except for Dick Angus, had retired or moved. This left a big gap. Dick approached the University of Maryland Collegiate 4-H Club for assistance, later hiring me to work in the office and assist 4-H programs. My four years at Maryland's state office and the summer internship gave me insights to the planning, team building, and detailed organization needed to have successful 4-H programs.

Louise Kilpatrick, new to the state staff, encouraged me to apply to several states for my first Extension job. She said, "You'll learn from the experience and discover how Extension systems function differently." Of course she was right. My choice was Rockingham County, New Hampshire, where I succeeded Beth Bourne, a Cooperative Extension legend and a wonderful person. She let me stay in her home while she traveled to Alaska in celebration of her retirement from a 43-year 4-H career.

The New Hampshire State 4-H leader who hired me was Jesse James, a tall Georgian. One of my first experiences was to take an International 4-H Youth Exchange visitor with limited English to the New Hampshire 4-H Camp. According to our camp nurse, the IFYE needed an immunization shot, so we traveled the back roads to Concord Hospital. I followed Jesse's directions, requesting the bill be sent to his home address: Jesse James, Old Stage Road. The hospital staff had quite the laugh. Thankfully, a phone call confirmed the details.

Later, life threw me its share of challenges. A car accident with a snowplow left me with limited mobility. Ten months of physical therapy worked miracles restoring my movement. Then breast cancer was discovered and the journey certainly had twists with a failed port, an allergic reaction to a chemotherapy drug, and a yearlong research project with weekly infusions. The life messages and lessons practiced in my family, church, and 4-H laid the foundation for surviving, coping, and then thriving.

Seeing the humor, beauty, and magic in everyday moments is such a gift. Hopefully, I have shared some of these life lessons with the families I have been fortunate enough to work with during my 39½ year Extension career in New Hampshire. I retired on May 30, 2008, and continue to serve as a volunteer, believing in the importance of "passing it forward" to the next generation of 4-H youth and families.

Erik's Sewing Adventure
Shawn Hokuf, Minnesota

Erik found himself in a particularly unusual situation that early August morning. As he waited his turn on the soapbox, there was a hint of mugginess that would soon overtake the Minnesota air, and the smells from food booths wafted through the open green doors of the enormous 4-H building. There he was, the only boy among nine girls who had gathered to display the hand-sewn garments they had constructed for the 4-H clothing design and construction project. Each of these 4-H members had entered their sewing project at their local county fair, and had won a trip to the state fair to participate in the judging competition. Soon the judge would decide which 4-H club members would receive the coveted purple ribbon. As he contemplated his minority position among the girls, he thought of the two biggest influences that had prompted his foray into this project category. Their guidance and his hard work and dedication had now landed this 11-year-old at the state fair conference judging table to showcase his purple, orange, and white nylon running suit.

The first influence, like so many other 4-H club members with supportive parents, was his mother. Besides being a 4-H leader, she kept busy with the domestic responsibility of raising her own four boys. Over the years, she had honed her sewing skills by constructing clothes for her own family, sewing clothing articles for herself, and mentoring other members of her rural, northern Minnesota neighborhood 4-H club. Not having a daughter to share her skills with, she was determined to have one of her sons expand his horizons beyond expected traditional gender roles. Perhaps her third boy would take an interest in her maternal craft. Another hugely positive influence was his mother's friend, Connie, a county Extension agent and champion of local 4-H programs. She was also a passionate promoter of young people; she could detect a spark of talent in a young club member and encourage them to dream big, follow their passions, and turn their "learn by doing" 4-H experience into a life-enriching experience or even a life-long career.

It was earlier that summer when Erik's mother taught him to sew a nylon running suit, which he later modeled in the local 4-H fashion revue. He picked up sewing quickly. He already possessed much manual dexterity from helping his father with mechanical projects around the farm. Later, at the county 4-H fashion revue, he displayed great poise and modeling skills. He felt a little out of place as the only male in the competition, as the girls blushed at his good looks and infectious smile as he strutted down the runway. Connie had lofty plans for this young boy. After he won the purple ribbon at the fashion revue, she encouraged him to develop his skills even more. She envisioned this young boy someday part of the fashion design scene, trading in his rural northern Minnesota roots for the fashion design studios and runways of New York. For now, this new 4-H project was all a bit overwhelming to him, and he was more concerned about the competition he was about to face at the state fair.

"And could you share with us about your project today?" queried the judge, jarring him back to the reality of having to give an oral presentation of his project experience. Erik, with much charismatic charm for an 11-year-old, explained why he chose the project, and what he learned from it. He shared with the other project participants the help and encouragement he had received to enroll in the project, what it cost, how it was constructed, and what sewing techniques he used. He told about the two adults who encouraged him to try this new project and who championed his efforts. The judge was impressed with the running suit itself. She was even more impressed by how much this young 4-H'er had learned through his exploration of the project, and how enthusiastically he shared his learning experience with others around the table. It also did not hurt that some of the girls were tired, having chatted the night away in the 4-H dormitory the night before. In the end, he walked away with another purple ribbon!

4-H leaders sometimes have little insight into how their encouragement will touch a life, and what great things it will lead to some day. Now 28, Erik is still sewing. He is known worldwide for his skills. His work has been showcased in numerous media, and people in his industry have heaped accolades on him for his talents. Today, as he methodically stitches a long swath of white fabric, holding a specially designed needle with a custom curved shape, he often smiles when thinking back to his first 4-H sewing project. Two of his assistants hold the cloth firmly at each side of their subject, as he leans over to cut out another swath of linen with pinking shears that he will use to hide a stitch line. "You need to orient the fabric at a 30 degree angle across her ribs, this provides the most tensile strength, and drapes better," he tells his understudies. They hang on every word, marveling at his skills for someone so young. He shares with his fellow artists where he first learned to sew, turning to the sewing machine he will use to fasten two leather shapes together. "Really?" they respond, "we would have never guessed!"

Erik did not end up in the fashion industry, but his 4-H experience, and the mentors who encouraged him, helped him to dream big. He now works around runways of a different sort. Today, Erik is the president and chief restorer of Air Corps Aviation, one of the premier vintage aircraft restoration shops in the world. His shop has garnered multiple national awards for its expertise. But of course, because of his 4-H experience, he is no stranger to the scrutiny of judges, and the pressure of competition. Now, instead of crafting garments, he cuts out fabric to cover the wings and control surfaces of the antique airplanes he restores for a living. He uses commercial sewing to fashion the lining for the landing gear bay and the interiors of airplane cockpits. He is not a fashion designer, but he has become an artist. His mediums now are fabric, leather, sheet metal, and wood. He still gains much satisfaction from practicing one of the fundamental premises of 4-H: learning by doing. Now *he* is the teacher and mentor, training other craftsmen to restore aircraft to museum quality. He ultimately went further in the 4-H aerospace model airplane project category, but he still uses the sewing skills he picked up to adeptly cover the skin of the vintage airplanes he restores. No one could have envisioned what Erik would someday do with his talents, but the role of his leaders and mentors in the 4-H program undoubtedly had much to do with his success.

Shawn Hokuf, who proudly wrote this story about his younger brother Erik, was also an active Beltrami County, Minnesota, 4-H member. Shawn now lives in Denver, CO.

4-H, My Foundation for Life

Terri Sturtz Licking, Nebraska

I would rank being a part of 4-H as one of the top ten positive experiences of my life.

My granddaughter, Hailey, showed livestock this past year (2009), making us a four-generation 4-H family. I was adopted at age seven, and moved to my folk's ranch where the main social summer activity for youth back then was 4-H. I was never a good athlete, so concentrating on 4-H was natural. One of the best things about 4-H is that you can be any shape, size, or physical ability and still excel. And while excelling, you learn skills you can fall back on for the rest of your life.

My parents became involved as 4-H leaders. Mom was one of the leaders for the home economics projects in the Cloverleafs 4-H Club. Dad was a beef leader of the Lone Valley 4-H Club. Mom also belonged to an Extension women's club that met once a month on a Sunday, and it always included a great potluck dinner at the women's homes. She also served on the county's 4-H council and Dad was livestock superintendent at the county fair, even after I went to college.

Mom insisted I take cooking, baking, and sewing projects. She was an excellent cook, and the family pie baker for reunions and community potlucks. My yeast rolls garnered purple ribbons at county fairs and blue ribbons at the Nebraska State Fair. My neighbor taught me sewing.

My real love was range management—the study of the grasses, soils, and proper grazing management of livestock. I also enjoyed showing beef. When Dad let me keep my first breeding heifer, Miss JS Technician II, it was the start of my herd. We raised purebred Herefords and I had ten breeding heifers by the time I went to college. The horse project was another favorite. Later, I met and married a rancher who lived 30 miles north and raised Angus. We have "Black Baldies," a combination of Hereford and Angus genetics. Those three 4-H projects have served me well, partnering with my husband on a Nebraska Sandhills ranch south of Thedford, Nebraska.

I enjoyed judging livestock—beef, hogs, and sheep. I made the county's team the last couple of years and went to the state contest. Range judging was my forte. In range judging, one had to identify 24 grasses; three different range sites consisting of a 3'x 3' staked-out plot where the contestant had to determine the soil site and the degree of use by the livestock. I won the 4-H division of the Nebraska State Range Judging Contest in 1972.

While growing up, I was shy, introverted, and a stutterer. It was through 4-H demonstrations, and giving oral reasons in livestock judging, that I gained self-confidence and increased my self-esteem. Speech in high school came easier to me than some of my non-4-H classmates, mainly because I had been speaking in front of audiences for several years.

4-H allowed me travel opportunities that I would not have had growing up. I won the first of two trips to Washington, D.C., to attend the Society for Range Management 25th anniversary convention. This was given to the top two participants at Range Camp. Back then, girls in range projects were a rarity. I flew for the first time at 17. While at the SRM meeting in D.C., I was elected secretary of their Range Youth Forum—more than 300 youth in high school and college voted for me. My 4-H public speaking experiences served me well, as the high school students had to give a presentation on their homes and how range tied into our lives. The following February the Nebraska delegation drove to Idaho to attend the national SRM meeting.

The second trip was to the Citizenship Short Course in Washington, D.C., four months after SRM. This trip took three weeks on a bus with stops at Henry Ford's birthplace and museum in Detroit, Niagara Falls on the Canada side, New York City, Gettysburg Battlefield in Pennsylvania, and the Amish communities along the way. 4-H gave me the opportunity to see nearly half of the continental United States before I graduated from high school.

After marriage, I moved only 30 miles into Thomas County. When our last child, our only son, was ready for 4-H he wanted to show beef just like Mom. Our two girls earlier were easier. They did the cooking and sewing projects with their paternal grandma's help. I went to the fair board and asked what they had for a livestock show. I was shocked when they said they had horse, but no beef. Thomas County, in the heart of the Nebraska Sandhills, the number one cattle producing area and no beef! They gave me the green light to organize one.

The 4-H Bucket Calf was a new project that paired 4-H'ers with an orphan calf. The 4-H'er became the calf's surrogate mother. At fair time, the pair was judged on their compatibility. The judge interviewed the 4-H'er on every aspect of care they gave. The calf is judged on cleanliness and showmanship.

This project may have been the beginning of interview judging for other projects.

That first year I sent out a plea to fellow ranchers and members of the Sandhills Cattle Association. The perspective "surrogate mother" and I would go and pick-up their calf and take it back to the 4-H'er's home. One of the extra things they had to do was keep in contact with the rancher who owned the calf. The animal was on loan unless the two parties made a contract otherwise. I had 12, 4-H "surrogate mothers" that first year with my son bringing home two calves.

When I learned that there was no livestock pen available, since there was no livestock show, the parents discussed setting up the rodeo arena using portable panels. But that would have required a great deal of effort. We decided we would "circle the trailers"—the pick-up trucks and their trailers in a circle to create a pen. We had classes for overall showman, heifers, and steer classes. The picture of that first show graced the cover of the *Nebraska Farmer* the next year to highlight their county fair issue. The following year we made a show pen with portable panels.

I enjoyed being a 4-H leader for 17 years. My kids stayed in 4-H until after junior high, when sports and sports camps took precedence. It is good to see my grandchildren becoming old enough to join 4-H. I hope they will enjoy 4-H and learn as much, or more, than I did. 4-H has changed to match the needs of the times, as it must. 4-H and the pledge it stands for is needed today more than ever. It is more than cows and cooking and literally has the sky as its limit.

Learning to Lead – Photo/Diane Russo

Becoming a Better Person
Rebecca Jackman, Rhode Island

This year has brought me a new level of understanding of the four "H's" in the pledge. I have learned how to help others and how to analyze the supplements that will work best for my horse. I have learned to keep better records of my horse's medical appointments and the events I have been involved in with my 4-H club. Being a member of the Cornerstone Crew 4-H Club since I was seven has helped me to develop skills I never thought were possible before joining 4-H. Now that I am 17 years old and looking at colleges, I still want to be involved with all things equine and some day to be as good a leader and role model as Beth Stone, my 4-H leader, has been for me all these years.

Head: As a result of my previous experiences, I realized I needed to keep better records so that when it came time to do my record book I would be better prepared. I kept track of everything my horse and I did on separate calendars and wrote in the cost and amount of time it took to complete each activity. By doing this, my records would be more organized, making it easier to find answers to questions. Another thing I had to work through this year was my horse's problem with her back legs due to having Lyme disease the previous year. I had tried many different supplements with little success until I found something that finally worked. I could see the difference in a couple of weeks as my horse began moving with more grace than before, when her transitions had been very choppy.

Heart: I learned more about sharing this year because of a pony I started riding when I was seven, but sadly had outgrown. Last year I let a younger 4-H'er ride my pony, J.R., and she did very well. She even received champion at most of the shows. My next-door neighbor had been looking for a horse or pony for her daughter to ride in the shows and I offered to let her ride J.R. She has been doing very well with my spunky pony.

I also learned to have more concern for others when my 4-H leader had hip replacement surgery. I wanted to help her and return some of the many special favors she had done for me over the years. My mom and I organized a program called "Friends of Beth" with each of our club's families providing meals for Beth's family during her recuperation. I not only helped Beth, but also learned to be a better organizer.

Hands: I have completed many community service hours with several different groups, including the Trudeu Center, my 4-H club, my brother's Scout troop, and others. I helped the Trudeu Center when they came to Beth's farm to ride some of her horses. Our 4-H club has completed many community service hours, including rides for children with special needs at Cornerstone Farm. When my brother's Boy Scout troop camped on our property, I taught many of the boys how to properly groom and tack a horse for Western and English riding. I also gave a demonstration on how to ride each seat and the different gaits. I made good use of my leadership skills by serving on most of my club's committees and am currently serving as secretary of the Cornerstone Crew and vice president of the Tristate Youth Group. I demonstrated responsibility by taking care of my three horses and by serving as a counselor at Cornerstone Farm, making sure all of the campers were observing important safety precautions when near the horses. I would not have been so motivated this year without the help of my trainer, Kristen McKenna, my mom, the 4-H'ers, and most of all Beth Stone, my 4-H leader. They all urged me to set my goals high and work hard to meet them. They also urged me to relax more.

Health: My self-esteem has really grown this year because I am now confident on not only my horse, but horses others have asked me to ride. I have also acquired a lot of self-discipline through working two jobs this summer and making the time to exercise three horses. That helped me improve my time management skills, which will really help in college. Last year, I found that stress was a problem for me, and I needed to focus on just working through the bad days and relaxing on the good ones. I learned the importance of personal safety in all situations and how to make better healthy life choices.

Through my 4-H activities I have become a better person. I plan to attend a college close to home and major in equine business management with a minor in equine massage. 4-H has really made a difference in my life and I want to thank everyone that helped me. The four "H's" are the foundation for our future leaders, as they become role models for younger members. I have learned so much from all the wonderful 4-H people who have taught and supported me. I cannot imagine my life without them. Thanks to my 4-H friends I have learned a lot about responsibility and what it takes to make the world a better place.

4-H: Lifelong Learning–Lifelong Friendships
Diane McLean Russo, Idaho

For some, learning comes easy, but for others it is a slow, grueling process. My childhood memories of school and learning are of the latter. There appeared to be so many unspoken rules. Only the bright would succeed. Teachers knew everything. People learned best in groups sitting in rows. Children with learning challenges were best placed in the back of the class or in the coat closet.

Learning within those parameters was nearly hopeless for me. I did learn what stale smoke or cat urine smelled like on coats, and that sitting in the back of the room could be fun as you could withdraw into your own world, letting your imagination and humor bring entertainment. I also learned humility, empathy, forgiveness, hope, and perseverance. It was the latter that made me successful in the end. And, I learned to keep striving, be curious, and to always be kind.

It was about this time that 4-H and I met. 4-H is a mode of experiential learning. What a wonderful world it opened up for me (to think that you could use your own passions as tools for learning). Learning made sense now. The personal interest of a topic now gave me a reason to want to learn. It was a big breakthrough for me which had many impacts. I academically excelled for the first time in my life. I became very involved in club projects such as teen leadership, dog, horse, photography, vet science, leather craft, sewing, cooking, and more.

Community pride was also instilled in us through 4-H. In 1976, I personally raised $2500 by making a 4-H community quilt to purchase panels for the only horse/livestock arena at the Clearwater County Fairgrounds (I went home for the fair this year, the panels are still being used). The last bidder on the quilt, Ester, my 4-H vet science leader, gave the quilt to me years later as a wedding present. To this day it reflects warm memories from the bed it is on.

I was not able to participate in too many statewide 4-H activities, as our club was located many miles from them. We did win an Idaho State award (Idaho Pride) for working on a Good Samaritan Project, which entailed rescuing from starvation and caring for approximately 20 head of livestock. I had the opportunity to represent Idaho at National 4-H Congress in Chicago, as well as winning the Security Bank Watch Award (state level) and the I Dare You Award (national level).

The awards were merely feathers in my cap; the real gem was the gift of learning and the lifelong friends I acquired. I have kept close contact with many of my old 4-H buddies, many of whom are successful, for which I think 4-H is partially responsible. Norm Fitzsimmons, the Clearwater County Extension agent at the time, attended my wedding, still sends Christmas cards 30 years later, and on grand occasions we still see each other.

David Pollock, one of the oldest volunteers in the county and I became good friends through 4-H. As fate would have it, Dave never married and did not have a family. We became family. We rode the range gathering up cattle in the fall crisp mornings, we taught other 4-H'ers about horses, and we shared the joys and sorrows of life. The days and lessons of life exchanged are irreplaceable. My kids called him Grandpa. Years later, as a family, we buried our dear friend.

Many years had passed from our original 4-H club meetings and fun when several of us got together. My brother was in town so he joined us, which was the beginning of his beautiful relationship with Lori Jo, one of my 4-H buddies. They are currently married, leaving me with a 4-H buddy as my sister-in-law. Yes, our 4-H buddies become many things to us as they always were. Many of my treasured friends of today were fellow club members of yesterday.

One cloudy day I found myself at a Washington State University function. I had invited 4-H'ers and FFA students to attend the Tree Research dedication, followed by a tour of the orchard as a possible career exploration. During the formal dedication, who would stand before me and squirm with delight but an old 4-H buddy, Caroline. We had not seen each other for years, but there we were, both employed by the same land-grant university. Quite possibly, WSU had employed the best, made better through 4-H.

Presently I work for Washington State University as an Extension educator. Previously I taught at the local community college for 17 years and before that taught elementary school. I find it interesting that I spent much of my life in the very process I disliked as a child. That dislike has motivated me to help others so learning can be more enjoyable. I believe I have made a difference. Today, I am thankful I can now give back a piece of what I gained through 4-H in order "To Make the Best Better."

Humor, the Fifth H

Horse Vandal Strikes at County Fair!
Donna R. Gillespie, Idaho

It was a typical second day at our county fair and things were starting to fall into place. The livestock market projects were entered and safely bedded down in the barns, judging was proceeding well inside the 4-H building and "so far, so good" at the horse show.

Even though we have all heard stories about "those crazy horse people" and the problems that can arise from too much parental involvement, out-of-control competition, and impulsive decisions, our 4-H horse program has always run pretty smoothly. Our horse leaders, youth, and family members are passionate about the program and strongly competitive, but I have always been grateful that we have not had some of the challenges that surrounding counties deal with. With that in mind, imagine my surprise and concern when a parent came running as fast as she could and pleaded with me to get to the horse show arena as quickly as possible. She was quite excited and blurted out several confusing statements including that a horse had been vandalized. Parents were starting to make accusations and tempers were on the rise.

Hurdling over the fence in the swine barn where we were taking photos, I hustled to the arena with several things running through my mind. The most obvious being, "What the heck is horse vandalism?" Did someone chop off one of those long flowing tails that were immaculately groomed and hung to the ground? Could someone really have caused pain or permanent injury to a competitor's horse? I could not even consider that as 4-H kids and their families love horses and, regardless of what had triggered this incident, I refused to believe someone had knowingly harmed an innocent animal.

I arrived on the scene just in time; the young owner was riled up and he and some adults suggested that teenage girls were jealous of the young man's success in the show ring and were "getting even" with him. I did not want to believe that and asked if we could all go to the trailer, take a look at his horse, and calmly discuss what might have happened. I still had not seen the vandalized horse and was somewhat apprehensive.

There, tied to the trailer, was a small leopard-spotted pony, covered with what appeared to be black paint that was still wet from the attempts to clean his soiled coat. The showman had won his last class and had tied up his pony for a short rest. When he returned "someone" had taken black paint and made a mess of things. It was obvious to those around me that this "someone" was a jealous, mean 4-H'er, or worse yet, a 4-H parent. And unfortunately, names were being thrown out for consideration.

Much to my relief the pony was not injured, but he did have more black spots and stripes than he was born with. Out of the corner of my eye, I saw a mom herding her five-year-old son toward the trailer. Low and behold he seemed to have black paint on his hands and clothing. It seemed the "jig was up" and we had found the culprit!

The mother was definitely mad, the pony's owner was staring at the little boy, the 4-H dad was shouting that his kids needed to keep their equipment and grooming supplies locked up, and the child was starting to cry. The scene did not seem to be a good place for positive youth development, so I asked the mom if I could speak privately with her son. The young man had met me on several occasions and seemed willing to share his story with me. He showed me where he found the hoof black paint and admitted to taking it. When I asked him if he used it on the pony, he guiltily looked down at the ground and said, "I was just doing dot-to-dot."

Things calmed down pretty quickly when everyone realized that a curious little boy with some free time on his hands was just having fun. The boy realized what he did was wrong, since the pony needed to look its best at the county fair, and the 4-H kids agreed they should be more careful about keeping their things put away. Apologies were shared between those who had been making accusations and the show went on.

When I returned to the swine barn I could not keep a straight face as I shared the story. Everyone had expected a serious problem and we all hoped no one could hear us howling with laughter about "those crazy horse people."

Whatcha Makin'?

Jim Kemble, Delaware

Like all field trips, a lot of planning takes place before the adventure begins. In the Delaware 4-H Engineering Program, youth participate in contests at the county level and then at the state fair in order to qualify for the National 4-H Engineering Event. The youth have always served as outstanding ambassadors of the Delaware 4-H Engineering Program. The trip in 2009 was like the others and filled with excitement from start to finish. However, one incident made things even more exciting.

Sometimes in the course of final preparation for the engineering competition, the excitement can lead to almost anything. Such was the case when we stopped to purchase some items to enhance the kids' small engine visual presentation. Hand cleaner, clean-up towels, rubber gloves, oil drain pan, a container to store the drained oil for proper disposal, fuel stabilizer, and a spark plug were needed for the demonstration. The young men then added some personal items including over $30 worth of "Hot Pocket" sandwiches and aluminum foil to wrap up leftovers. There were also some personal hygiene items including deodorant and toothpaste in the cart.

One group took the items for the engineering demonstration to a register as the other group with the personal items arrived at a neighboring register. As the demonstration items were rung-up, the personal items were being placed on the neighboring conveyor belt. That is when things began to get interesting. One of the young men, who had lagged behind, walked up to the register, saw what was on the belt and blurted out, "Whatcha makin', a bomb?"

Almost instantly the register was frozen along with the registers on either side. Two store managers appeared out of nowhere, reviewed the items, made a decision, and said the registers were out of order. The young men had to leave all of their "stuff" at the registers and leave the store. The adult leaders were waiting in the parking lot when they came out and they excitedly explained what had happened. "We can't go back in there," "We were probably filmed," and "They may hold us to determine our intent for buying those items," were among the comments blurted out in their excitement.

It was all the adult leaders could do to keep from breaking out laughing.

While it could have been a very difficult situation, the store officials handled it well. That evening I left a message on the 4-H office phone about keeping the bail money handy until we got back home. When we returned to the store for dinner, the young men had disguised themselves with hats, coats, and glasses. It was good for them to realize the potential seriousness of what had happened, but the adult leaders could not resist giving them lots of good-natured ribbing. The rest of the trip went very well with our youth representing Delaware 4-H far beyond our expectations.

Drawing by Maria Barga

The Mare Who Wanted to Jump
Nancy Valentine, West Virginia

While 4-H horse shows usually bring a great deal of excitement, they can also bring unanticipated anxiety and stress, particularly for the Extension staff charged with managing the event. One year during the West Virginia State 4-H Horse Show, we had a young man competing with an overweight, unconditioned gray mare named Lucy.

Well, it was just not Lucy's best show. She would not stand still in the showmanship class. In the western pleasure class she would not stay in the gaits, tossed her head, and when they asked for a lope (slow canter) she took off running like she was in a timed event.

The young man also had her registered in the gymkhana (or timed) events. The first event was the pole bending class. Lucy did not negotiate the course very well and the young man got hit in the mouth with one of the poles. That required a trip to the emergency room.

The next day was the last class in which he had entered—barrel racing. The horse show management staff was in the show stand, which was elevated above the show ring. The staff had full view of the classes. Lucy turned the last barrel and we knew we were in trouble.

She grabbed the bit in her teeth and took off for "home." She was heading straight for the entry gate. You have probably guessed it—she tried to jump the gate. Of course, she was so heavy (and had certainly not been trained as a hunter or jumper) that she did not clear the gate.

The young man went flying over her head, did a triple summersault in the air, and landed so hard on the ground he literally bounced up with his feet under him, still holding the reins. What a sight to see Lucy hanging on the gate with her front quarters on one side and her hindquarters on the other. We had to finish breaking the gate in order to get her off. For the first time during the entire show she was calm and cooperative. This was certainly not Lucy's finest moment! It is a 4-H horse show memory!

Dr. Nancy Valentine, Ed.D., currently serves as a National Program Leader, 4-H National Headquarters, NIFA, USDA. She was a West Virginia 4-H agent when this story occurred.

Arizona 4-H Teen Road Trip

Curt Peters, Gerald Olson and Bryan Chadd, Arizona

What happens when you put 20 teens, three vans, and a mountain of camping gear together? *4-H Road Trip!*

For one week each summer for the last five years, 4-H teens in Arizona have traveled across the state and beyond, seeing sites, absorbing different Native American cultures, learning about history, applying technology, building community, and helping others on the Arizona 4-H Teen Road Trip. During the travels, teens were followed by others from across the country via the Internet, sharing the sights and sounds of such different places as the Chiricahua Mountains, Las Vegas, San Diego, Salton Sea, Biosphere, a Titan Missile silo, Gila Bend Desert Shrimp Farm, Chaco Canyon, and the Four Corners. Each sunrise and sunset on the road was filled with new challenges, new experiences, and new discoveries. Here is the story of one such trip—one that was filled with moments of learning, fun, and moments when the learning and fun were impossible to tell apart!

The day started early after a very long, very hot night at Roper Lake in southeastern Arizona. Even at 7:00 a.m. it felt like the temperature was already 100 degrees. It would be a long July day out in the Arizona sun. We ventured to the Phelps Dodge copper mine, the largest open pit mine in the world. There we found such incredible sights such as tires on the earthmovers that were 20 feet tall and tractor buckets that could hold all 23 of us shoulder to shoulder! Huge pieces of equipment moved huge rocks from a huge hole in the ground. The magnitude of the equipment was spellbinding.

Eventually we made it back down the slope to Clifton, a small mining town, for lunch. The lunchtime routine was choreographed with everyone playing a part. First the tables came out of the van, followed by the ice chests that held the sandwich meat, cheese and vegetables; then the bread, fruit and drinks. The small city park lacked anything that faintly resembled shade so by then it *really* was over 100 degrees! The playground equipment was hot enough to fry an egg. Our only hope for a respite from the heat was to get back into the vans and crank the air conditioning to high. Looking into the eyes of everyone, it was clear that they were whipped. Lack of sleep due to the heat the night before, then spending the morning climbing on the mining equipment, and then eating lunch under the brutal sun—it just zapped all of the energy out of us.

We all begged, "Let's go back to camp so we can jump in the lake and try to cool off!" Our pleas were ignored; there was still one more appointment scheduled that day.

We turned the corner and into the parking lot of the Safford Sewage Treatment Plant. This was a sick joke, right? We were going to the Sewage Treatment Plant? Yuck! Sure enough, that was the stop. We slowly dragged ourselves out of the vans, griping as we shuffled slowly to the front door, hoping that maybe this was just a bathroom break—conveniently located at the sewer plant. "Go ahead and wait in the conference room. Steve will be with you in a minute," we were told.

The room was big, the chairs comfy, and the AC was cranked up. Attitudes changed to "This is OK; at least it's a decent place to chill." After about a 10-minute wait, Steve burst into the room, full of energy, and asked if we were ready to learn about waste. He was greeted with a combination of blank stares and rolling eyes. No doubt, this would be a tough crowd.

Steve started by explaining the brief history of the new, state-of-the-art plant and how it is different from other sewage treatment plants. "Come on, let's see the lab," he called over his shoulder and we obediently followed.

The lab was full of dials, test tubes, and pipes. "This is where it all happens. We monitor the whole operation from here. One person can run the entire plant from here," Steve announced. Some eyebrows raised and a few heads shook. Sounds impressive but was it really possible? Back into the heat, we went to see the rest of the facilities. First stop was the large-item screen. Steve lifted a trap door so we could look into the area where the sewage first arrives and see where all the big items are filtered out. "Sunglasses, dentures, and many other items, some too gross to mention, get filtered here. These items have to be removed, otherwise they clog the process," Steve said with enthusiasm.

The water looked nasty, but surprisingly there was little smell. Hmm, that is impressive. We worked our way through the rest of the facility—the algae ponds, stirring ponds, additional filters. At each step Steve managed to tell a lively tale of what really happens. Still no smell and the water kept getting clearer. By this time we were all mesmerized looking at the water and equipment. Suddenly we broke out of our trance and began firing questions at Steve, excited about what we were seeing.

Finally Steve brought the tour to its end by filling a glass with crystal-clear water. "Cleaner than the water you drink out of the tap, but by law we can't deliver it to your house. We just pump it into the river bed and let it soak in so we can pump it back up, treat it, and then let you drink it." That brought more quizzical looks and questions for Steve. "It's all public perception—no one wants to drink "treated" water. But just wait, in 20 years it'll be in your drinking fountain."

Despite the heat, we briskly walked back to the conference room for final comments. Steve asked what we thought. "Amazing what you do to clean up that s@#$ water! Whoops, sorry 'bout the language." After a loud and excited "thank you" and handshakes, we piled into the vans and headed back to camp. The vans were lively with conversation, both about the treatment plant and the rest of the day. The evening campfire discussions focused on the changing world of science, engineering, and technology, and ended with the discovery that a seemingly "crappy" job could be administered with great passion and skill.

It was an "Ah-ha" moment that came at the strangest of times as the result of a visit to the strangest of places with the strangest of topics. Just goes to show, when 4-H is involved you just never know when learning and discovery will happen! So be ready, it can happen at any time. Even on a *4-H Road Trip*!

Drawing by Maria Barga

Manure Happens
Laura Hietala, Connecticut

For those who have grown up in 4-H, that final year—when we are 18 and find ourselves looking back knowing that it is our last year as a 4-H member—is bittersweet. We have spent so much of our lives as a part of this amazing program, but now it is time to leave and become a part of what 4-H has prepared us for—the real world. You are ready for it, but it is hard when you know while you are prepping your project for that last 4-H fair that you will never do it again. For me it was no different.

The 2003 Hartford County 4-H Fair in Somers, Connecticut, was one of the most memorable for me. I had the best 4-H project animal I had ever worked with. Spirit, a Holstein fall yearling I had been working since shortly after her birth on September 13, 2001, was the best. But it wasn't because she was the best behaved and the easiest to train. In fact, she was quite the opposite. She lived up to her name and made me work for every bit of progress I made with her. It was because of this that I was so excited to show her off in showmanship. I had worked hard, and I knew that it was going to pay off. Of course, I was not the only 4-H'er who was in her final year. My friend Diana, who was in a different dairy club, was my toughest competition, as always. It was her last year too, and she wanted that trophy as badly as I did. It all came down to a few hairs on our heifers' top lines, but I came out on top. My first blue ribbon at a 4-H fair was my only one, but I could not have been more proud.

The Eastern States Exposition (the "Big E") was coming up. I wanted a repeat performance, and Diana wanted one with a slight alteration in the order of placing.

A month later we were getting ready for the show yet again, but in a different setting. The "Big E" in West Springfield, Massachusetts, was one of my favorite places to show. The competition was tough, I worked hard non-stop for four days straight, and went home exhausted at the end of the show each year. I loved it. Showing with some of the best 4-H dairy showmen in all of New England was one of the best experiences, and one of the most challenging. The highest placing I had managed to date was a third-place finish, and I was ready to top my class there at last. It was my last 4-H show, and I was going out with a bang. It did not, however, go quite as I planned.

Finally, with our heifers buffed and polished, our whites sparkling, and our show halters shining, we were ready to lineup for the final show. Diana and her heifer were right in front of me and Spirit, entering the ring slowly after the class before us had filed out. My eyes were on the judge, who was watching the exhibitors lead the animals in. Spirit was in top-form, she was groomed to perfection. Nothing could go wrong, or so I thought.

I was not even entirely in the ring when it happened. One second, I was getting Spirit's head a little higher, making sure she looked her best, and the next, I felt something unpleasantly warm and smelly hit the calf of my left leg. As I felt the manure from Diana's cow ooze into my freshly polished boots, I looked back in a panic: was I following too close? No, she was a half a cow-length away. Where had it come from? Had the judge actually seen it happen? What should I do now? Brown cow manure does not exactly go unnoticed on white pants. My mind was racing. I did not know if I should laugh or cry. All my hard work! I managed to keep it together, though I do not know how, since it felt like I had warm play-doh in my left boot, squishing with every step. I tried very hard to pretend it was perfectly normal to have a dinner-plate-sized cow pie splattered down your leg. Spirit, thankfully, did not seem to be insulted, so we managed to do pretty well. I do not remember exactly where I placed—somewhere in the upper-middle of the class, with Diana either a place below or a place above me. I just remember the disappointment I felt that something so out of my control could cost me my top placing. Of course, manure or no, the top finisher would have placed where he did. I think the judge may have seen it happen, or he had turned around at the audience's mixed reactions of laughter and horrified gasps, so he knew it was out of my control. Either way, the best showman had won and I knew it. Still, I led Spirit out of the ring with mixed emotions. All my hard work had been sabotaged, but I had still managed to hold it together and had done a respectable job.

Probably the most memorable part of that day happened after the show was over. I had just sat down on my tack box to remove my ruined show boots when Diana's father came up to me laughing hysterically, video camera in hand to show me what had really happened. I watched on the tiny screen as Diana entered the ring, followed by me. A few steps in, her heifer's tail began to rise, which was a telltale warning to stay out of the way. As she was about to deposit her pile safely in the shavings at her feet, she coughed, and the stuff flew a good three feet. The look on my face was priceless! I asked Diana how long it took her to train her animal to do that, since it had only been a month since I had won over her at the 4-H fair. I got to watch the video at least three more times, even in slow motion. It got funnier each time.

I am now a 4-H leader for the same club of which I was a member. With 20-plus 4-H'ers, one or two are bound to come out of the show ring a bit upset. Their heifer laid down in the ring, or the animal was in heat, or something else completely out of anyone's control occurred to cause them to place lower than they had hoped. Whenever that happens, I have found an easy way to get a laugh from a disappointed 4-H'er. I just say, "Well, at least the animal in front of you didn't poop on your leg."

Banned From the Barn
Vivian Hallett, Illinois

I have served as a Cumberland County, Illinois, 4-H leader for 33 years and also started a 4-H club in Pinal County, Arizona, in the 1970s. One of my favorite 4-H experiences was being "Banned from the Barn."

I was to give the "Thank You" at the leaders' banquet and had read an article titled "Confessions of a 4-H Mother" from the *Prairie Farmer* magazine. I had found Alumbaugh's article to be humorous and very thought provoking. It inspired me as I composed that thank you message over 18 years ago.

I remember vividly my son's first year at the Cumberland County 4-H Show. Throughout the summer I shared his enthusiasm for his swine project, recalling my own experiences as a 10-year 4-H member. The memories of learning to care for animals, making new friends, trips to new places, and the county fair came rushing back like a patchwork quilt, lovingly pieced together.

For those 4-H'ers with animal projects, their hard work culminated with the last full week in August at the Cumberland County Fair. The 4-H'ers and leaders had waited in anticipation for months to see how their animals would place, how the judges would evaluate their animal's grooming, and how well the 4-H'ers would show their animals. It was finally time to load the projects and head to the fair. The following scenario may be familiar to other 4-H'ers, leaders, or parents. I was "banned from the barn" by my own children and husband that first year because of the following...

It appeared everything was going well at the county fair. That is, until the hog show was about to begin. Then it happened. Almost unconsciously I slipped into the role my parents played so many years ago. "Do you have your brush? Tuck in your shirt. Get rid of that gum. Now, make sure you keep the pig between you and the judge. Always keep your eye on the judge." I kept going like a drill sergeant, barking orders to him as he moved a little further away with each statement. The moment there was a break in my instructions, he scurried off to one of the far corners of the barn.

That was okay because I knew I would have another shot before he went into the ring. But time was running out. There were only 15 minutes remaining before his class was to show. Should I go back to the pens and see if his pigs were washed and ready to go? It was almost as if I was possessed, a demon-driven 4-H mothering machine.

The judge was beginning to make his final "sort" in the class right before ours. Now it was time for action. I headed down the alley, not noticing the glances of other leaders and parents around me. Yes, there he was, opening the gate to his pen. He started down the alley at a leisurely pace. "You'd better hurry up," I said. "There are already a lot of pigs in the show ring."

He began to move more quickly. "Now just slow down," I cautioned him. "There's no need to get in too big of a hurry. Stay cool." I should have taken my own advice, but I could not help it. I was on autopilot. He finally made it to the show ring, but the judge just was not paying attention to his hog. "Bill," I hissed from the sidelines, glancing around to see if anyone noticed my bizarre behavior. "Keep your pig moving, keep your hand off of his back, and get rid of that gum!"

Was it this hard for my parents and my 4-H leader? I wanted to jump over the fence and help, or hit the judge with a spit wad so he would look towards my son.

My usually calm manner was gone and in its place was a stressed-out bundle of nerves. Even a disgusted look from my husband followed by a jab in the ribs could not deter me. One class down and two more to go. Before the second class, I cornered my son like a fight manager in the boxing ring between rounds to give him a little praise. "You really did a good job showing your pig." But, the kicker was when I asked him, "Would you like to know how you could improve?" He looked up at me and apprehensively said, "I guess so."

All the information I had been storing up for just that moment came gushing out. My son waited patiently until I got it all out of my system. When the show was over he did not have a champion pig, but he had a really good time and was so proud of those ribbons…and he had learned a lot. You know, I learned a lot too. Mainly that I should try to keep my mouth shut. I was also learning my children were growing up and could figure things out for themselves.

As my daughter became 4-H age, I tried to remember the things I had learned from my son's first year 4-H member experiences. I became the parent in the bleachers and tried to let her take care of the things she needed to do as an exhibitor.

There is a new pledge for 4-H leaders and parents. "We pledge our head to clearer thinking, to keep from giving all that unsolicited advice; our hearts to greater loyalty, to stay out of the way as our children learn the good and bad of competition; our hands to larger service, like working at the 4-H barbeque or lemonade stand, or covering our mouths while our children show their projects; and our health to better living, which will surely improve if we won't get so stressed out at the project show or county fair." (Author unknown)

I learned that being "banned from the barn" was not all that bad. It gave me a chance to just sit back, relax and do some needlework to relieve my over energized *stress*.

Poultry Judging
Joe Hune, Michigan

I was well over halfway through the procedures of examining my chicken for the poultry showmanship class, which includes a few dozen steps of examining a bird while showing how well the bird is handled, when the unthinkable happened.

One step is to turn the bird upside down to examine its rear end. I had my little Cochin Bantam upside down and, as I completed a thorough examination of the bird's bottom area, I felt the bird begin to stiffen up and twitch. Thinking nothing of it, I continued with my memorized steps, while explaining to the judge exactly what I was looking for. Suddenly, my poor chicken's wings began to flap and it vomited all down the front of me. I knew that something was desperately wrong as I flipped the bird right side up—only to find that the poor thing was dead. Its head dangled right down to the ground, and the judge, Stan Miller, said, "Joe, I think your bird's dead."

I said, "I think so too, Stan."

"Would you like to get another bird?" he asked.

Knowing there was no way in the world this lifeless, little bird would ever squawk or act up, I said, "Can I just finish with this one?"

The judge agreed and I proceeded to complete my showmanship class. The last procedure is to tip your bird right side up and display to the judge that you can properly control the animal. Well, I did just that and I certainly displayed complete control over my animal. After I was finished with my class, another 4-H'er asked if he could borrow my chicken because it was much calmer than his.

At the end of the day the judge checked and rechecked the rules, but there was nothing in them that said the bird had to have a pulse in order to win! So, I received the big, blue rosette ribbon for first place in senior poultry showmanship! Later, I also received a big, *black* rosette ribbon. We had my poor little chicken that gave its all for my sake stuffed by a taxidermist and it now sits proudly on the television at my parent's house.

Joe Hune formerly served as a Michigan State Representative.

What's Wrong With My Apple Tree?
Jim Rutledge, Oregon

As state 4-H program leader, I always tried to find an evening for the 4-H staff to come to my home for a reception and some casual get-acquainted time during the annual Extension conference at Oregon State University. When the weather cooperated we would gather on the back deck with refreshments and sometimes a fire in the portable fireplace. Over the years I had established a garden and orchard that nearly filled my small backyard. I had apple, peach, and cherry trees, and several varieties of blackberries, raspberries and blueberries. But one apple tree just would not produce. It was large enough to bear fruit but for two years had only yielded one or two apples. As it happened, Roy Hamilton, one of our experienced 4-H agents, had joined us at our reception one evening. Roy had plans to go into the apple business when he retired and knew a lot about apple trees.

Roy was energetic and enthusiastic about anything and everything he did, so I asked him to check my apple tree. That is when things got interesting. A small group had gathered to hear Roy's response to my question, "What's wrong with my apple tree?" First, he suggested a good beating might make the tree produce. He was serious. Roy advised, "Next spring take a baseball bat and beat the trunk with it. The tree will be stressed and realize for the survival of the species it will have to produce seeds and the only way to do that is to produce apples." He insisted he had seen this approach work on apple trees in the past. I was not too sure he had given me good advice, but as he said, "What have you got to lose? It's not bearing fruit now; if you beat it to death, you haven't lost anything."

Roy asked which tree it was and offered to take a look. It was already late fall and the tree was bare so I did not think he could determine very much, but I pointed out the tree anyway. Roy climbed the hill up to the tree that had a trunk about three inches in diameter and was about eight feet tall. None of us bothered to climb along with him, expecting Roy to take a quick look and return with a diagnosis. But that is not exactly what happened. Roy looked around, brushed the leaves from the base of the trunk, and then in a voice loud enough for everyone to hear, proclaimed, "I think it's dead." He then grabbed the tree's trunk and wiggled it around. Then he got a good grip and pulled it out of the ground saying, "Yeah, I was right, it's dead." By now he had everyone's attention, and many of the younger agents were wondering how I would react. Those who did not know Roy very well were quite alarmed, while those who knew him fairly well were not all that surprised. I had invited a veteran agent to take a look at my tree and he ended up pulling it out of the ground. Of course it was dead; it was out of the ground! Roy asked if there were problems with any of the other trees and, fearing a repeat performance, I quickly assured him the others were doing just fine.

He brought the tree down and showed me that something had caused all the roots to die. Roy was not sure if a mouse had girdled the trunk or a disease had gotten into the soil, but he knew it would not survive. Roy retired a couple years later and moved to Washington State where he is now working with his brother-in-law raising and selling apples.

As a group, in Oregon and nationwide, 4-H educators possess a great deal of knowledge on a wide variety of topics and equally impressive skills and talents they are quick to put into action. When dealing with this group it is important to be careful what you ask for. I did not expect my simple question to lead to my apple tree being unceremoniously yanked from the ground. But after years of working with these energetic, talented, and dedicated youth professionals I should have known to expect the unexpected.

Dr. Jim Rutledge has retired and is living in his home state of Oklahoma.

Who Would Steal a Cane?
Robert A. Brown, Pennsylvania

It was my first county fair running the livestock shows as Bucks County 4-H Extension Educator. I did not have "to do" lists left from my predecessor, so I tried to think of everything, knowing full well that something was going to "bite me." Well, it did not take long. I did not have something we needed the first evening of the first day. The hog show was about to begin when a few kids that were about to show asked me where the canes were to show the hogs. Apparently the club had bought about 10 wooden canes a few years before for everyone to use. The canes were stored somewhere in the office and I was supposed to have them. News to me! There was no time to go and get them.

Some kids had their own canes, but several just practiced with a stick and used the club's canes for the show. Well, it just would not be right for some kids to enter the ring for a showmanship contest using a tree branch and others the traditional cane. So I gathered up a bunch of 4-H members and told them the plan. We would cover the fairgrounds looking for "elderly" people who were walking with a cane. We would tell them we really needed their help by letting us borrow their cane to use in the swine show. These kids thought I was nuts until I saw a man walking by us with a cane. I told him our predicament and he laughed so hard I thought he would fall over. Then he told us he would be glad to help as long as we could give him a chair, or a wall to lean on. My initial success got the kids excited about finding their own "cane provider."

The kids scattered across the fairgrounds and within about 15 minutes there were a lot of "mature" people walking with canes toward the hog arena, laughing and being escorted by smiling 4-H members. They happily let us borrow their canes and had a great time being part of the show. We even introduced each of them as a "sponsor" of the Bucks County 4-H Swine Show. They left with our appreciation (and a freshly washed cane), saying they had the best time. Kids and parents still remind me of the year I "stole" canes from old people.

Heads Up
Nancy Valentine, West Virginia

Many years ago we were in the process of building the West Virginia 4-H Horse Program. While there were youth enrolled in 4-H horse projects, there was no equine specialist at West Virginia University. Some of us started providing technical assistance to youth, volunteers, and county Extension staff who had limited knowledge and experience with horses. We traveled the state to conduct clinics on a variety of topics, assist county agents with organizing and conducting county and regional horse events, and promoting the West Virginia 4-H Horse Show.

During one particular regional horse show we were working with people whose hearts were in the right place, but were terribly lacking in knowledge of how to organize and conduct a horse show. The facility was lacking in some basic elements, like a gate for the show ring and equipment to conduct the events.

Using all of our creativity and hard work (the signature of Extension workers) we got through the show, but not without some laughs along the way. Nicholas County 4-H Agent Rush Butcher went to his farm and got an aluminum gate for the ring. Of course, there was no time to fasten the gate to the post, so we assigned a program assistant to manually open and close the gate and hold it shut during the classes.

A common term in the horse show world is "hold the gate" which means keep the gate closed until the judge is ready for horses to enter the ring. The first time the announcer said, "hold the gate," we looked down and the program assistant was literally holding the gate in the air over his head. I guess our quick in-service training needed work.

There was a pole bending class scheduled. This is a class where poles are anchored to a base and set in a straight line. The horses are timed as they weave in and out of the poles. The fastest horse completing the course wins. When we got to the show grounds there were no poles. Again, using our creativity, Rush went to his garden and pulled the beanpoles out for us to use. Needless to say, his wife Ruby was not at all happy to find all of her bean vines on the ground. We found some old coffee cans and started scraping up muddy gravel to put into the cans that would hold the poles in place.

One of my friends who was a state specialist with a doctorate degree was helping. This included scraping up the muddy gravel. On top of all the other things we were dealing with, it was raining quite a bit. It was interesting to see the look on the faces when Dr. Reita Marks from West Virginia University was introduced as she crawled out of the drain covered in mud.

Another common term at horse shows is "heads up." This is used to alert people to get out of the way when a horse is fast approaching or if there is a horse-related emergency of some kind. During this same horse show there were a few "cool dudes" dressed in cowboy hats and boots roaming around the grounds. It was obvious they did not have too much experience around horses and were really just curious spectators.

As we opened the gate for the class to enter, one of the horses became rather unruly near the gate. The announcer immediately said "heads up." When we looked around, there were the cool but clueless "dudes," standing in the middle of the gate looking up at the sky, completely oblivious to the potential danger of being trampled by a misbehaving horse.

Dr. Nancy Valentine, Ed.D., currently serves as a National Program Leader, 4-H National Headquarters, NIFA, USDA. She was a West Virginia 4-H agent when this story occurred.

Why We Do
What We Do

You Can Do Anything
Ron Drum, Massachusetts

Katie was just a little girl when I first met her in 1988. I know it is cliché, but she actually *was* hiding behind her mother's skirt! As each year passed, she moved further and further out from behind that skirt, taking on more and different roles and responsibilities—which I knew, as the county 4-H agent, was mostly because of her experiences in 4-H.

Then one day she came to me and asked, "Can we have a teen conference in our county?" "Sure!" I answered. "Let's figure it out!"

She raised the idea at the next teen council meeting. She described the problems she had noticed and had heard others complaining about. She described how her idea could help with these problems. Then she explained what she wanted the teen council to do. Her presentation resulted in one of the longest, most involved teen council discussions I could remember. In the end they voted her down. It was going to be too hard, too costly, too much work.

After the meeting she just sat there, stunned. "Give up?" I asked.

"What choice do I have?" she answered angrily. Then she glared at me and said, "And *you* said they would help."

"Yes. I did, didn't I?" I said. "Well, I guess I was wrong. Does that mean we give up?"

"Do we have a choice?"

"Yup."

"WHAT?"

"We do it anyway."

"But, *how*? *They* voted it down. Remember?"

"We'll just have to get them to change their minds! Let's talk to some of them individually."

She spent the next week doing just that, trying to win them over one at a time and she made a few successes. In the meantime, I contacted a friend who worked at the local YWCA. She had mentioned to me once that she wanted to work closer with 4-H, maybe collaborate on a project. I thought this might be just the thing and she agreed.

That summer a group of 4-H members and YWCA members worked together to plan and implement the county's first teen-planned and teen-run conference. They called it "Escape to Teen Mountain" and it was a resounding success. All of the teens were proud of their success—but none more than my friend Katie.

"I feel like I made the impossible happen!" she said as we hugged at the end of the day.

"You did." I whispered in her ear. "You did." Then she pushed away, spun around in a spiral, and said, "I feel like I can do *anything*!"

"You *can*!" I answered. "You can do anything you put your mind to!"

I was proud of her and I was proud of myself. I thought I had taught her a great philosophy for life! That is until she came to me after high school graduation to say that she wanted to be a veterinarian, specializing in horses. I knew that, at that time, this choice was one of the most difficult fields of study to get into, let alone be successful at because so many young people were making that same choice. Even the best of the best were finding it difficult to get into veterinary school. Had I set this young woman up for failure?

One school after another turned her down. After multiple turndowns from all across the country, she decided to look at schools outside of the United States. She was thrilled by her acceptance into one in Glasgow, Scotland. It was a tough school to get into and even tougher from which to graduate.

She struggled. There were days we did not think she would make it. There may even have been days *she* did not think she would make it! But in the end, she did. One of my greatest regrets is not having been able to attend her graduation.

A few months later that year I received the following letter:

Hey Ya Ron Drum,

Yep. I am really Dr. Katie now. I graduated from Glasgow Vet. School on July 7, 2001. I cannot believe after all these years of struggles I made it. Some wise person told me, "You can do it; you can do anything you put your mind to!" I want to thank that wise person. Thank you very much. I really wanted to share my happiness with you. I am now an Equine Ultrasound Intern. I am loving it. I have never been so happy with life. Things are finally working out. Hopefully, next year I will get my radiology residency…Fingers crossed.

You can do it; you can do anything you put your mind to! Maybe that is not such a bad philosophy for life after all—fingers crossed or not!

Ron Drum was a Massachusetts 4-H agent when this story occurred. He currently serves as a National 4-H Council Resource Development 4-H Science Accounts Manager.

The Story of Billy
Dale Leidheiser, Colorado

Billy bounded up the bleachers when he spied me sitting alone. I was on the top row of the bleachers as far away from people as I could get, sipping a chocolate milkshake and watching dairy cows parade around the ring. I was taking a reprieve from the challenges after five days of Columbia County Fair activities in rural Wisconsin. I was exhausted by the long hours and non-stop activities of the event.

Billy had been to camp a few weeks earlier and *loved* it! He was nine years old and had just completed his first 4-H overnight camping experience. He wanted to talk about "Exploring Camp," a camp with hiking, nature study, recreation, crafts, and campfire all packed into two days. At the end of this one-sided conversation he asked, "Do you know what I want to do after that?" I said, "No, what do you want to do after that?"

Billy said that next he wanted to go to the five-day summer camp for 10- to 13-year-old 4-H members. He could spend a week doing the things he experienced at the Exploring Camp and lots more. He could hardly wait to have that experience the following summer. Again he asked, "Do you know what I want to do after that?" I said, "No, what do you want to do after that?"

Billy had done his research and knew all about the camps I organized. He wanted to go to the Primitive Camp for 14-year-old teens. This was a special camp for that odd age that does not fit with preteens or with older teens. The appeal for Billy, and what he talked about, was spending five days canoeing down the Wisconsin River, doing water and aquatic life study, setting up camps on beautiful sandbars, and preparing his own meals. Once more he asked, "Do you know what I want to do after that?" I said, "No, what do you want to do after that?"

Well, after that Billy wanted to be a camp counselor. He admired and looked up to those older teens for their leadership, communication skills, and the care they took with all the campers under their supervision. It was a position he aspired to achieve and a feeling he longed to share. And yet another round of "Do you know what I want to do after that?"

Next, Billy wanted the experience of the Junior Leader Canoe Trip. A three-day canoe trip focused on leadership development and teamwork. After that he wanted to go to the Winter Camp where teens would cross-country ski, snowshoe, toboggan, and participate in a variety of workshops. Then he asked a final "Do you know what I want to do after that?" I said, "No, what do you want to do after that?"

"Well, after that, I want to be you." I was so startled I almost fell off the bleachers. Billy both caught me off guard and taught me a lesson. While I was busy planning educational activities for young people, this nine-year-old reminded me that he was watching, paying attention to, and learning from the behaviors of the adults in his life. The sense of belonging we create for youth and making them feel valued is one of the most important gifts we have to offer. And, one of our greatest responsibilities is always to act with character, because children are always watching.

Learning Skills for a Lifetime – Photo/Diane Russo

Eternally Grateful
Sharon Miller, Illinois

The following story is about a young man named Larry who credits 4-H and his club leader with changing his life.

I was a troubled youth in the fourth grade. My parents had just gotten divorced and I was a bully at school. Nobody liked me and I did not care.

My mom had heard about a group of kids starting a 4-H club. I did not know what 4-H was, and I really was not too interested in finding out. The mom of one of the kids I had picked on at school was in charge of the club. My mom decided it would be good for me to go and see what 4-H was all about. I went, but I was kicking and screaming all the way. I sat pouting in the chair, and every time someone tried to talk to me I would snap and scare them to death. I was miserable and so was everyone there. The 4-H leader tried to be nice to me and wanted to include me in everything going on, but I was not cooperating. We did not stay long at that first meeting, but my mom told the leader we would be back for the next one.

By the time the next meeting rolled around I was ready to take them all on—I brought my BB gun. My mom dropped me off and went back home until after the meeting. I took the gun and shot out the window on the front door. It was totally by accident, but I knew the 4-H leader was going to kill me. I ran and hid, taking the BB gun with me. When she found me, she tried to hold me on her lap and talk to me. I kicked and screamed, but when she told me that she was not angry and that accidents happen, I was shocked. I finally calmed down and we went on with our 4-H meeting.

I was elected as the chairman of the refreshment committee, a job I figured I could do well. There were many other incidences, but they became fewer and fewer. I began to kind of like this 4-H thing. I was making this club my own and becoming part of something I had never had. I was becoming part of something that made sense. My leader's husband took all the boys and did a woodworking project that year. We made birdhouses and later put them up outside. Our club went to the Illinois State Fair with our 4-H projects. We also won a state award and my 4-H leader's husband took us to a football game at the University of Illinois where we received our award. I was very proud to be a part of the Ridge Runners 4-H Club. When I had a problem, I started going to my 4-H leader and she would talk me through it, and what she would say made sense.

To make a long story short, I finished high school and went into the army where I became a chaplain. I now work in Springfield, Illinois, for the Illinois Department of Conservation. Years after my time in 4-H, I ran into my 4-H leader in the grocery store in Grand Chain. I told her if it had not been for her not giving up on me, I probably would have gone to prison for hurting someone. I am eternally grateful for her and 4-H.

Many 4-H leaders likely have stories about their own Larry. Some members are just more of a challenge than others and often that is the child who needs 4-H the most. We may never know how much impact we had but if even one troubled youth becomes a caring, contributing citizen, all of the work will have been worth it. I know Larry's story is true because I was his 4-H leader.

James' Story
Arch Smith, Georgia

4-H Project Achievement has long been one of the most positive learn-by-doing experiences that the Georgia 4-H Program offers to young students. 4-H Project Achievement allows young people in grades five through 12 to demonstrate their knowledge gained through their project work.

Fifth and sixth grade 4-H'ers are referred to as Cloverleaf 4-H'ers, and in order to participate in Project Achievement they must develop a six-minute illustrated talk on a project area in which they have an interest and/or have done some 4-H work. As 4-H'ers move through junior high and high school, the illustrated talks become longer and 4-H'ers are required to keep project records and submit a 4-H portfolio.

From 1985 through 1987 I served as a Carroll County, Georgia, county Extension agent. We would go into school classrooms and encourage fifth and sixth grade 4-H members to become involved in 4-H Project Achievement. Many young people would get excited about the chance to participate.

A young child said to me at the conclusion of a club meeting, "Mr. Smith, I would like to participate in project achievement and give a 4-H demonstration." I told him, "Come by the Extension office one afternoon and I'll work with you and we'll get your 4-H project started." He responded, "I do not have a way to get to the 4-H office after school." I asked him, "James, where do you live?" He told me the address, which I quickly recognized as being in a low-income, subsidized housing, so I told him that I would come by his house and work with him. A few days later I went to his house, discovering that his father was disabled and his mother worked to support the family. Both parents were appreciative that I had come to help their son with his 4-H project. We worked a little while and I left him some things to do and told him I would be back in a few days. When I returned he had accomplished the tasks so we were able to get his demonstration together. Over the next few weeks he practiced and prepared for the 4-H Project Achievement contest. The event was held at a school in Marietta, Georgia, one Saturday morning in late spring. After the contest was over, we would take the children to the White Water Theme Park to reward the young 4-H'ers for successfully completing the 4-H Project Achievement process.

We had a couple busloads of children and as we were about to depart the school and travel to White Water, a little boy stuck his head out the window, held up a white ribbon, and said, "Hey, Mr. Smith! I won third place!" There was a wide, bright smile on his face and great pride in his accomplishment. He was proud of the work he had done to prepare for 4-H Cloverleaf Project Achievement.

Since there were about 20 or 25 other children in the room when James presented his project, he never knew that he placed third out of three contestants. He thought he was competing against the entire group. I will never forget the sense of accomplishment on that young man's face. James was successful because he did his own work and was able to get up in front of the group and deliver his project.

It is the positive impact we have on children like James that is my motivation to get up and go to work every morning.

Arch Smith currently serves as Georgia Interim State 4-H Program Leader.

Today I Lived
Kendyl Sullivan, New Hampshire

"You can't control the length of your life. Just the depth." Anonymous

I can still remember staring at the purple and white checked fabric, wondering how that material would ever turn into anything that even resembled a skirt. Up to that point, my sewing experience amounted to piecing together doll clothes with a needle, thread, and some fabric out of my mom's scrap box. A sewing machine was as foreign to my nine-year-old self as a car. I had seen one, but operating it was a mystery. Just as I was about to give up before even trying, Dotty came to my rescue.

Dotty was, and still is, the 4-H educator in my area. She is the person who introduced me to sewing and, thanks to her, I actually did finish that skirt. I also quilted with her for years and can honestly say that all I know about stitching, cutting, tying, and quilting, I owe to her. Even when I made mistakes that were seemingly irreversible, Dotty taught me that there is nothing a seam ripper and some time cannot fix. She was always ready to help me, teach me, or simply listen to whatever poured out of my mouth. Dotty was the best.

Then, the spring before my fourth year of quilting with her, the unthinkable happened. Dotty's husband passed away suddenly. They had been married a great many years, and I was sure this huge tragedy would change Dotty tremendously. If only I knew how right I was.

One day a couple of years after Bud's death, I sat talking to Dotty. She was seventy pounds thinner, had recently bought a sports car, and had a newly renovated house. I was talking to her about Bud and how she managed to get along so well after his passing. I asked why she did all of the seemingly "fun" things after Bud was already gone. This is what she said to me: "When Bud died, I realized something. He would not want me to just sit around here missing him. He would want me to keep living and have a good life. But I also realized something else. Life is not as long as everyone seems to think it is. His life ended so suddenly that it got me thinking about what I wanted to accomplish before I died. I have been taking chances, having fun, and doing all of the things I said I always wanted to or have previously been too scared to do. I have been living."

This was the most inspirational conversation any 16-year-old could have had. Dotty really made me think. What do I want to accomplish in my life? One hundred years from now, when my grandchildren look back on my life, what do I want them to see? What do I want to do? These questions are a little much for me to try and answer right now, and they are a little much for most people to try and answer during the span of their whole lives. I know that I want to go to college, get a job I love, have a family, travel the world, and go bungee jumping. But those are relatively miniscule goals in the whole scheme of things. Who knows what I am going to be or do in 20 years. These are not things I need or want to know right now. What Dotty has taught me is that all I need to do to have a really happy life is never hold back, because I may never get a second chance to do something amazing. At the end of the day, when all is said and done, I do not want to say, "Today I made $100," or "Today, I got an A in a class." All I really care is that everyday, I am able to say, "Today, I took a chance. I tried something new. I looked fear square in the eye and laughed in its face. I helped somebody, I smiled, and I laughed. Today, I lived."

Kendyl was 17 and soon to be a freshman at Colby College (Waterville, Maine) when she wrote this story for her college entrance essay. She is now a senior at Colby and as this book goes to print is traveling in Europe. The Dotty who so inspired Kendyl is Dotty Burrows, her 4-H agent who served Carroll County from 1986 to 2008. Dotty retired in 2008 and lives in Center Sandwich, New Hampshire, where she is happily engaged as a 4-H volunteer in her hometown and county and as a volunteer with the Agricultural Science and FFA Program at the Region 9 Vocational Center in Wolfeboro, New Hampshire.

The County 4-H Agent's Job
Brevoort C. Conover, New Jersey

The year was 1959 and at that time most county 4-H agents were men. There had been a succession of men in the Warren County position before me and each of them had their own idea of how the work should be done. Learning my job would be a challenge.

Several 4-H volunteers were invited to participate in my interview. One of the major concerns was access. Would I have my home phone number unlisted as the previous agent had done, which to them was very upsetting. I assured them my phone number would be listed and needless to say, they were very pleased.

The county 4-H agent job is multifaceted. There are so many aspects to it; you have to use your best judgment to prioritize what you do and when you do it. Meeting and getting to know the volunteer adult leaders seemed to me the best place to start. I viewed the job as "hands on" because these were the people who were working with the youth. Most of them had 4-H club meetings in their homes, and as I met the volunteers I was also getting to know my way around this new territory.

In a rural county in the northwest part of urban New Jersey, I quickly learned the volunteers did not want too much changed in their county program. This was going to be a challenge! Of course, the senior agricultural agent told me the same thing. Take things slow and do not make any drastic changes right away. He had been the county 4-H agent in that county some 20 years before and knew the people well.

Program planning was a priority. As I saw it, my job was to help young people learn, grow, and mature into more confident citizens. The 4-H program was to provide the ways and means to do this with the help of volunteers. I saw a need for program planning committees composed of leaders, members, parents, and others. Involving everyone in the planning process gave them a stake in these events and activities. The adults and older members could also serve as chairs or superintendents of the events. This was leadership training at its best and allowed me the time to oversee the activities to ensure that they were properly organized.

When I arrived you could say 4-H was all "cows and cooking," as the program was strictly rural. During the '60s, the push was on to expand 4-H into urban areas. Introducing my plans for including youth from the town of Phillipsburg was a touchy proposition. The senior agent did not want me to publicize it too broadly for fear of "stirring up a hornet's nest," and upsetting the traditional farm families who were viewed as the backbone of the program.

The primary promotional efforts to attract new members were through the schools. We targeted areas of the county that did not have a large 4-H membership and conducted assembly programs using demonstrations and other visuals, such as slide shows. After the projects had been briefly described we would talk about the "fun" side of 4-H, including the county fair, camp, and a variety of group activities. The teachers and administrators were generally supportive and cooperative.

In Phillipsburg, a town of more than 20,000 people, we visited the Firth Youth Center. Gaining their cooperation was important because they had meeting rooms and volunteers who worked with the boys and girls. We targeted several 4-H projects we thought would be attractive to the urban young people, such as archery, electricity, food preparation, woodworking, skiing, and automotive care and safety. We conducted programs in a number of schools and we were off and running. Locating volunteer adult leaders was a challenge, but through newspaper promotion and school newsletters, we managed to find enough to cover all of the interest groups.

Helping young people develop is the heart and soul of a well-rounded 4-H program and required active participation of the members. The local club meeting was the vital first part where the boys and girls learned-by-doing. Here they did things with their hands, such as sewing, cooking, sawing a board, etc. They took part in the teaching process too, by performing demonstrations and developing leadership skills by conducting club meetings as officers. All of these things were done under the watchful eye of the adult leader.

County events were a step up from the club level. Demonstrations and illustrated talks were performed at the county public presentation night by the 4-H'ers. Completed projects were displayed at the county fair and this included the variety of animals which also had their own shows. Decision-making was taught through judging activities, whether with animals or a variety of home economic projects. The year's activities culminated in member recognition at the county achievement night. Families were encouraged to attend and view each of these events to support and witness the growth of their 4-H'er.

Camping, or outdoor education, was a separate, but vital part of the county program. Both adults and teens served as counselors for the 150 to 200 members who traveled to the state 4-H camps in a neighboring county. The weeklong event took a great deal of planning to be successful. The attendees met new friends, took part in new experiences, and learned a great deal about nature. I served as camp director, but the successful camps were largely due to the creativity and hard work of the volunteer counselors.

Vital to the success of the program was the county 4-H leaders' association, made up of all the adult volunteer leaders. They elected their own officers and served as a sounding board for the various events and activities conducted throughout the year. They met four times a year with educational and informative programs, an important part of most meetings. Program and project committees were appointed by the association president. Leaders were encouraged to volunteer for the committee of their choice with project training emanating from these groups.

Leader education was a high priority. New leaders received orientation followed by training related to teaching methods, program philosophy and the expected results. Emphasis was placed on member participation at both club and county levels. As teen members matured, junior leaders were appointed by the adult leader to assist with project education and club management.

As the program grew, I found it necessary to appoint experienced leaders as area coordinators. I divided the county into areas, primarily using towns or municipalities, and recruited a coordinator. The coordinator served as a local resource a new volunteer could call on for advice or assistance. I included the coordinator in the new volunteer's orientation to help develop a positive relationship. This new organizational pattern proved to be very successful.

Older members were part of the senior 4-H council. They met monthly with an adult advisor. This group had responsibilities for several activities, but its primary function was leadership development. They elected their own officers and planned their own program each year. This group was also involved in a number of community projects, such as beautification and stream cleanups.

The county 4-H agent job changed a great deal over the 19 years I was involved. I just loved attending the dairy judging events and going to camp for the week. I tried to visit every 4-H club in the county at least once each year and visited some clubs more often. I presented educational programs at club meetings when asked by the leaders. Providing support to the volunteers was a priority and I was committed to that premise, even if it meant being out five or more nights a week. Many people thought I was crazy, but I really loved my work.

The county fair was a great deal of work, with long hours. It required detailed organization and planning if it was to be a meaningful, successful event. While adults and senior members chaired and supervised the various exhibits and shows, involvement of the members was essential. I played an active role in overseeing the rules and requirements for each of the activities. These regulations were designed to include rather than exclude to encourage maximum participation.

Program promotion and visibility were key elements to attracting boys and girls to 4-H. I became an amateur photographer, learning how to take, process, and provide finished prints, along with providing readable copy, to each of the county newspapers. This allowed 4-H leaders and members to be on display in these papers almost weekly throughout the year. It was very effective.

Environment Education became a "hot topic" in the early '70s. I adopted the National Wildlife magazine's taped program on the problems we faced with pollution, especially with soil, water, and air quality. This was very useful for school programs. It led to the highly successful Youth Art Poster contest, which had an environmental theme and was conducted throughout the county school system for several years. At its peak, more than 1000 students submitted entries.

Serving as county 4-H agent was extremely satisfying. I especially enjoyed the close association with the many volunteers who truly loved working with young people. It was a dream come true, I could not have asked for a better career.

Breve Conover served Warren County for 19 years followed by his election and appointment as New Jersey State 4-H Department Chair, Cook College (now School of Environmental and Biological Sciences), Rutgers University, retiring in 1989. Breve's dedication and service to 4-H was recognized with his induction into the National 4-H Hall of Fame Class of 2010.

Always Check Your Markers
Carol Schurman, Pennsylvania

As Extension educators, we often work long hours and too many nights and weekends. Sometimes we wonder if it is all worth it. One day last summer I received a note from Jasmyn, a former 4-H member we had hired as a summer assistant for three summers. Her note made my day and really lifted my spirits! Jasmyn gave me her permission to share the following message.

Dear Carol,

As I sat in my office getting ready for summer camp that afternoon, I was checking a box of markers for any ruined ones and my co-workers questioned what I was doing. No one thought it was important to check and I thought I was pretty smart for doing so. I realize that I learned that from you.

It might seem like a miniscule realization to some, but it got me thinking more. I want you to know that even though I was pretty well grown when I became your summer assistant, you and 4-H continued to teach me a lot, and helped me become who I am now. My early college years were difficult for me, and something was missing. That is why I contacted you about volunteering for 4-H. Being in 4-H as a kid and teen had given me confidence in myself, and gave me a sense of belonging. I wanted that back, and I wanted to give that feeling to other kids.

Becoming your summer assistant was the best thing that happened to me. I know that I grew so much during those three summers. You were one of the first people to treat me like a woman, not a girl. You saw something in me that I did not realize was there. In a short time working with your 4-H program, my confidence came back. I found my passion again. I found friendships that I know will last a lifetime. I found that feeling of belonging. I also learned important things like the difference between a pony and a mini, bacon comes from a pig's stomach, you should always have a box of well-sharpened pencils on hand, and before camp you should always check your markers!

Thank you so much for seeing something in me and asking me to be your summer assistant. Thank you for teaching me.

Sincerely, Jasmyn

Youth development professionals work with so many people that we often are unaware of the positive impact we have had on the lives of others. Our work is not always exciting or glamorous, but making a difference in the life of a child will always be important. And, while we may not give much thought to the real difference we are making, the occasional thank you note or a few heartfelt words means more than most of us would ever admit. 4-H is more important now than ever, and I am proud to be part of it, even if I do have a 4-H meeting every night this week!

Jasmyn graduated from college and is now working with workforce preparation in Union County, Pennsylvania. She became interested in this career while a summer assistant. Jasmyn continues to use her 4-H skills as she helps her clients prepare presentations and public speeches!

Lessons for Life
Lynne M. Middleton, Tennessee

When I became a 4-H agent in the spring of 2000 I had exciting goals. I intended to increase enrollment in my county program, encourage volunteers to become more active, teach youth new skills, and offer programs to youth they would never learn about outside of 4-H. Now, eight years later, my goals are much the same but my success has been greater that I could have imagined.

My mother, who taught English for 42 years and is my role model, retired in June 2005. More than 300 people attended her retirement party. There was a line of people to hug and thank her for what she had taught them during her career. Some she remembered; many she did not.

One person stood out in my mind even after the party was over. The lady was in her 40s and was dressed in ragged clothes. Her hair was long and ratty and she smelled of smoke, but the thing that stood out most to me was her captivating smile. She was a happy person and one could tell it by looking at her. I crossed the room in time to see her reach my mother.

My mother taught this woman in a creative writing class when she was a college student. The woman explained that she was a writer now and adored her "job." She explained that in the average person's eyes, she was probably not successful. She had published 12 books, but had very little money and was not able to splurge like some would like. In her own mind, however, she was successful and looked forward to accomplishing her goals. She had been writing since graduating from college, was still enjoying it, and did not care if she made any money. The thrill for her was in writing a story to share with others.

When she heard about my mother's retirement party, she thought about the gifts that she might give her favorite teacher. The lessons my mother had taught her, according to the woman, were priceless and no gift could ever thank her enough. After puzzling over what to buy, she realized that nothing would be better than to give back something that my mother had taught her. She wrote a book and dedicated it to her favorite teacher, the person who encouraged her to write and helped her learn what she needed to know to be successful. The gift she gave my mother was the first printed copy of her newest novel.

After the party, as we cleaned her office out, my mother found awards, trophies, and presents that students had given her throughout her 35 years of teaching. Many of them were expensive gifts, but she placed them in a box for a thrift store. She joked that it had taken her seven years to begin receiving gifts from students because the first years were her "practice years." Out of all of the gifts, the one that she treasured most was the book that the woman had dedicated to her.

My mother reminded me of a Chinese Proverb that says, "Give a man a fish, and he will eat for a day. Teach a man to fish and he will eat for a lifetime." What that English teacher had taught that writer was the best thing she could have done for her.

That conversation came back to me recently. One of my 4-H members, Deanna, graduated from high school in 2006. Last month she came to visit me. She was registering for her college classes and wanted to know what classes I suggest she take. I did not know what career she would pursue so I asked what she wanted to do after college. She sat quietly and then said, "I want to do what you do, Ms. Lynne." That morning I had taught six classes of students and I was exhausted. I laughed out loud at Deanna's comment and said, "You want to plan programs for kids who do not appreciate you, write pages and pages of reports, and deal with other people's children all day long?" She responded, "No. I want to touch people the way you touched me. I want to give kids the kind of opportunities I would not have had if it had not been for you. I want to take kids on trips, like you did for me, and show them things they may never see otherwise. I am 19 years old and I had never left the state of Florida before I met you. I had never flown on a plane or ridden on a train before you took me to Indiana that one summer." As touched as I was at that moment, I told her, "Taking you on a trip is something that anyone could do, Deanna." She responded with, "But teaching me lessons that I will need for life isn't something anyone could do. No one else had. You may not think you have done much for me, Ms. Lynne, but I know you have and I appreciate the person you have helped me become!"

As soon as Deanna left my office that day, I wrote our conversation down. Not because I ever thought her thoughts would be published, but because it meant so much to me that she appreciated what I was doing for the young people I work with.

Teaching youth is what 4-H agents do. We plan educational experiences that youth would not experience anywhere else. We take them on trips, teach them skills, and have fun with them. Most of all, we give them memories that will be with them for the rest of their lives. Whether it is one 4-H member or one hundred who have been positively impacted by something I have done, that impact is the whole reason I wanted to be a 4-H agent and it is why I still love my job!

My Momma Needs a Husband
Robert Ray Meadows, Virginia

We may never know how we impact the lives of children and youth through 4-H, or how they impact our lives. As a career 4-H youth development professional, I have been privileged to witness a variety of firsts in the lives of youth involved in 4-H—firsts that many of us take for granted.

Among these include a 16-year-old experiencing her first milkshake, an inner-city 4-H club visiting a farm with each member getting the opportunity to milk his/her first cow, an older teen taking his first airplane ride, and others. While these memories provide personal satisfaction that all the long hours of 4-H work made a difference in the lives of thousands of children and youth, it is true that young people often impact our lives as well. Such is the case of a nine-year-old girl who participated in a residential 4-H camp a few years ago.

During the time I served as Program Director of Airfield 4-H Educational Center in Wakefield, Virginia, the campers gave me the affectionate name of "Bubbly Bob," a name that is dear to me. I am often called by this title even today. Directing ten- to 12-weeks of 4-H camp each summer, with a different group of counties and cities represented each week, it was my practice to eat lunch and dinner at the tables of campers (breakfast was always with my staff). Believing that we should "stay close to the customer," it was important to me to listen to campers to determine how they were doing, what they thought about camp, what areas needed improvement, their perspective about the staff and counselors, etc. Each day I chose to sit at a table and eat with seven or eight of the campers. It was also my habit to sit at a different table each meal, thus eating with different campers. By doing this, I ate with hundreds of campers over my eight years at Airfield.

One day, a nine-year-old girl begged me to sit at her table at dinner. I politely replied I had already sat with her and needed to meet with other campers. She began to plead with me, "Please, Bubbly Bob, sit at my table one more time. I need to tell you something." How could I say no to a little girl with those big brown eyes? I said okay.

That night at dinner, I sat directly across the table from this camper. Noticing that she was not eating and sitting there with her head resting on her hands, I asked her, "Aren't you hungry?" to which she replied, "Bubbly Bob, do you need a new wife?" I said I was flattered, but was too old for her. I commented that there were plenty of good-looking lads in camp her age. She immediately stopped me and said, "No, no, no! My Momma needs a husband."

This was an awesome experience for me. I realized that this little girl thought I was good enough to be her dad. I soon learned she had no father and was starving for the attention of a dad in her life. When a child thinks enough of a person to believe that he/she is good enough to be a parent, *Wow*! I had tears in my eyes and was humbled by her comment.

During the last night's campfire, she stood to claim an honor (an opportunity to recognize someone who has made a difference during camp or somewhere in life). She again impacted my life by telling the entire camp, "Bubbly Bob is the greatest man I know." For several months after camp, she called me just to see how I was doing. Having no idea what ever happened to that little brown-eyed girl, I am grateful that I took the time from a very busy schedule to sit with and listen to a group of campers during mealtime. By doing so, I not only showed that I valued them, but I myself came away feeling valued, blessed, and richer for the impact it had made on my life. We need to take more time to listen to children.

Following his years at the Airfield 4-H Educational Center, Dr. Robert Ray Meadows served as Associate Director, 4-H (State 4-H Leader), Virginia Cooperative Extension and is now retired.

4-H Shooting Sports – Photo/Conrad Arnold

The 4-H Agent
Mark Tassin, Louisiana

A friend, a teacher, a motivator
A coach, a fitter, a mediator
Sometimes you are called to be substitute mom or dad
To brighten the day when it looks real bad

Anger and frustration are common emotions
But you must be ready to come up with one of your potions
To wipe a tear from an eye and create a smile
On the saddest and most troubled child

When seas become rough don't give up the ship
Still in store for you many a trip
So right the vessel and set sail into the wind
To ready yourself for the journey that will see you prosper in the end

Your skills you can not obtain from any book
Because in times of need you have taken a look
They don't teach them in any class
They're obtained as time will pass

You've been criticized and that's no fun
But you realize you are the one
That can help a child grow and reach the top
And because of this you will never stop

In this world today people so easily quit
But you refuse to stop until all the pieces fit
Your success is not measured by ribbons achieved
It is scaled against your drive to succeed

Your time and devotion are hard to measure
Only you know the amount of pleasure
Derived from the satisfaction of a job well done
Knowing that in many eyes you are number one

Honest and integrity are qualities you do possess
Although your patience is put to the test
You take a deep breath and put a smile on your face
Because in a child's heart you've earned a special place

You bleed green and white and that's okay
Because in the future there'll come the day
When boy becomes man and you had something to do
With his success he attributes to you

We Want Your 4-H Story

We know the stories in *4-H Stories from the Heart* represent only a small fraction of all the wonderful 4-H stories that exist. We want your story for the next book!

Submitting a story is easy. Just follow these simple guidelines:

1. We want stories of 1000 words or less that are inspiring, funny, "tear-jerkers" and more. We want heartfelt stories that document 4-H's positive impact on your life or the life of someone close to you. Stories written in first person are usually best.

2. We are primarily interested in stories that have not been previously published.

3. Stories must be submitted as a MS Word document and sent as an email attachment. We prefer stories that are single spaced and written in a 12-point font with 1 inch margins.

4. Please provide a title for your story and include something about the setting (approximate year or years, location, state, activity or event, etc.).

5. At the end of your story provide your contact information including your name (as you want it listed), phone number(s), mailing address and email address.

We cannot promise all stories submitted will be used. Selected stories will be edited for "readability" and for punctuation, grammar, and spelling. Authors of selected stories will be asked to review and provide written permission to use the edited version of their story.

Please send your story to: dantabler2@gmail.com.

Tell Us What You Think

We would like to know what you think of *4-H Stories from the Heart*. Please tell us if any of the stories really touched you and we will share your comments with the author(s). And, if you have suggestions for improving the next book we sincerely want to hear your ideas. Communication is always a challenge in big organizations and we know it is likely only a small fraction of current and former members, parents, volunteers and faculty/staff were aware of the opportunity to submit a story. We did our best to "spread the word" using every communication method available to us over several years. We are sorry if our message did not reach you and look forward to receiving your 4-H story for a future publication.

Please send your comments to me at dantabler2@gmail.com or by mail to: 705 East Laurel Street, Ext., Georgetown, DE 19947.

We look forward to hearing from you. Dan Tabler, Editor